ENGAGED WRITERS AND DYNAMIC DISCIPLINES

Research on the Academic Writing Life

Chris Thaiss
Terry Myers Zawacki

Boynton/Cook
HEINEMANN
Portsmouth, NH

Boynton/Cook Publishers, Inc.
361 Hanover Street
Portsmouth, NH 03801–3912
www.boyntoncook.com

Offices and agents throughout the world

Library of Congress Cataloging-in-Publication Data
Thaiss, Christopher J., 1948–
    Engaged writers and dynamic disciplines : research on the academic
writing life / Christopher Thaiss and Terry Myers Zawacki.
        p. cm.
    Includes bibliographical references.
    ISBN 0-86709-556-3 (acid-free-paper)
    1. English language—Rhetoric—Study and teaching.   2. Interdisciplinary approach in education.
3. Academic writing—Study and teaching.   4. Scholarly publishing.   5. Academic writing.
I. Zawacki, Terry Myers.   II. Title.
    PE1404.T4717 2006
    808'.0420711–dc22   2005030415

Editor: Charles I. Schuster
Production Service: Lisa S. Garboski, bookworks
Production Coordination: Patricia I. Adams
Typesetter: Aptara, Inc.
Cover design: Joni Doherty Design
Manufacturing: Steve Bernier

Printed in the United States of America on acid-free paper
10   09   08   VP   3   4   5

Contents

Preface   v
Acknowledgments   ix

Chapter One   What's Academic? What's "Alternative"?   1
What Is Academic Writing? What Are Its Standards?   4
What Constitutes an "Alternative" to Academic Writing?   8
Disciplines, Genres, and Research on Alternative Discourses
    and the Academy   13
Our Methods and Materials   24

**Chapter Two   Faculty Talk About Their Writing, Disciplines,
and Alternatives   32**
Disciplinary vs. Academic Standards   36
The Analytic Academy: Tension Between Reason, Emotion,
    and the Body   38
Allowed Alternatives   41
Working Outside Disciplinary Boundaries   45

Chapter Three   How Our Informants Teach Students to Write   58
"How to Think Like a Scientist": Teaching the
Tools of the Discipline   62
"Good Writing Is Good Writing": Perceiving the
Universal in the Disciplinary   67
Neither This Nor That: Alternative Exigencies, Alternative Forms   75
New Media, Hypermedia, Multimedia   80
Faculty Expectations in Department Assessment Rubrics   83
Conclusion: The Standard vs. the Alternative   88

**Chapter Four   Students Talk About Expectations, Confidence, and
How They Learn   95**
Our Sources of Data   96
Student Expectations for Writing in Their Disciplines   101
Passion and the Discipline   112
How Students Learn to Write in Their Disciplines   121

How Student Perceptions Relate to the "Taxonomy
   of Alternatives"   129
Conclusion   134

Chapter Five   Implications for Teaching and Program Building   136
   Conclusions   136
   The Discipline and Passion   136
   Alternative Discourses   137
   Five Contexts for Writing Assignments   138
   Stages of Writing Development "into" a Discipline   139
   Tension Between Individual Desire and Academic Convention   141
   Practices for Teachers   142
   Practices for Faculty and Program Development   156
   Directions for Future Research   167

   Work Cited   171
   Index   181

Preface

This project began in 2000 with a call for papers for a collection on "alternative discourses in the academy." For many years, each of us had been studying academic writing environments, primarily through administration and faculty development in our university's writing-across-the-curriculum program, which had begun in 1978. We had read and analyzed hundreds of portfolios from students across many majors, and we had worked with hundreds of faculty in workshops, frequently hearing colleagues' opinions about standards in their disciplines and how students either met them or didn't.

At the same time, each of us had been reading the literature on "alternative discourse," and had pondered the ramifications of contrastive rhetoric and of feminist and other "identity" scholarship on our teaching and program direction. In our own ways, each of us had confronted the tension between the "standard" and the "alternative" not only in our day-to-day responsibilities but also in our writing. Terry had directly addressed this tension for feminist scholars in a 1992 essay "Recomposing as a Woman." In a 1997 collaboration, an essay on WAC assessment, we had noted the diversity of styles and voices in student portfolios from different disciplines: while the received wisdom seemed to be that the "academy" hindered individual diversity and expression, we were seeing personality, engagement, and passion in assigned student work in many fields.

Nowhere had we seen systematic empirical study of this tension in academic writing in disciplines. When the call for papers came along, we took it as an opportunity to look closely at a range of data sources from our institution in order to achieve a research-based idea of the relationship between the "academic standard" and individual variation. Could we reach a sound definition of "academic writing"? How did disciplinary differences and commonalities contribute to this definition? What roles did the individual scholar/writer—faculty or student—play in shaping and changing the standard? How did our students grow to fluency in academic and disciplinary discourses, while realizing their own ambitions for learning and expression? How could teachers help students—and themselves—more fully achieve these intertwined, but sometimes conflicting, aims? The first stage of our research, interviews with faculty, produced the article for the 2002 collection *ALT DIS: Alternative Discourses and the Academy*. This new book, *Engaged Writers and Dynamic Disciplines*, grew out of three subsequent years of research with faculty and students; that research is described, analyzed, and applied in the chapters that follow.

We direct this book to teachers, to writers, to scholars and researchers, and to writing program administrators. We have tried to strike a balance between meeting scholarly expectations and meeting the practical needs of teachers and program administrators across disciplines. As we show in the chapter descriptions that follow, we begin with a review of theory and research and describe our methodology, proceed through analysis of findings, and conclude with recommendations for teaching and program development.

We also wanted this academic book to resound with voices, to display the rich, diverse personalities of the students and faculty we came to know or came to know better through this research. This is a book of hypothesis and analysis, but it is also a book of stories: thumbnail portraits of lives and ambitions expressed in each person's words and our brief narratives. Conversely, as a collaboration between two writers, the book also blends our voices into a single "we." Readers of scientific research will find the "we" an aspect of the academic standard; for humanities people like us, the "we" of collaborative writing is still an alternative discourse, one that involves a good deal of risk for the untenured in those disciplines, as we discuss in Chapter Two.

The Chapters

Chapter One: What's Academic? What's "Alternative"?

What compels us in this chapter, certainly, is our sense, shared by some scholars in rhetoric and composition, that "academic writing" is not as stable, unified, and resistant to alternatives as others often assume it to be. Some of those who perceive academic writing as unnecessarily narrow propose alternatives as ways to acknowledge and honor diverse voices and cultures. Our goal in this chapter is to examine these differing perspectives: we explore definitions of the key terms, "academic writing," "alternative discourse," "discipline," and "genre." We trace summarily the recent history of theory on these key concepts. In so doing we reflect on the scholarship on gender, race, and ethnicity, and the field of contrastive rhetoric. We then introduce our five-year investigation, describing our research methods and materials.

Chapter Two: Faculty Talk About Their Writing, Disciplines, and Alternatives

In this chapter, we report the results of our research with faculty colleagues across disciplines. We present their voices and views in regard to the writing conventions and expectations in their chosen fields. We devote considerable space to their thoughts on the range of alternatives possible for scholar-writers, with special focus on several faculty who have been wrestling with their own places amid the changing expectations in their fields. Next we turn to those informants who—for different reasons and with varying emotions—have embarked on writing that they know falls outside academic conventions. We report their motives, experiences, speculations, and assessments. Our presentation of findings is conditioned by the extended definitions of key terms from Chapter One. Also instrumental is our discussion of the tension between reason and emotion/sensation in academic prose.

Chapter Three: How Our Informants Teach Students to Write

Here our faculty describe and illustrate their goals for student writers in their disciplines. These goals to a remarkable extent follow from their own values as writers; while all acknowledge the need for writers to learn standards and conventions in the discipline, all also appreciate to varying degrees the need for the individual student to engage personally with their studies, to find their passion in the discipline. We describe the diversity of approaches and assignments that result.

As we will show in this chapter, our data confirm that there is an academic way of conceptualizing writer, reader, and task, and that these follow the academic principles we've laid out in Chapter One. But, as we will also show, the common terminology about writing that faculty use hides basic disciplinary differences in argumentation, epistemology, style, form, and tradition—differences that are revealed when faculty elaborate on their assignments and values.

Chapter Four: Students Talk About Expectations, Confidence, and How They Learn

Student voices predominate in this chapter. We focus on the stories students across majors tell about their goals as writers and how these coincide with perceived conventions for writing in their disciplines. Relying on survey results, focus groups, and reflective essays in advanced writers' proficiency portfolios, we build a sequence of student academic writing growth through three stages of increasing sophistication. We show the diverse ways in which students feel bound by perceived conventions and how they come to understand—if they do—what it means to participate in shaping the discipline, whether writing conventionally or in alternative ways. Our data also lead us to an explanation, based in part on activity theory, of why students misunderstand faculty expectations.

Chapter Five: Implications for Teaching and Program Building

In this final chapter, we summarize principal conclusions we have drawn from our research. These conclusions provide the basis for seven applications to teaching both by faculty across the curriculum and teachers of English composition. These are followed by five recommendations for faculty development programs in the uses of writing in teaching. Suggestions for future research conclude the chapter.

Acknowledgments

The research reported in this book could not have been undertaken without the help of the following people:

Undergraduate research apprentice Erica Wilmore, who painstakingly collated survey responses, summarizing and highlighting key comments. Graduate research assistants Darcy Hood and Anna Habib: Darcy for making sure that our bibliography matched in-text citations and Anna for the hours she spent transcribing faculty interviews and student focus group tapes. We also appreciated Anna's insights into the themes she saw developing in the transcripts.

Our faculty informants, all colleagues at George Mason University, who generously gave us several hours of interview time and whose careful reflections on their writing and teaching enriched our work.

All those faculty across the disciplines who participated in departmental assessment workshops that led, in turn, to the discipline-specific rubrics we discuss in Chapter Three.

The faculty teaching advanced composition courses who conducted the survey and helped us to recruit focus group participants.

The students who participated so thoughtfully in a series of focus groups with their only reward being a free lunch.

Those students from across disciplines who allowed us to use excerpts from their portfolio essays written to attain proficiency credit for advanced composition.

Our spouses, Bob Zawacki and Jean Thaiss, for their ongoing support and encouragement of our project.

We also want to acknowledge the support of the following organizations:

The Center for Teaching Excellence at George Mason University for our undergraduate research apprentice; the English Department for our two graduate research assistants; the College of Arts and Sciences and the Provost's Office for one-semester research leaves; and the Council of Writing Program Administrators for a grant to pursue this research.

Finally we want to thank the faculty and administrators at George Mason University, who, day by day and year-in and year-out, create an environment in which students can develop as writers. Their ongoing commitment inspires us every day.

Chapter One

What's Academic? What's "Alternative"?

Whenever we feel that we have achieved some certainty about standards that our colleagues across the curriculum will apply, we receive a fresh surprise. Recently, for example, we co-led a workshop on assessment standards for student writing for faculty representatives from many departments, who would then go back to lead similar workshops for their own departments. As material for the assessment session, we had selected for review four sample student papers, each from different majors but all written in response to a "review of the research" assignment. In building this sample, we made our own preliminary judgments of the relative quality of the papers. We chose papers that seemed to us to represent a clear range from poor to excellent. The "poor" paper, in our view, lacked organization, was short on evidence to support its thesis, and was marred in its effectiveness by errors in Standard Edited American English (SEAE) syntax and punctuation. The best paper, in our view, had a strong thesis, argued it with evidence from reliable sources, was clearly organized, and used SEAE with no errors. When we conducted the cross-curricular session, we kept our preliminary judgments to ourselves, since the object of the session was to help faculty establish their own judgments, not to have them replicate our views. To our surprise, the "poor" paper was judged by a plurality of the participants to be the best in the sample—because they regarded it as having the "freshest voice" and "taking the most risk" in its approach to the research—while they downgraded the "excellent" (in our view) paper as "conventional, saying nothing new even though competently written." Where we had expected this mixed group of business, science, social science, and humanities faculty to prioritize formal and logical properties usually invoked as defining academic prose, many of them had prioritized a creative, personal criterion almost never named in lists of academic writing conventions.

This incident occurred while we were in the midst of *one* phase of the research for this book; that is, interviewing a variety of faculty on perceived standards and alternatives for academic writing in their disciplines. The incident, as it defied a stereotype, reinforced for us the value of our investigation for fellow scholars and its potential usefulness for teachers and program developers. Still, we did not realize the degree of interest in our subject by other teachers and program developers until our first presentation of this research at a Conference on College Composition and Communication (CCCC) convention. Our session on this research, which we'd written about for the collection *ALT DIS: Alternative Discourses and the Academy*, drew a standing-room-only audience. It was gratifying to know that others considered the questions we were asking as important as we did. But what, we wondered, accounted for the increased interest we were seeing in this topic, as evidenced by other filled-room sessions on alternative discourses?

What compelled us, certainly, was our sense that many people in our field realize that "academic writing" is not as stable, unified, and resistant to alternatives as we often theorize it to be, and that they wish to learn more about the complexity of what we call "academic writing." Yet we also know that many others in composition and rhetoric do perceive academic writing as unnecessarily narrow and are interested in alternatives as ways to acknowledge and honor diverse voices. What these two groups have in common is their concern for student writers, for giving them an accurate sense of what they need to know in order to succeed as writers in school and the broader community: writers who can meet others' expectations and also articulately express their individual and communal identities, desires, and understandings. A more precise understanding of these complex terms—"academic writing" and "alternative discourse"—is important because thousands of teachers across the country are responsible for giving accurate and helpful guidance to students; they are also responsible for evaluating student writers to determine whether they meet certain literacy "standards." We will give elaborated definitions of "academic writing" and "alternatives" to it later in this chapter. The research we have undertaken for this book uncovers perceptions—through interviews with faculty and student informants—about characteristics of academic writing and what might constitute alternatives—both acceptable and unacceptable. Based on our research findings, which we report in Chapters Two through Four, we make recommendations for teacher practice, course design, and faculty and program development.

Our Research Plan: Aims and Methods

As part of our teaching and scholarship, each of us has been interested over the years in the meaning and uses of alternative rhetorics, as these have appeared in arguments advocating students' right to their own texts, feminist arguments for the need to disrupt patriarchal texts, linguistic cultural analyses of contrastive rhetorics, and critical pedagogy and cultural studies arguments for alternative discourses as a way to challenge cultural hegemonies. Our research plan was driven by these interests, as well as by our many years of research and experience in writing across the curriculum and writing in the disciplines (WAC/WID) program development and teaching, which have led us to question some assumptions of the scholarship on alternative rhetorics, as well as assumptions often made about academic writing. We therefore wanted to shape and pursue a study that would help us further understand (1) the nature of academic writing, as it is perceived by academic professionals across disciplines, and (2) the attitudes of these professionals toward what might be called "alternatives" to that writing. As we reflected, we became particularly curious about how these definitions of "academic" and "alternative" had been developed through our potential informants' own writing careers. How had they developed their ideas of what was "standard" in their fields? Had they in their growth felt pulled in other directions, toward alternatives from the standard, and, if so, how had they worked with those conflicting desires? Finally, how had their own histories as writers influenced their teaching of students, particularly in how they assigned and responded to student prose?

In addition to our projected work with faculty across disciplines, we also wanted to hear from students—undergraduate majors from a variety of fields. Would their responses, in surveys, focus groups, and proficiency exams, in relation to the same issues reveal similar perceptions to those of faculty? How well could these undergraduates talk about the "standards" and "conventions" of writing in their majors? What could they reveal to us about tensions between their goals and desires as writers and what their professors expected of them? Did they perceive that their professors were as accepting of—or resistant to—alternatives as the faculty informants said they were? We hoped that by finding answers to these and similar questions we could reach conclusions that would enrich our teaching, our program administration, and our work in faculty development.

A third major source of data emerged from the assessment workshops that we alluded to in the opening incident. These workshops are part of a state-mandated assessment of student writing competency in higher education; they have allowed us to extend our investigation of faculty perceptions of criteria for successful academic writing in disciplines.

We believe that these varied sources of data, described in detail later in this chapter, give us a rich view of faculty and student attitudes toward and practices around academic writing, a view that offers what we see as a more balanced, contextual, dynamic view of academic discourse.

What Is Academic Writing? What Are Its Standards?

"Academic writing" is one of those terms that is often invoked, usually solemnly, as if everyone agreed on its meaning, and so is used imprecisely yet almost always for what the user regards as a precise purpose; e.g., commonly by teachers in explaining what they want from students. For our purposes as researchers, we'll define "academic writing" broadly as any writing that fulfills a purpose of education in a college or university in the United States. For most teachers, the term implies student writing in response to an academic assignment, or professional writing that trained "academics"—teachers and researchers—do for publications read and conferences attended by other academics. In this second sense, "academic writing" may be related to other kinds of writing that educated people do, such as "writing for the workplace," but there are many kinds of workplace writing that would rarely be considered "academic"; indeed, as the research by Dias et al indicates, the distinctions in audience and purpose between academic writing by students and writing for the workplace greatly outweigh any perceived similarities. The distinction is important, because the teacher who is assigned to prepare students for the kinds of assignments they're likely to receive in other classes should distinguish between the characteristics of truly academic writing and characteristics of writing in other venues.

Most textbooks used in introductory composition classes either attempt to define or imply a definition of academic writing, but most of these definitions are abstract and are not based in research. These writers may or may not consider differences in standards and expectations among disciplines and among teachers. Some texts do attempt the somewhat easier—but still problematic—task of defining standards and characteristics of writing in particular "disciplines" or groups of disciplines, e.g., writing in the "social sciences," but these do not bring us closer to a workable definition of academic writing as a whole.

Further, scholarly writers with an interest in "alternatives" to supposed standards and conventions in academic writing will invoke it in various ways, thereby assuming a definition. A few of these writers have attempted explicit definitions—for example, Patricia Bizzell in her introductory essay in *ALT DIS*. As opposed to a careful statement such as Bizzell's, most of what a student is likely to receive about academic writing, especially in the informal atmosphere of the classroom, relies too much on a teacher's limited personal experience of particular classrooms or on commonplaces that have been passed down. For example, one common assertion about academic prose—"It avoids the use of the first person"—continues to be made in classroom after classroom, even though many teachers across disciplines routinely accept first-person writing, and journals in every field accept articles with more or less use of the first person.

There are exceptions to almost every principle an analyst can identify as a characteristic of academic writing. So what can we say with confidence about its characteristics, regardless of differences among disciplines and individual teachers? Our reading, observation, and research suggest the following:

1. *Clear evidence in writing that the writer(s) have been persistent, open-minded, and disciplined in study.*

   The concept of the discipline—and of "discipline" without the "the"—is central to the university, because academics have learned so much respect for the difficulty of learning anything sufficiently deeply so that "new knowledge" can be contributed. What the academy hates is the dilettante, the person who flits whimsically from subject to subject, as momentary interests occupy him or her, and who assumes the qualifications—merely because of that interest—to pronounce on that subject of the moment. Whether they are reading student papers or evaluating journal articles, academics are invariably harsh toward any student or scholar who hasn't done the background reading, who isn't prepared to talk formally or off the cuff about the subject of the writing, and whose writing doesn't show careful attention to the objects of study and reflective thought about them. Of course, standards for fellow professionals and for introductory students differ monumentally, but even the most neophyte student will be penalized for shallow reading and for lack of careful thinking about the subject. Persistent, disciplined study can be shown as well in a personal narrative as in a lab report, so this first characteristic of academic writing is not restricted in style or voice, although disciplines and subfields of disciplines do vary in customary ways of thought and in traditional modes of expression. We'll address in more detail later in this chapter the concept of "the discipline" and will describe disciplinary variations in subsequent chapters when we report the responses of our informants.

2. *The dominance of reason over emotion or sensual perception.*

   "And I wonder anew at a discipline that asks its participants to dedicate their lives to its expansion, but that requires a kind of imperial objectivity, a gaze that sees but rarely feels"

   Malea Powell, "Listening to Ghosts" (16)

In the Western academic tradition, the writer is an intellectual, a thinker, a user of reason. This identity doesn't mean that emotions or sensual stimuli are absent from academic writing: indeed, the natural sciences have always depended on acute sensate awareness, detection of subtle differences in appearance, fragrance, flavor, texture, sound, movement; moreover, the arts and humanities would not exist without the scholar's intense and highly articulated sensual appreciation. As for emotion, every discipline recognizes at the very least the importance of *passion* in the ability to dedicate oneself to research, acknowledged as often tedious. But in the academic universe the senses and emotions must always be subject to *control by reason*. Political thinkers, for example, may be motivated by their passion for a system of government, even by their anger at opponents, but the discipline of political science demands, as do all disciplines, that *writing* about these issues reveals the writer as a careful, fair student and analyst of competing positions. The sociologist may describe in passionate detail personal experience of poverty or family dislocation, but the *academic* writer must not stop with the appeal to emotion (what Aristotle called *pathos*); the responsible sociologist must step back, as it were, almost as if he or she were a separate person, and place that emotional, highly sensual experience in a *context* of the relevant experiences of others and of the history of academic analysis of the topic. The literary or art historian, to cite one more example, might write about, and describe in great sensual detail, work that was intended by its creators to be pornographic, but the academic writer must be able both to appreciate the sensual power of the work and step back from the sensations to evaluate the work rationally.

With students, perhaps the most common instruction by teachers in regard to the control by reason of emotion is to avoid "impressionism": merely expressing "feelings" or opinions. The various formulations of the principles of the "personal essay" (e.g., Newkirk, Heilker), a popular assignment in composition classes, all countenance the telling of "personal experience" narratives that include the expression of emotion, but all demand of the writer an analytical persona that reflects on and evaluates the narrative in some way. The "discipline" of which we speak is largely this ongoing process by which scholars learn through practice to cultivate both emotion and the senses and, necessarily, to subjugate them to reason. It's not coincidental that "discipline" has been associated so often in education with, as the *Oxford English Dictionary* notes, "mortification of the flesh," the scourging of the body that is an extreme form of the subjugation of the senses to reason that is basic to all academic discipline.

3. *An imagined reader who is coolly rational, reading for information, and intending to formulate a reasoned response.*

> The academic writer may wish also to arouse the emotions to agreement or to sympathy, as well as to stimulate the senses to an enhanced perception, but the academic writer wants above all to inspire the intelligent reader's respect for his or her analytical ability. The writer imagines the reader looking for possible flaws in logic or interpretation, for possible gaps in research and observation, and so tries to anticipate the cool reader's objections and address them. When an analyst such as Bizzell, in the essay mentioned earlier, calls the writer's "persona" "argumentative, favoring debate," we should understand "argument" not as an explicit form; after all, there is much academic writing that appears benignly descriptive, not "argumentative" in the formal sense. But all academic writing is "argumentative" in its perception of a reader who may object or disagree—e.g., the teacher who may take off "points" or the fellow scholar who may sit on a review panel; the writer's effort to anticipate and allay these potential objections is also part of the broadly "argumentative" ethos.

While the three "standards" we have described for academic writing might appear simple, they are devilishly hard to teach and even to observe in any given piece of writing. Would that the standards were as straightforward as "avoid the first person" or "use correct English" or "have a clear thesis." As our findings chapters will describe in detail, our informants tended to speak vaguely about what they regarded as "standards" and "conventions" in their fields, even though none of them had any hesitancy to say that they knew what the standards were. What their stories imply to us is that their knowledge of standards accrued over time, through coursework, reading, attempts to write and reactions to that writing; through regular talk with fellow students and fellow researchers and teachers. It's no wonder, given this gradual trajectory of initiation, that newcomers to academia, such as undergraduate students, often feel that teachers' reactions to their writing are mysterious, perhaps motivated by social and personality differences, rather than by factors clearly attributable to academic quality. (One of our student findings, as we'll describe in Chapter Four, is their perception of teacher standards as idiosyncratic and unpredictable.) But, as we will discuss in the next section, perceptions of academic quality often have a great deal to do with social—and cultural—differences among writers and their readers, not only with actual analytical and rhetorical control of a person's writing. In the next section, we make a distinction between an alternative text that is acceptable to academic readers and one that is unacceptable unless or until it is somehow revised through negotiation between writer and teacher.

What Constitutes an Alternative to Academic Writing?

We suggested three features we can confidently say characterize academic writing: disciplined and persistent inquiry, control of sensation and emotion by reason, and an imagined reader who is likewise rational and informed. Can the same confident assertions be made about the characteristics of alternatives to academic writing? Here, we think, we're on much more slippery ground, as the following anecdote from one of our informants illustrates. "My goodness, aren't I daring," anthropology professor Roger Lancaster told us he remembered thinking when he had finished writing *Life Is Hard: Machismo, Danger, and the Intimacy of Power in Nicaragua*. The book is comprised of journalistic and impressionistic passages, raw field notes, chapter-length interviews, life histories, newspaper articles, and letters. In the book he also discloses his sexual orientation and describes his partnership with a military man opposing the Sandinistas: he questions whether his research will be compromised by this relationship. The collage-like quality of the book and the self-disclosure were both very different—"daring"—approaches for him; he felt he had created a truly alternative text. Yet, when he reread the book a year or so later, he recalled this reaction: "Oh my god, it's a standard ethnography." For us, Lancaster's shifting perceptions about his work illustrate the difficulties of talking about alternatives and academic writing. When academics talk about writing alternatively, often they mean they are including what has previously been excluded—voices, structures, styles, formats, genres, personal information. Still, they are writing for other academics, in an academic forum, and, if they are being published and read, are no doubt displaying the features we described above.

Though he was experimenting with new forms and with—what might be considered by some—risky self-disclosure, Lancaster's book certainly demonstrated these features. The variety of material he includes both broadens and deepens a reader's understanding of the culture. His disclosure that he is homosexual occurs in the context of his work in the field and in his analysis of the larger issues around homosexuality in Nicaragua. When he first perceived his work as "daring," he may have been most uncertain about how his imagined readers—anthropologists—would respond. Yet anthropology's tradition of stylistic experimentation—from Malinowski on—no doubt reassured Lancaster that his "daring" work would still provoke a reasoned response from academic readers, who had already been constructed by the discipline as readers who readily accepted "alternative" texts as long as those texts were still performing disciplined academic work. The fact that his book is now required reading in some introductory anthropology courses seems to confirm Lancaster's changed perception of the book as "standard" ethnography, not particularly alternative in this discipline.

Just as arguments and advice about "academic writing" are often based on assumed meanings, so too are arguments about "alternative" discourses. In these arguments, certain kinds of texts (and voices) are labeled "alternative" because they do not conform to some analysts' expectations for standard academic writing. Because they do not conform, the argument proceeds, they are marginalized and/or go unheard. But, as the example of Lancaster's book illustrates, an alternative text may be widely accepted if the writer conveys to the reader a conscious awareness that he or she is constructing a different kind of text and if the reason for using an alternative form is clear. Lancaster, for example, described to us the "organic relationship" between a text and its writer; he needed an alternative form, he said, "to mirror the discombobulation of a failed revolution." As we will show in our research, professional academics often find that alternative forms and methodologies can perform rigorous and disciplined inquiry at the same time that they may uncover knowledge not available through more traditional discourses.

An "alternative" may also be employed for political purposes in order to call attention to those voices that have historically been marginalized or silenced by dominant discourses, as, most notably, feminist and African American scholars have done. In her essay "Recomposing as a Woman—An Essay in Different Voices," for example, Terry joined a conversation among feminists that had been in progress for a number of years, as the title indicates in its echo of two landmark publications; that is, if women do think, write, and speak in voices different from men, then their different voices should be as valued as the patriarchal voices that had been dominating academic discourse. Terry purposely claimed a marginalized space by using an alternative style and format to suggest what a "woman's voice" might sound like if she wrote according to the characteristics being theorized by "difference" feminists. While the essay was intended to show that genre and gender are both socially constructed categories, Terry also argued that women should not have to speak from the margins of their discipline if they happen to write in ways not generally recognized by disciplinary insiders. Her readers—other academics—are expected not only to follow the logic of the argument but also to see that it is possible to reason in this alternative form.

But what about those writers, typically our student writers, who are not aware that the texts they are producing are linguistically and/or culturally quite different from traditional academic writing? Take, for example, a paper, written by one of our students, a young man from Sierra Leone. The student spends the first half of his paper, the topic of which is the political turmoil in his country, describing the beauty of the country and its people. There is no introduction and no thesis related to the ostensible topic; he instead conveys in heartbreaking detail his longing for the land he'd left behind. It is not until well into the third page of an eight-page paper that he begins, with no transition, to describe the strife in neighboring countries. Around page 7, he mentions—almost casually—that this strife endangered his own country. Then he returns to a description of the country and concludes the paper. While this student seems to be unaware that he is writing from a different cultural paradigm, one that values indirection and subtle implication, he may also have had good reason to fear writing in a more direct style. In other words, he may have been quite conscious of constructing an alternative text for the readers he is imagining, readers who may be very different from the "coolly rational" academic readers Terry imagines in her essay.

How will an academic reader—say, a professor in the student's major—receive the Sierra Leone essay? In *Listening to the World*, Helen Fox is concerned with the misunderstandings and misreadings that occur when teachers are confronted with these kinds of culturally different texts. She, along with many others, argues that western academics reject these texts because of the radical disjunction between "the dominant communication style and world view of the U.S. university" (xxi) and that of the writer who produces a text which seems "obscure, or digressive, or overly descriptive, or disturbingly unoriginal" (126). These writers—especially since they are students—may be perceived to lack the discipline and control expected in standard academic writing in the western tradition and so the argument will be dismissed. Yet, interestingly, our political science informant told us she would not automatically reject the Sierra Leone paper nor ask the student to take out the descriptions of his country; rather, she would ask him to include a statement of purpose to help focus his intentions for the reader. Her response indicates a degree of openness to a nontraditional text, but, while she is accepting much of the student's work on its own terms, she is also demanding revisions that will make the text more familiar to traditional (western) academic readers. We cannot assume, then, that teachers will reject nontraditional forms as long as they can relatively easily be made to fit within the three principles we have identified.

While many readers/teachers may be open to culturally alternative texts, there's another kind of disjunction between a writer and reader that we haven't yet addressed, that is, the disjunction caused by texts that are what we might call "syntactically diverse." It's often postulated that among the flaws the "coolly rational" academic reader will most strongly object to is "incorrect" usage of the grapholect (in this case, SEAE). Certainly composition programs and standardized tests that place primary emphasis on syntactic and mechanical correctness illustrate this assumption about academic readers. Within our schema of standards in academic writing, this emphasis would fit as follows: the academic reader objects to flawed use of the grapholect as evidence of lack of control by reason, perhaps also evidence of superficial preparation and lack of attention to the published literature. This projected reader is embodied in the stereotyped professor (of which there are, of course, some outspoken examples) who loudly complains, "Why, they can't even use commas correctly!"

However, as our anecdote about the assessment workshop at the beginning of the chapter illustrates, it is easy to overestimate the importance to the academic reader of the student's adherence to syntactic and mechanical "correctness." In other words, academic readers may indeed accept in student writing some amount of error in use of the grapholect as an allowed alternative to academic prose. There are several reasons to believe that academic readers may be more tolerant of these kinds of "error" than the stereotype suggests. First, the scholarly community is increasingly international, and conscientious readers of all nations need to develop an ability to read across dialects and linguistic blendings. As one of our research informants, a mathematician, noted in reference to the international community of math scholars, the structure of articles in math is sufficiently uniform across the international community so that one can understand much of the argument in an article written in a language one doesn't understand. Because of (1) the customary sequence of sections and (2) the use of symbolic language, the content of the argument, or "proof," should be clear. Moreover, the growth of English as a lingua franca provides a different kind of example of acceptable diversity. As English continues to spread in international influence, there has developed a range of "Englishes" that differ in aspects of syntax, and certainly of lexicon. Each has its own "correct" features. The differences between the British and American grapholects are one instance of this divergence.

Second, as American schools have accommodated more and more students and faculty of diverse linguistic backgrounds, the variety of acceptable Englishes grows. In a highly linguistically diverse university such as ours, it would not be practical or productive to place primary and equal emphasis on all aspects of SEAE as a "standard" of academic writing (though one of our informants from economics insists on such a standard). The standards described above indicate that students must be sufficiently fluent in a language, regardless of dialect, to carry out the logical operations that show reasoned control; but some of the most common "errors" made, for example, by those who are learning SEAE—e.g., lack of agreement in number between subject and verb or idiomatic use of articles—often don't affect the logic of sentences. The same is true of so-called "nonstandard" dialects of American English (e.g., Black English Vernacular).

In Chapters Two and Three, we will briefly return to this issue of "syntactic diversity" within academic writing, reporting what our faculty informants said about their expectations regarding student "correctness" and the results from our assessment workshops.

The foregoing discussion of various alternatives suggests a possible taxonomy of alternatives that can help writers/analysts speak more specifically about what they are seeing when they categorize a piece of writing as alternative to "standard" academic writing:

- *Alternative formats*, as exemplified in Lancaster's *Life Is Hard*, with its use of journalism, field notes, interviews, letters, autobiographical detail, etc.; these may also include unconventional layouts and typography; shifting margins; overlapping text and text boxes; creative use of sentence and paragraph structure.

- *Alternative ways of conceptualizing and arranging academic arguments*, as exemplified by the paper written by the student from Sierra Leone.

- *Alternative syntaxes (language and dialect differences)*, which we have characterized as varying in their acceptance by academic readers.

- *Alternative methodologies*, which entail experimenting with methods and ways of thinking outside one's disciplinary tradition.

- *Alternative media* (email, hypertext, blogs, digitized text and images, video), which we recognize as having the potential to change utterly the way "academic writing" gets written and read.

We recognize that these categories overlap and encompass each other in many complicated and interesting ways and also that other scholars might configure them differently depending upon their research interests and political agendas. If we try to categorize the literature on alternative discourse according to this taxonomy, for example, we can quickly see how many categories a particular piece of writing might fill depending upon the writers' motives, the effects they want to achieve, and their sense of the stakes involved in writing alternatively.

Thus far in this chapter we've attempted to define "academic writing" as broadly as possible in order to suggest that the term is not so narrow as is often theorized in the literature. Similarly, we've explored a taxonomy of alternative models that given readers might or might not accept as legitimate options within their conceptions of "academic writing." We and our informants have much more to say about these alternatives in the following chapters.

We have not included in our taxonomy of alternatives to academic writing thus far an alternative strategy that is almost never accepted as "academic writing": when an academic chooses to write about his or her disciplinary specialty for a nonacademic audience. This alternative is definitely not academic writing because the decisions that writers make for the nonacademic reader typically run counter to the overt complexity and the impersonality demanded by the academy. While it is sometimes possible for a single work to appeal to both the academic and the popular audiences, the distinctions are often so basic that these occurrences are rare. In the next chapter on our faculty's professional writing, we discuss informants who do this kind of writing even though they recognize that such work risks not being taken seriously; nevertheless, they consider it important for political advocacy and community education. Further, as we will discuss in Chapter Three, many of our informants, even those who do not do this kind of writing themselves, give undergraduates assignments that require them to connect what they are learning in the major with their own experiences and/or topics in the popular media and to write about these for audiences outside of the academy.

Disciplines, Genres, and Research on Alternative Discourses and the Academy

We can't proceed to the description and analysis of our research findings without first defining other key terms and summarizing the research that has led us to our particular takes on them. Therefore, in this section, we probe the key concepts "discipline," "genre," and "alternative discourse." By way of clarifying these terms, we look at three research areas—writing in the disciplines (WID), feminist theory and critical pedagogy, and contrastive rhetoric. Our review of work in these areas also illuminates the theoretical bases of our own study.

Discipline

We'll begin with a discussion of the term "discipline", which, in WID research, is most often used as synonymous with "such fluctuating administrative expediencies" as "the departments" or "the majors" (Thaiss, "Theory" 314). Hence, most WID studies give names such as "history," "chemical engineering," and "landscape architecture" to the rhetorical setting for the research. As we will show, and as Chris and others have argued, disciplines are much more fluid and elusive than the programmatic names suggest. So too are academic genres, which arise from the shared aims of disciplinary discourse communities, but which also give rise to and shape those communities.

We find Stephen Toulmin's definition and discussion of disciplines in *Human Understanding* useful in understanding this fluidity and also why some disciplines seem more open and dynamic than others. Toulmin describes disciplines as "operative niches" (28) made up of sets of concepts, within which standards for rational thought are determined. A discipline, he states, can be summarized as follows:

> A collective human enterprise takes the form of a rationally developing "discipline," in those cases where men's shared commitment to a sufficiently agreed set of ideals leads to the development of an isolable and self-defining repertory of procedures; and where those procedures are open to further modification, so as to deal with problems arising from the incomplete fulfillment of those disciplinary ideals. (359)

Depending upon the level of consensus about intellectual goals, Toulmin says, some disciplines might be called "compact," there being a high level of agreement about the processes of intellectual inquiry; others "diffuse" with concepts still evolving, and others "quasi," with unity and coherence preserved across ever changing techniques (396). Toulmin goes into much greater depth about the characteristics of disciplines, including those enterprises he calls "non-disciplinable" because it is not possible or desirable to "isolate certain classes of issues" for specialized study (405). In our work, however, we are most interested in his understanding of "compact" and "diffuse" disciplines, as we'll explain shortly.

Also useful to us is Toulmin's explanation of the role of factors beyond the discipline in influencing how a discipline is constructed as these pertain to the work our faculty informants are doing and their perceptions of disciplinary standards and expectations. Toulmin argues that, in addition to the activities that characterize a discipline, we must also look at the "ecological relationships" that govern the enterprise; that is, the wider interactions that affect how and why ideas, procedures, and techniques evolve (360–61). While disciplines may share fundamental concepts, methods, and aims, they are not immutable, he says. "Intellectual novelties" are always being introduced, and, given the conditions to prove their advantages, the degree to which they are taken seriously and integrated into disciplinary processes is "balanced against a process of critical selection," which considers not only the merits of the novelty but how well it meets the "specific 'demands' of the 'local intellectual environment.'" It is this critical selection process that accounts for the relative stability or transformation of disciplines (139–41).

What Toulmin's discussion of disciplines shows, we believe, is that research on academic writing practices and products should not be bound up in rigid conceptions of disciplines nor should disciplines be viewed as synonymous with traditional departmental structures or majors. In our research, for example, when we asked informants to describe their disciplines and standard writing within that discipline, as we will discuss more fully in Chapter Two, they could easily name their discipline, but, depending upon the "compact," "diffuse," or "quasi" status of their discipline—to use Toulmin's terms—their responses either correlated or did not with the name of the department in which their discipline lodges. Similarly, their descriptions of the standard writing for their disciplines fell into a Toulmin-like continuum, with informants from diffuse or quasi disciplines using general terms like "logical arguments" while those from compact disciplines named generic templates like the experimental report as standards for the academic writing they produce and assign to their students.

Research on workplace writing, which is based on multiple contextual factors rather than on professional categories such as engineering or law (see, for example, Odell and Goswami; Bazerman *Shaping*; Dias, Freedman, Medway, Pare), can also be helpful in understanding the term "discipline," as Chris Thaiss suggests in "Theory in WAC: Where Have We Been, Where Are We Going?" (315). This is the opening move that Anson makes in his 1988 review of over 300 WAC/WID-focused studies, "Toward a Multidimensional Model of Writing in the Academic Disciplines," which begins the *Writing in the Academic Disciplines* collection, edited by David Jolliffe. The distinction "academic" and "nonacademic," on which much of our research relies, Anson argues, glosses over the social and organizational contexts that influence writers and writing practices. In both professional and academic communities, writers' goals, the characteristics of their texts, and their instructional practices[1] stem from a wide array of variables that makes strict identification of both genres and disciplines difficult, if not impossible. These variables

---

[1] Anson's review of studies of teacher attitudes and ideological positions related to their instructional practices correlates to our findings, as we explain in Chapter Three. According to Anson, these studies suggest that teachers work from tacit, generalized beliefs about the nature of academic writing, and that, while they may have thought about their own writing processes, they tend to hold "monolithic conceptions" of writing, reflecting "highly subjective elements as well as more objective, shared characteristics that define their field" (17). Similarly, the writing tasks teachers assign are influenced by their knowledge of the discipline, their curricular agendas, institutional mandates, sociopolitical movements, and their attitudes and responses to all the foregoing. The ways students understand and carry out these writing tasks are likewise influenced by a complex array of variables, including prior knowledge and experience, sociopolitical, cultural, and ideological views, beliefs about writing, and career goals (Anson 17–24). (For a very good overview of the research on students' acquisition of disciplinary conventions, see David Russell's "Where Do the Naturalistic Studies of WAC/WID Point? A Research Review.")

include, for example, writers' knowledge of the discipline, their political and institutional position within the discipline, and their attitudes towards their position, the institution, their colleagues, and their readers (7–10). Anson's "multidimensional model" is useful for explaining not only the "contextual relativity" of academic writing—what Toulmin calls the "ecological relationships"—that account for the stability or fluidity of disciplinary structures, but also its disciplinary forms or genres.

Genre

An ecological or contextual understanding of disciplines and disciplinary writing is integrally related to the concept of *genre* as "social action," the substances and forms—to use Carolyn Miller's words—that comprise academic discourse and, in turn, relay the shared values of the discourse community. As we will discuss, genre is yet another term that resists a fixed definition. While genres are described in many composition textbooks as static forms (such as "term paper" or "lab report" or "critical analysis") inscribing (and prescribing) the work of a discipline, most current literature understands genre as "social action," arising from social motives and contexts, but also shaping motives and contexts as they are reproduced by communities sharing common communicative purposes (Miller 1984; Swales; Bazerman 1988; Pare and Smart 1994; Devitt 2004[2]). Miller's "Genre as Social Action" has offered one of the most important formulations of this view. Miller argues that genres are "typified rhetorical actions based in recurrent situations" (159). At the "core" of situation is "exigence," a "set of particular social patterns and expectations" that translate into motive and provide "a socially recognizable and interpretable way" to enact one's intentions (158). Motive, then, becomes "a conventionalized social purpose, or exigence, within the recurrent situation." It is for this reason, Miller says, that certain "recurring situations seem to 'invite' discourse of a particular type" (162). While a community establishes discourses so that individuals can "act together," discourses also shape the community by establishing that there are shared motives and naming what these might be. As Miller argues, when we learn genre, we are learning more

---

[2] In *Writing Genres*, Amy Devitt notes the "circularity" problem that arises when genre is equated with form: "A genre is named because of its formal markers; the formal markers can be identified because a genre has been named" (10). In Devitt's theory of genre, genre may be "visible in classification and form" but always exists as "a nexus between an individual's actions and a socially defined context" (31). She offers six principles to guide an analysis of genres in social settings, which attempt to capture the complexity of the work. There is not space to summarize them here (33–65).

than "a pattern of forms or even a method of achieving our own ends. We learn, more importantly, what ends we may have" (165).

An excellent example of how conflict in exigence produces very different conceptions of genre is presented in a study by David Russell and Arturo Yanez, who use activity theory in their analysis of writing in an introductory history course to explain why the teacher and the students may have differing conceptions of what constitutes successful writing. The students in the general education course were unwilling to produce the genres the "specialist teacher" had assigned; they were not interested in becoming historians so did not see why they should be asked to write what they perceived to be a history discourse. The history teacher, on the other hand, was unaware that he was working within a deeply embedded, highly professionalized "genre system"—history writing; rather he believed that his assignments would elicit generalized critical thinking practices that would serve the students well no matter what their course of study. (In an earlier article "Rethinking Genre in School and Society: An Activity Theory Analysis," Russell lays out the potential of activity theory for understanding the dynamic and multilayered contexts around genre formation.)

A much broader application of genre as social action is that presented in the comparative studies of academic and workplace writing captured in *Worlds Apart: Acting and Writing in Academic and Workplace' Contexts* by Patrick Dias, Aviva Freedman, Peter Medway, and Anthony Paré. These writers hypothesize that the differences in motive between student and workplace writing are so basic as to invalidate the assumption that most academic writing is preparation for writing in the workplace. Student genres are characterized by two social motives: first, faculty intend for student assignments to be "epistemic," in that they should enable writers "to take on stances toward and interpretations of realities valorized in specific disciplines"; at the same time, this epistemic motive is constrained by the fact that students are being "sorted and ranked" according to their ability to produce these genres (44). Two very different exigencies, then, might motivate the same piece of writing. These academic motives, Dias et al argue, are nowhere present in the writing of workplace professionals, whose writing is motivated by practical needs of the organization and so is evaluated on its effects, not on its conformity to pre-established criteria.

Even as genres proliferate through differences in exigency, they are stabilized through the power of discourse communities, John Swales argues in *Genre Analysis.* Swales defines discourse communities as "sociorhetorical networks that form in order to work towards common sets of goals." Members of discourse communities can be characterized by their familiarity with the genres used to further those goals, by their ability to "process" the genres (encode and decode), and their range of experience with appropriate processing tasks (9–10). "Genres belong to discourse communities, not to individuals," Swales argues. While in his conception of genre, this point seems apparent, it is one Miller did not pursue in "Genre as Social Action" but now finds particularly persuasive when she returns to the topic in "Rhetorical Community: The Cultural Basis of Genre." Though not as influential as her earlier essay, we include Miller's reconsideration of genre and community because of its significance to discussions of alternative discourses.

Miller's later essay, which appears in *Genre and the New Rhetoric*, takes up the concerns of other contributors to that volume; that is, genres—because they are socially and culturally determined—must be "tied to an analysis of power" and taught as "culturally contingent" forms (x). Miller acknowledges that her original view of genre fails to take into account the powerful role of institutions in the reproduction of genres, the same concern expressed by those who theorize that alternative discourses can be used to resist these hegemonic discursive structures. Institutions are powerful, Miller says, because they systematically direct our individual memories and perceptions while hiding their influence. As individuals (actors), we rely on known structures to interpret the situations in which we find ourselves. In turn, institutions, though they do not have "minds of their own," instantiate and reproduce these structures, meaning that we—the social actors—by our recurring actions, reproduce the structures of the institution (71). Though rhetorical communities may be structured by institutions, Miller argues in her conclusion, they are not to be characterized by "comfortable agreement or a dominating majority." Rather, because they are made up of different members, they are "fundamentally heterogeneous and contentious" (74).

Yet, as Charles Bazerman points out in "From Cultural Criticism to Disciplinary Participation: Living with Powerful Words," the fluidity of disciplines, disciplinary communities, and their representative genres does not mean that they are not also always responsive to "the powerful but nonetheless fluidly interpreted and reconstituted social facts of disciplinary institutionalization and control" (63). The many qualifications in Bazerman's phrase imply the constant tension between definition and fluidity, the institution and its component groups, that makes it so difficult to determine at any moment just where power lies and to predict change.

Research on Alternative Discourses and the Academy

In our discussion so far, we've shown that academic genres, like disciplinary discourse communities and disciplines themselves, evolve and change in response to a complex range of variables, including the motives underlying their production, the contexts in which they are produced, and the institutional and ideological agendas that help to shape both motive and context. As we've also discussed, however, institutional and ideological agendas are similarly responsive to competing social, cultural, political, and economic interests, albeit not without struggle. This brings us back to a question we think is central to discussions of alternative discourses and the academy: How does this dynamic of disciplines occur in practice? How does it affect how teachers teach and students learn?

In her preface to *ALT DIS: Alternative Discourses and the Academy*, Bizzell tries to answer this question. She is optimistic about the potential for "hybrid forms" (a fraught term, she recognizes)—to the extent that they accomplish valued intellectual work—to blend with other discourses "to produce new forms with their own organic integrity" (ix). In another piece in the collection, however, Bizzell rethinks her optimistic position: "Valuable intellectual work for whom?" she asks. This is the hot-button political question that drives most conversations about alternative discourses and to which so many of the alternative voices are responding. In this section, we'll discuss responses to this question by those who have claimed various stakes in the debate (a debate that many date from the publication of "Students' Right to Their Own Language"). The complications, however, really begin with the meaning of the term "alternative discourse" itself. Not only, as we will show, is the meaning contested by those who have a significant stake in the debate by virtue of their scholarly identities and subject positions, but also by those, like us, whose work focuses on the multiplicities inherent in writing in the disciplines.

For us, as WID scholar-practitioners, one way to define "alternative" is in opposition to a standard discourse that is clearly recognized and articulated by participants in the discipline, a point we explore in our article "Questioning Alternative Discourses: Reports from Across the Disciplines." However, "alternative" can also be synonymous with "variant," merely different options without a clear sense of a dominant one. When we talk about alternative discourses, then, we need not be talking about oppositions or resistance. So, for example, those disciplines that in Toulmin's formulation are less "compact" would entertain many alternatives. To illustrate, one of our informants, who defines herself as a political scientist, stated that she could identify 40 branches of the field, each with its own journals and discursive and methodological expectations.

Moreover, alternative forms and styles, we suggested based on our research with faculty informants, often grow organically out of the research agenda scholars set and their sense of the best way to present the findings to the audience they envision. Among our informants were faculty who were confident that their disciplines would accommodate their interests and methods although these were not necessarily in the mainstream as they saw it. Others, conversely, had a sense that the work they were doing or wanted to do would be resisted by those whom they considered more conventional. For example, an informant from nursing felt she was not able to explain the phenomenon of nurses' "intuition" using traditional quantitative methodology. Resistance to traditional methods and discourses, we argue, may not need to be overt or dramatic to help effect change, as we will discuss in Chapter Two in regard to faculty's definitions of writing "standards" in their fields.

There isn't room in this chapter to discuss all the important work that has been done on alternative discourses. Here we describe three general categories into which the literature can be organized along with a brief review of some of the better-known scholars/scholarship in each area.

The "Alternative" as Resistance to Stable Convention

As we have noted early in the chapter, these kinds of alternative discourses might be characterized by their use of autobiographical details, personal stories, unconventional syntaxes, and other unconventional ways of making arguments. Typically the writers are motivated by a need to make visible the identities and ways of knowing that, they argue, have been silenced by traditional academic discourses. Their texts argue that dominant discourses can be changed, or at least resisted, when different voices are allowed to speak and to be heard.[3] As we also noted, among the most notable voices in this argument have been feminist and African-American scholars, whose activism emerged from the liberatory movements of the 1960s and '70s. They have since been joined in their concerns by those professing critical/cultural pedagogies and those interested in the study of contrastive rhetorics.

Feminist and Cultural Theory

In their early efforts to find common ground as women writing in the academy, many feminists argued that women share particularly feminine ways of knowing—whether biologically or socially constructed—and should not have to "write like men" in order to be heard in a patriarchal academy (see

---

[3] An example of the recognition by a discipline of deliberately alternative work is provided by the February 1992 special issue of *College Composition and Communication—In Focus: Personal and Innovative Writing*—which was devoted to essays and articles that editor Richard Gebhardt hoped would help redefine "'acceptable forms of academic publication'" in composition studies (9). Gebhardt was responding to criticism of the journal for being "restrictive" in its editorial choices.

Elizabeth Flynn's "Composing as a Woman," for example). Gesa Kirsch pursued these ideas in *Women Writing the Academy*. Interviewing academic women from different disciplines and professional ranks, she concluded that disciplinary boundaries need to be "redefined" to make room for writers—both women and men—who want to write in nonmainstream or interdisciplinary forms (134). During this same period of time—the 1980s and early '90s—feminists in a range of disciplines were arguing for alternative research methodologies and ways of presenting their work (see Sandra Harding, Lorraine Code, and Patricia Williams, for example).[4] Others experimented with presenting their arguments in a gendered style (see Tompkins; Zawacki "Recomposing"; and Bridwell-Bowles, for example).

It was difficult, however, for feminists to get around the "essentialist" problem, i.e., the assumption that women all write their gender in the same ways. In fact, disagreements appeared early on with many feminists making the case for argument (Lamb, Jarratt, Worsham) and other feminists—lesbians, women of color—claiming alternative textual orientations (Anzaldua, hooks, Rich, Royster "A View"). By the mid-'90s, the focus for most feminists had shifted to an examination of the processes by which the subject position "woman" is constituted; this kind of analysis still entailed, for many, the inclusion of the first-hand accounts as a way to establish a politics of location (Brodkey "Writing on the Bias"; Lu "Reading and Writing Differences"; Zawacki "Telling"; Hindman; Fleckenstein; see also Kirsch and Ritchie for a discussion of the term "politics of location").

Writers and teachers of different races, ethnicities, and economic classes overlap with feminists in their arguments for the inclusion of the autobiographical as a way to locate themselves in relationship to dominant discourses. Whether purposely constructing alternative discourses from what they perceive to be the margins of a discipline or writing in a more conventional academic manner, they question the connection between identity and genre. Among composition scholars Mike Rose, Victor Villanueva, Keith Gilyard, Jackie Jones Royster, Barbara Mellix, Min-zhan Lu, and Malea Powell come most prominently to mind. In first-hand accounts, many of these writers describe their uneasy positions as outsiders who have had to negotiate the languages and ways of thinking in their home cultures with those of the academy. Often, as Gilyard's and Mellix's narratives vividly show, they have felt a profound sense of loss on their way to acquiring mainstream discourses. (For

---

[4] These arguments continue to be persuasive to feminists. Witness the theme of the 2001 Third Biennial International Feminism(s) and Rhetoric(s) Conference—"Feminist Literacies: Resisting Disciplines."

related discussions, see essays in *Negotiating Academic Literacies: Teaching and Learning Across Languages* and *Cultures; Genre and Writing: Issues, Arguments, Alternatives;* and *ALT DIS: Alternative Discourses and the Academy.*)

That disciplinary discourses are definable and entrenched and, furthermore, must be challenged, dismantled, or transformed is taken as a given in most of the feminist and cultural work on alternative discourses; indeed, several essays from this perspective explicitly criticize WID and WAC (writing across the curriculum) pedagogy for instantiating traditional, exclusionary disciplinary discourses. Victor Villanueva's essay in *WAC for the New Millennium,* for example, criticizes the "assimilationist" politics of WAC, which he sees as "more repressive than mere accommodation" (166). Donna LeCourt's frequently cited essay "WAC as Critical Pedagogy" also criticizes WAC for silencing alternative literacies and advocates resistance. Similar to LeCourt, Harriet Malinowitz, in "A Feminist Critique of Writing in the Disciplines," calls on WAC to join with other critical pedagogies (such as women's studies) to "dismantle existing systems of knowledge production" if it is serious about the claims made by many scholar-practitioners that WAC plays a subversive role in exposing assumptions about writing in the disciplines (293).

Contrastive Rhetorics and Alternative Syntaxes

The field of contrastive rhetoric originated out of the attempt to describe how different cultures conceived of the aims of discourse and created rhetorical structures to enact them. In recent years, some contrastive rhetoricians, emphasizing the relationship between culture and ways of thinking and writing, have taken up the argument of alternative as resistance. Unlike the alternatives we've been discussing, the differences that emerge in nonnative English speakers' writing are not purposely enacted. Rather they grow out of assumptions about what constitutes good writing in their home cultures. Often, in fact, their assumptions are at odds with the alternatives employed by those speaking out of race and gender positions. Writing about themselves, for example, may be anathema to many students coming from cultures where the emphasis is on the group rather than the individual. Because many nonnative students come from homogeneous cultures, they may have incorporated a "reader-responsible" style that relies on a shared understanding of the proper way to make an argument. Their arguments, then, in their indirection may look very different from the explicit "writer-responsible" style prevalent in western discourse (Hinds). Nonnative students' ideas about critical thinking and the concept of originality may also be quite different (Fox *Listening*, Pennycook, Johns "ESL Students"). Some non-native scholars have explored these kinds of cultural disconnects by writing about their own experiences with literacy in the U.S. educational system (see Lu, for example).

The recent collection *ALT DIS: Alternative Discourses and the Academy* presents a range of perspectives that unite in calling for a broadening of standards and conventions in acceptable academic discourse in the United States. For example, coeditor Helen Fox, whose book *Listening to the World* is perhaps the best-known statement from this perspective, bases her argument in the essay "Being an Ally" on broadening what she regards as the U.S. university's "powerful, but at the same time, extremely narrow concept of thinking and communicating" (64). Other essays explore specific traditions in detail and question their relationship with what their authors see as the dominant discourse in the academy. For example, Malea Powell explores her own path as a Native American in the academy, and sees the connections and disjunctions between alternatives and academic discourse by juxtaposing images from native and academic cultures. Emphasizing syntax rather than rhetorical forms, Peter Elbow draws an important distinction between what he sees as a "recent rhetorical flowering" of alternative options for academic writers and "the virulent stigmatization of dialects that attaches more to grammar and syntax than it does to rhetoric." He offers to teachers a range of techniques for "inviting" students to try out their "home dialects" in school assignments, with suitable caveats, and shows how the process of drafting, revision, and editing can be adapted to help students translate, if they wish, or if the teacher requires that a final draft be in Standard Written English.

Among the earlier essays Elbow cites is Lisa Delpit's "The Silenced Dialogue: Power and Pedagogy in Educating Other People's Children," which caused controversy when it appeared in 1988, as it ran counter to the prevailing arguments of advocates for educational methods that would present and sanction a wider array of voices. Taking to task such "well-intentioned White liberal" innovations as "dialect readers" in classrooms, Delpit, author of the 1986 essay "Skills and other Dilemmas of a Progressive Black Educator," argued strongly for direct teaching of the "linguistic aspects of the culture of power" (571). Though not by any means advocating resistance to "the rules," the essay shares with the "alternative as resistance" literature an unquestioning sense of a discursive split between those "within" and those "outside" the power structure.

"Alternatives" as Options in a Fluid Mix of Disciplines and Genres

Other scholars wonder, however, just how resistant to change the academy and individual fields of interest might be. If disciplines are as hard to define as the research posits, and if genre is being constantly reinvented as exigencies change, then how do we most productively regard the roles that new and different voices—the categories of our taxonomy—might play in a changing landscape? *ALT DIS: Alternative Discourses in the Academy* also includes several articles that address this issue. For example, in her essay, coeditor Patricia Bizzell notes that "'Alternative' invokes a sort of countercultural image"; she suggests that the term "mixed" or "hybrid" might better convey what is alternative about the discourse, i.e., that it is a blend of "stylistic, cultural, and cognitive elements" and/or of traditional and nontraditional forms (ix). Jackie Jones Royster places the emphasis on "alternative *assumptions*" about discourses held by "the *people* who shape the discourses, use them, monitor them, and enforce their values. . ." (26). While these arguments over terminology are interesting, we find particularly useful the definition Paul Kei Matsuda gives in his concluding synthesis to the *ALT DIS* collection. Alternative discourse, he says, is "a marked form of discourse use within a particular site of discourse practices and in a certain sociohistoric context" (192).

To us, this definition acknowledges the existence of, and perhaps struggle among, different voices, patterns of arrangement, language standards, etc., in any given rhetorical situation, academic or otherwise. But it also acknowledges the fluidity of the scene and the many factors that research has shown make definitions of "discipline," "academic writing" and "genre" so difficult.

Our current research, then, takes place amid this ongoing debate. We wanted to find out how faculty defined "academic writing" in the disciplines and whether they sensed any of the tensions around disciplinary "standards" and "alternatives" as we've described these in our review of the literature. We also wanted to learn how they interpreted academic writing in their assignments and responses to student writers/writing. Similarly, we wanted to know how students interpreted their teachers' expectations and whether these interpretations might be in conflict with their own goals for college writing. The following chapters describe, interpret, and apply our findings.

Our Methods and Materials

Our research sources include the following:

- Interviews, each lasting approximately an hour and a half, with faculty from 14 different disciplines, all successful writers and teachers. Our questions fell into three clusters:

  1. How do the informants define "standard" writing in their disciplines and what do they perceive as "alternatives" to that discourse?

2. Have our informants sometimes written in alternative forms? If so, how and why? If not, why not?

3. What writing assignments do our informants give to students, and to what extent are those assignments intended to teach the standards and conventions of the discipline? Do our informants give assignments asking for alternative ways of thinking and writing about the discipline? How open are they to students' writing in alternative ways to the assignments they give?

- A survey of 20 short questions about writing in the disciplines administered to 183 students enrolled in nine different sections of a required upper-division advanced writing course. These sections vary according to the designations "Natural and Technological Sciences," "Business," "Social Sciences," and "Humanities," giving us a representative sampling of majors (40 in all) across the university;

- Six student focus groups and one individual interview, consisting of a total of 36 students from a variety of majors, in order to deepen and clarify survey results;

- Assessment data from 12 departmental/college workshops in which faculty evaluated the writing competence of their upper division students based on papers from writing-intensive courses. Faculty derived evaluation criteria through a holistic scoring process.

- Timed (2-hour) essays by 40 undergraduate students from 22 majors, written as the final part of a credit-by-proficiency process by which self-selected students apply for exemption from a required advanced writing in the disciplines course.

Though we have limited our research to only one site, that being our own institution, we intend to create a kind of multidimensional model of academic writing—albeit partial—that takes into account the motives of writers working within a local institutional context (see Anson "Multidimensional"). We are well aware of other limitations of this kind of qualitative research, one being that researchers are always implicated in their research findings, possibly even more so when working at their own institutions and bringing—as we do—their own prior experiences and subjective understandings of the institutional culture to the scene of their research. That said, we would also argue that one of the givens of qualitative research is that the whole process is unavoidably subjective, from the design of survey and interview questions to the construction of meaning from the data that "emerges," including the analytical categories for coding that data, which are themselves derived from prior knowledge and experience. (For a good discussion of coding, see Grant-Davie's "Coding Data: Issues of Validity, Reliability, and Interpretation.")

Another given is that conversation as a research tool—whether interviews or focus groups—is necessarily dynamic and "intersubjective" (Mortensen). Participants in focus groups, for example, are always responding not only to the researcher's questions but also to one another's contributions as well; in the process, they are continuously expanding their subjective understandings of both their past experiences and their present experience of the conversation at hand. Similarly, interviewees expand their understandings as the questions lead them from one topic to another. Add to this dynamic the informants' goals for participation, their orientations toward the researchers and the research topic, their individual frames of reference, and the shifts that occur in these frames as the conversation proceeds. Another aspect of the intersubjectivity of our process, of course, is our collaboration itself. Each of us participated in all aspects of the research. In particular, in regard to the dynamics of interviews and focus groups, we didn't so much take turns asking questions as observe the flow of questions and answers and jumped in as inspired, making observations from our experience that seemed to bear on what the informant was saying and inviting the informants' responses to these as well.

To explain how these dynamics might affect what gets said in the conversation, we'll turn to our own student focus groups for an example. The students who participated in our focus groups were self-selected; they came from sections of a required advanced writing in the disciplines course in response to our request for volunteers. (For the informed consent forms, see Figure 4–2 in Chapter Four.) Out of the 300 or so students who heard the request for volunteers, only 36 responded. Why these 36? What were their goals and motives for participating? Were they in any way representative of our overall student body? Were they generally good writers? Did they have generally good relationships with teachers? We could go on with this line of questioning, but the point is that we didn't ask these questions in the focus groups, nor did we think it was necessary to do so given that our purpose in conducting focus groups was to deepen our understanding of the survey data we'd already gathered.

Thus, while we are assuming certain ethnographic limitations, we nevertheless believe that we can make claims about the contexts in which we conducted the investigation. In turn, we believe readers will find these claims relevant to understanding the contexts in which they work. We want to turn to a more detailed explanation of our research processes, including a description of our institution—the local context—our faculty informants, the assessment workshops, our survey instrument and the proficiency exam, and the makeup of the student focus groups.

George Mason University

George Mason is located in Fairfax, Virginia, in the fastest-growing, most diverse, and affluent part of the state, the burgeoning suburbs of Washington, D.C. GMU itself is one of the most culturally and linguistically diverse universities in the country, with more than 25 percent of students nonnative speakers of English, a rich mix from around the globe (more than 100 language backgrounds represented). Growth and diversity have always been the main facts of life at GMU and, in fact, were the catalyst for WAC. George Mason teaches 29,000 students (two-thirds undergraduates), offers 60 bachelor's degrees, 62 master's degrees, 16 doctoral degrees, and one professional degree in law. It is a Carnegie Research II institution.

Faculty Informants

We interviewed 14 faculty members from a diverse array of disciplines, though only one is from a preprofessional field. We decided from the outset that we wanted to talk with faculty from across the disciplines whom we knew to be successful writers in their fields as well as teachers committed to student writers and writing. We gave priority to experienced writers who had achieved the scholarly success of tenure at the university, knowing that they had made decisions about their work based on expectations for tenuring in a research university, although two were tenure-line at the time of our interview (one has since achieved tenure). We determined their commitment to student writing based on our encounters with them in workshops, in various WAC projects, and in informal conversation. We'd known many of these faculty for years and relished the opportunity to talk to them systematically about their writing and teaching.

Our choice of faculty was motivated by several other factors as well. We knew that some were doing work that might be characterized as alternative, as we explained earlier. We wanted to know how aware they were of arguments about writing to resist or writing on the margins. We wondered, too, how they had developed their ideas of what was standard and alternative in their fields. We also wanted to be able to apply our findings to course design and to our work with faculty, so we were interested in talking with faculty who had taught writing-intensive or writing-infused classes. As we noted, we do not intend for these faculty to be taken as spokespersons for their disciplines although, as we will show, each could easily note either a formal center of their discipline in terms of ways of thinking, standards of evidence, and format, or a clear range of acceptable styles.

All the faculty we selected agreed to be informants for our research, and only one asked that we not tape-record his interview. We conducted all the interviews together, beginning with the same list of open-ended questions we have described earlier. We each took careful notes during the interview, and, after each interview, we wrote up and compared our notes, reviewed the tapes, adding and clarifying points, and then each of us coded our notes according to themes we saw developing. Although we have read pieces by almost all our faculty informants, we have not done a systematic analysis of their writing as part of this research for two reasons; one, we are primarily interested in their perspectives on their work overall and on the nature of writing in their chosen fields, and two, we felt that our interpretation of their writing might get in the way of a clear presentation of their perspectives.

We interviewed:

Debra Bergoffen, professor of philosophy; author of *The Philosophy of Simone de Beauvoir: Gendered Phenomenologies, Erotic Generosities*

Keith Clark, associate professor of English and African-American studies; author of *Black Manhood in James Baldwin, Ernest J. Gaines, and August Wilson.* Also edits *Contemporary Black Men's Fiction and Drama*

Dina Copleman, associate professor of history; author of studies of 19th- and 20th-century London life

R. Christian Jones, professor of environmental sciences; author of numerous studies of wetlands ecology

Roger Lancaster, professor of anthropology; author of *Thanks to God and the Revolution* and *Life Is Hard*, his study of life in Nicaragua during the Sandinista regime, and, most recently, *The Trouble with Nature: Sex in Science and Popular Culture*

Linda Miller, professor and department chair of dance; choreographer and writer about dance although now her writing is predominantly administrative

Victoria Rader, associate professor of sociology; author of *Signal Through the Flames*, her study of the homeless advocacy of Mitch Snyder

Priscilla Regan, associate professor of political science; author of *Legislating Privacy*, on federal debates regarding privacy vs. freedom of information and the new technologies

Lesley Smith, assistant professor, author of hypermedia

Robert Smith, professor and chair of psychology; author or coauthor of many articles and reports on the effects of substances on animals and humans

Jeanne Sorrell, professor of nursing and director of the Ph.D. in nursing; author of many articles on writing in the nursing profession; coproducer of videotapes on primary care

Daniele Struppa, associate professor of mathematical sciences and dean of the College of Arts and Sciences; author or coauthor of articles and books on differential equations; a nonnative speaker of English, his first language is Italian

James Trefil, professor of physics and Robinson Professor of Interdisciplinary Studies; contributing writer to *Smithsonian Magazine*, and author or coauthor of popular books on science, typically reviewed in the *New York Times*

Walter Williams, professor of economics; author of numerous articles in economics and also a syndicated columnist

Student Survey Instrument

Since we were relying on the good graces of our composition colleagues to administer the survey in their advanced writing classes, we attempted to develop a survey that would take no more than 15 minutes to answer and that would make sense to students at the same time that it was specific enough to yield useful information about their perceptions of assigned writing in their major courses. The survey consisted of 20 short answer and Likert Scale questions, including four questions asking the student's major, number of courses he or she had taken in the major, a particular area of interest or concentration within the major, and whether English is a first language. The remainder of the questions focused on students' awareness of the characteristics of good writing in their majors, how they had learned those characteristics, the kinds of writing tasks they'd been assigned in their major, whether they were given what they perceived to be atypical assignments, and the degree to which they perceived their teachers to be strict on conventions or accepting of alternatives. (For the full survey, see Figure 4-1 on pages 97–98.) Although we received 183 responses to our survey from students in 40 different majors, we quickly saw the gaps and ambiguities in many of our questions when we began collating the results.

Student Focus Groups

We decided to conduct focus groups as a way to help clarify and deepen our understanding of the survey results. As we've mentioned, only 36 students, of the approximately 300 who were invited, volunteered to participate in our focus groups. We consulted about our procedures with our Director of Institutional Assessment, who told us that such a small yield is not unusual. Even when students are offered incentives for participating (like the free lunch we provided), those who volunteer tend to be the more engaged and committed learners. We conducted six different focus groups (and one individual interview) to accommodate these students' schedules. Each group consisted of a variety of majors with a total of 12 different majors represented. Because each focus group yielded somewhat similar information, albeit with a few surprises, we feel confident that we would have received much of the same data had we been able to include more students and/or a more diverse group of students. While we had asked the participants to fill out a form listing their major, number of courses taken in the major, and total number of credits, we did not ask for other kinds of demographic information, such as GPA, preferred learning styles, or aspects of their personal identities, for example. We did not necessarily need such information—though it might have been interesting—nor did we want to seem intrusive. We can say, however, that, apart from their varied majors, our participants do not reflect the diversity of our student body: 11 were females, four were of non-Anglo race/ethnicities (Chinese, Iranian, Latina, African American), and only one was a nonnative speaker. Our institution, on the other hand, has a much higher proportion of non-Anglo/nonnative students and is over 50 percent female.

Essays Written for Course Exemption

Another source of data, described in more detail in Chapter Four, derives from timed (2-hour) essays written by upper-division students seeking exemption from a required writing-in-the-disciplines course—English 302. From a pool of approximately 60 essays responding to questions about the papers in the accompanying portfolio and what the writer had learned about writing in the major, we selected 40 essays by students from 22 majors.

Criteria from Departmental Assessment Workshops and Faculty Surveys

Over the same time period that we were interviewing faculty and surveying students, the university Writing Assessment Group, of which we are a part, was also engaged in a departmentally based assessment of students' writing competence in response to a state mandate. A full description of this process along with some of the departmental results, is available on the George Mason University WAC website at: http://wac.gmu. edu/program/assessing/phase4.html. While these workshops were not part of our research design, they've given us valuable insights into faculty expectations for students' writing in the upper-division courses in their majors. Prior to conducting the departmental workshops, the assessment group distributed a university-wide survey to determine what faculty viewed as the most important writing skills for students to acquire in their disciplines, the kinds of assignments they gave related to these skills, their perceptions of the students' proficiency in these skills, and strategies they use to teach with writing in their courses. We will be referring to some of the criteria that faculty derived in these workshops in Chapters Three and Five.

Chapter Two

Faculty Talk About Their Writing, Disciplines, and Alternatives

When I was at UVA the best I could hope was that nobody would hold my Smithsonian *writing against me, that they'd say 'Oh, he's still doing regular physics, so this popular writing is no worse a hobby than building furniture in his basement.'*

—JAMES TREFIL, PHYSICS

When we began our research with faculty in spring 2001, we wondered how readily our informants could answer questions about the conventions of and expectations for writing in their disciplines. Had they given explicit prior thought to the concept? Were they, as David Russell postulates, so imbued with the idea of the "transparency" (2002, 10) of writing in research fields that they did not recognize the rhetorical peculiarities of discourse in their own disciplines? We were in fact doubtful that scholars from outside rhetoric and composition, which studies such differences, would readily respond to our queries about "alternative discourses."

We need not have doubted. While certainly not all our informants could speak with equal facility about nuances of the discourses they used or that they felt were standard in their fields, none hesitated to answer our questions, and all spoke thoughtfully. Their comments about their own writing and writing in their fields revealed a fairly sophisticated level of rhetorical knowledge, particularly given that we were trying to keep the interviews manageable in terms of the informants' time and we had many topics to cover. To some extent, their rhetorical awareness may be the result of our selection process: all our informants (except one) have written with sufficient success in their fields to achieve tenure in a research university, and we chose several who have had writing success with popular as well as academic audiences. Moreover, many of our informants had taken part in WAC faculty development workshops and/or had written for our program newsletter, so we knew they had reflected on the characteristics of student writing and how to teach students to write in major courses, undergraduate and graduate.

We did not predict—but were not surprised—when their answers revealed significant differences among them in a range of categories:

- Sense of disciplines and of standards and expectations for writing in them
- Range of allowed alternatives for scholarly writing in their chosen fields
- Their own practice (and confidence) in writing "alternatively"
- Sense of objectives for student writing
- Assignments to students
- Responses to student writing
- How they deal with "alternative" writing from students

The differences in their responses were sometimes stark, but more often subtle; some responses they rationalized in terms of what they perceived to be disciplinary or academic norms, but many were based on their individual or local institutional situations—their own desires as writers or the shape of a program in which they taught. Their answers reveal tensions between perceived norms, what they want to write vs. what they actually write, and what they think students need to write.

In this chapter, we report the results of our research with faculty, focusing on the ways in which our faculty informants talked about the writing conventions and expectations in their chosen fields. We devote considerable space to their thoughts on the range of alternatives possible for scholar-writers, with special focus on several faculty who wrestle with their own places in the dynamic of changing expectations in their fields. Next we turn to those informants who—for different reasons and with varying emotions—have embarked on writing that they know falls outside academic conventions. We report their motives, experiences, speculations, and assessments.

Our presentation of findings is conditioned by the extended definitions of key terms—"academic writing," "alternative discourses," "disciplines," and "genres"—from Chapter One. For example, when we refer to "alternatives," we would expect the reader to keep in mind the taxonomy of alternatives offered in Chapter One as well as the distinction between "alternative" as "departure from a standard" and "alternative" as "one among several roughly equal options." Also instrumental is our discussion of the tension between reason and emotion/sensation in academic prose. Overall, our extended definitions and our review of several research traditions in the introductory chapter are intended to broaden the meanings of the terms and highlight areas of debate. We see the informant data, in this chapter and the ones that follow, as helping to clarify issues while also enriching the concepts.

We began our interviews by asking informants to define their disciplines and the "standards, conventions, and expectations" for writing in them. Our next group of questions concerned what the informants perceived as alternatives to those discourse standards and conventions.

Disciplinary Names

In Chapter One we put forward the idea of a "discipline" as dynamic and heavily nuanced; we suggested that departmental names, though often used in WAC research as synonymous with disciplines, are not sufficient to address the multiple contextual factors that scholarly writers face. We asked informants to name their disciplines in order to contextualize their comments about standards and the scope of the scholarly audience they were addressing. As we anticipated, their responses did not follow a predictable pattern.

Struppa (mathematics), R. Smith (psychology), Rader (sociology), Bergoffen (philosophy), Sorrell (nursing), Miller (dance), Williams (economics), Lancaster (anthropology), Regan (political science), and Copelman (history) consistently used the familiar names of these fields to identify the disciplinary framework of their comments.

But when some informants elaborated, more specific research fields emerged. For example, Struppa, although consistently identifying himself as a mathematician, repeatedly talked about writing in "my field," by which he meant differential equations. This distinction became crucial when he spoke about different styles and audiences in mathematical writing. Regan, although naming her discipline "political science," said she could identify 40 distinct branches of the field, each with its own journals and standards, and saw her own work as "technology studies," distinct, say, from "policy studies." Jones, who chairs a new department of environmental science, variously spoke of himself as an "ecologist," "biologist," and "scientist." L. Smith, with an M.F.A. in poetry, a Ph.D. in history, and a tenure-line appointment in an interdisciplinary degree program, initially named "history" as her dominant discipline, since "my training in history has taught me to contextualize all my ideas and make connections"; but as she spoke she reconsidered. "If I have to identify a discipline, I'd say it's 'writing,' because it's not only what I do, but also what I conceptualize about."

We could have added, even though she didn't say, that multimedia design may be her primary field, since this is what she does: she teaches such courses as "writing in multimedia" and "information in the digital age" and edits an online teaching journal. Clark was the only one of our informants who named a specific research field—literature and African American studies—rather than "English," his department, to define his discipline. Trefil was the only other exception in that he used a broader-than-departmental term to name his discipline. Though tenured as a physicist, he consistently spoke of himself as a "scientist."

Standards and Conventions

As happened when they named their disciplines, our informants initially responded to our questions about standards and conventions by describing expectations for writing in rather broad and imprecise terms. These terms tended to match the general features of academic writing we outlined in Chapter One. As informants elaborated on those expectations, however, especially in reference to their own writing, their responses became more nuanced and particular, reflecting, in many cases, distinctions between form/format and the way genre emerges based on exigence. And, as we will show in the next section on allowed alternatives, some interesting variations emerged.

In their initial responses, most of our informants easily identified standards for writing in their fields and ticked off a few general features— "clear," "logical," "reasoned and linear"—that roughly match the model we present in Chapter One. As L. Smith quipped, "You have to show off in the beginning that you've read the relevant literature, explain how you're different, and then it's just simply a matter of writing out your analysis bit by bit." The most precise among them, Struppa, provided in conversation what he called a "template" for the typical article in mathematics, "regardless of field":

> So you say, "As is well-known, this such and such a topic is interesting, so and so has said this and these other guys have worked on it, and these couple of questions remain open. In this paper, we try to apply this theory to solve this thing." This is almost a template. Then you go to definition one, say a couple of words, give an example, say some more words, go to the theorem. So language is really very, very minimal.

In his initial remarks, Lancaster gave an even more simple definition of the "typical ethnography" in anthropology: "seven to eight chapters, brief intro and conclusion, recognizable rubrics—kinship, etc." Jones made passing reference to the well-known arrangement of the experimental lab report: "methods, findings, and all that," and noted its stylistic features:

"terse, compact, lots of numbers, jargon—very technical." Sorrell's reference to the "early" paradigm for articles in nursing was judgmental, as well as descriptive—"deadly boring, no first person, template—methods, findings, favors experiments."

Other informants spoke to certain approaches or procedures, rather than formats or arrangements, that they considered standard. R. Smith several times noted "data-driven" as the generic motive in writing in psychology, regardless of specialty. Copelman, by way of contrasting standard history writing with a newer approach that we describe below, gave this explanation, "…at the heart of historical writing is the notion that you have a problem on the one hand and a question, something that you're testing and investigating, on the other hand, and you bring to it some evidence." Also in contrast to the work she is currently doing, Bergoffen noted that traditional philosophical writing makes "no appeal to emotion"; the emphasis is on logic—"this follows from that."

A few of our informants did not even attempt to find a single, dominant paradigm. Regan, whom we've already mentioned, is one. Miller stated that dance has no academic tradition of writing, and that her voluminous writing as a teacher, choreographer, and administrator was a constant effort to "adapt" dance to the written word for diverse audiences that had little knowledge of the field and that in some cases were hostile to it. Multimedia theoretician/teacher/designer L. Smith reacted to our questions about convention with a laugh. In her field, standards are constantly evolving with advances in technology, and conventions are rapidly formed and then disappear. Perhaps the convention is anticonvention. "I'm always thinking about new possibilities. I don't push my students to strive for what is, but to imagine what never was, but could be." Nevertheless, she was also careful to note "precision," "making every word count," and "contextualizing" as goals in all her work.

Disciplinary vs. Academic Standards

To the limited extent that these faculty named dominant conventions of approach, arrangement, and style in their fields, their comments for the most part confirmed our general definition of academic discourse, as described in Chapter One. That one standard is careful, thorough study respecting the precedents of past researchers was illustrated by all our informants: such terms as "evidence," "beginning with the text," "data-driven," "rigorous," "contextualizing," and "footnotes" typified their language. Williams's frequent mention of "the King's English" as a standard for writing in economics illustrates particularly sharply this academic drive to precision and to respect precedent. Indeed, respect for discipline and careful study characterizes not only those discourses and methods that our informants named as dominant or traditional, but the many alternatives that they also identified, as we'll detail below. For example, although Regan mentioned that there were 40 distinct subfields of political science, each differing rhetorically, she characterized all of them as stressing "good scholarly writing": clear, hypothesis-based, and logically and systematically argued.

Moreover, our informants thoroughly corroborated in their answers our principle regarding audience: that academic writing presupposes a skeptical, coolly rational readership whose objections should be anticipated. In describing their own writing histories, the faculty frequently mentioned both the reception of their work by fellow scholars and their anxieties about response. For example, Bergoffen told the story of how her paper on theories of deconstruction had been praised by a conference audience, only to be rejected by a panel of "more traditional" readers when she submitted it for the volume of conference proceedings. Regan spoke of her anxiety in stepping out of her field to submit an article to a policy journal. Trefil, in explaining the impersonality of style in scientific articles, noted the seriousness of many issues and the competitiveness of researchers; hence, the convention of an impersonal style, as he sees it, is an effort to reduce the potential for animosity.

Some of our informants implied audience concerns when they drew a contrast between academic prose and writing that "might be perceived as too popular." "The idea of engaging the reader is often viewed with suspicion," Lancaster said. "One of the most insulting things you can say in academics is that it reads like journalism. If it's too readable, it's not taken seriously." Historian Copelman also mentioned the academic reader's "suspicion" of texts that are too "seductive." If historical writing is "totally gripping and easy," she said, readers won't be likely to see the complexity of events and the differences in interpretations. Academic historians say "wait a minute, it's more complicated than that." Untenured faculty, she noted, *should* "run away" from any demand by a publisher to write what she called "history without footnotes."

Indeed, the anticipation of a skeptical, critical audience leads almost all our informants toward a narrowly cautious attitude in regard to advice they would give to newer scholars hoping for that most important achievement of career academics: tenure. While acknowledging the riskiness of all scholarly efforts, all of them urge untenured colleagues to avoid unnecessary risks. For example, Struppa spoke at length about variations of style in mathematics articles, with one fairly frequent rhetorical flourish being the inclusion of short excerpts from poets or other writers in a preface. He spoke about a doctoral student of his who was fond of including sayings from Sufism. "I allowed these," he commented, "because his math is good. But if his math was less solid, I'd have told him to take them out." Clark, who was in the midst of his tenure-decision year when we interviewed him (he received tenure later that year), spoke admiringly of the conservative training in textual analysis that he'd been given in graduate school. He distinguished carefully but clearly between the originality of both his subject matter and his critical views of it and what he regarded as "circus acts," i.e., writing differently for its own sake rather than because the material demands it. He went on to describe (detailed in the section on allowed alternatives) less traditional work he's beginning to do now that he has published two books.

The Analytic Academy: Tension Between Reason, Emotion, and the Body

The third of our three principles of academic writing in Chapter One was also confirmed by our informants' comments; the next section shows many ways in which the tension between reason and emotion/sensation is being played out in the academic writing of our informants. As the examples of alternative discourses in Chapter One demonstrate, writing that foregrounds passions and sensual richness may still exhibit the analytical control that the academy puts first, but this tension is an issue for some of our informants in their own work. Our informants ranged from those who strove in all their writing for analytical objectification to those who were struggling to balance the claims of systematic analysis, of emotion, and of the life of the body.

The faculty who were most comfortable with the academy's emphasis on impersonal analysis were R. Smith, experimental psychology; Jones, environmental science; Regan, political science; Struppa, mathematics; and Copelman, history. Physicist Trefil and economist Williams might also be included in this group, but their significant alternative careers as nonacademic writers qualify their inclusion. Neither quarrels with the need for "rigor" and objectivity in their academic disciplines, but that each has devoted years and many writings to reaching nonacademic readers and developing a less rigorous style demonstrates their desire as writers to work outside of academic strictures.

Psychologist Smith, for example, is fully at home in the genres he has most cultivated: the experimental report and the funding proposal. In his answers, he was unwavering in his stance that all students of psychology, regardless of specialty, need to be driven in their thinking by what the data reveal; they need to practice and learn experimental design and the skills of careful observation and recording. Writing should be dispassionate and impersonal, guided by the APA Manual. In emphasizing his discipline's commitment to the "data-driven" model and its only limited tolerance of alternative forms, he told us of one colleague, a clinical psychologist, who had built a successful career as an advocacy writer on mental health issues but who had only recently been recognized as a serious scholar in the field for this kind of work. His own careful research on the long-term effects of controlled substances, Smith argued, is no less passionately engaged for being written in a dispassionate style and it, too, serves the wider community.

In the context of reason vs. emotion, we stress the distinction between the passion with which a scientist such as Smith conducts his work and the dispassionate methods and rhetorical forms he uses. Similarly, while to be a good observer of his subjects' behavior he must cultivate a highly nuanced sensory awareness, he must also strive for a method of sensory perception that ensures consistency and reliability, and he must use a rhetoric that emphasizes his reasoned control.

Chris Jones, too, is passionate about his and his colleagues' work, their focus the freshwater ecology of the Potomac River basin. As an environmental scientist and activist, he gives part of his time to writing public policy statements and testifying to regional governments. But he carefully distinguishes between this nonacademic writing/speaking and the writing by which he conducts his experimental research in the scientific community. Jones in particular rejects the idea of using "I" in his research prose: "'I this' and 'I that'—that's prissy," he said. His main concern is that research documents be "quality-controlled and quality-assured," and he expects of himself and of his students a traditional formal consistency that reinforces and exhibits the care of the research design and procedures. He does acknowledge formal differences among poster presentations (the least formal), journal articles (the most), and books, but in all these venues he prefers a basically impersonal, dispassionate style that mirrors his concern for quality assurance.

Political scientist Priscilla Regan took a slightly different stance toward uses of the personal in academic prose. Like Smith and Jones, she sees her academic prose as focused on the objects and themes of her research, not on her experience nor on her feelings about her topics. To illustrate, she noted that even though the expertise for her book, *Legislating Privacy: Technology, Social Values, and Public Policy*, came in part from her five years as a technology specialist for the U.S. Congress, she does not mention this experience in the book and does not use her experience as evidence for the recommendations it makes. She built the arguments in her book on the findings of other researchers and on her own data collection following her government employment. This separation of perspectives carries over into her observations on appropriate style. She does not use "I" in her scholarly writing. Like Struppa, she does, however, distinguish between the text of the book or article and its preface, where, she says, she permits herself to use the first person in acknowledgments.

Struppa, in his elaboration on the "template" for articles in mathematics, gave examples of how personal emotion enters, usually shyly, into the systematic and highly conventional style of the writing. In further illustration of the use of the preface noted earlier, Struppa spoke about one of his articles, in which he included a dedication to an uncle who had attempted suicide. Without mentioning the context for the dedication, Struppa merely inserted into the preface a quotation from the Japanese writer Yukio Mishima. "Human life is limited, but I would like to live forever." Mishima's words, Struppa said, "were a message from me to my uncle that I knew what he was going through. This is as personal as I get. And that is allowed. But it's not very typical." As another example of the slight intrusion of emotion, he cited an article by a Japanese scholar in his field, who had concluded a proof with a metaphorical expression of his scholarly satisfaction: "How beautiful is the view from the top of the mountain."

This confluence of reason and emotion, of the impersonal and the "I," appears in still other ways in our informants' words. Although Copelman denies the academic validity of using the personal in her writing of history, she recognizes the influence of personal background and experiences on her work. Since Copelman identified herself as a feminist historian and is also a member of the women's studies faculty, we wondered whether and how she might mark her identity as a woman in her scholarly work. "I find the use of 'I' annoying in academic writing," she said, but, later in the interview, she told us about a conference paper in which she combined "a lot of very different material—fiction, historical documents, autobiography—to explore marginality in the immigrant experience." The paper was "purely an indulgence," she said, "not even recognizable as a history genre" but rather a chance to address something she cared deeply about as an immigrant herself. That immigrant aspect of her identity, perhaps even more than her feminism, is, she said, a pervasive influence in her work, "a kind of a hum in the background," but one which she plans "someday" to address explicitly. In that she characterized the conference paper as "serious intellectual work," even though indulgently alternative, we see that her immigrant experience informs and inspires her research and writing even while she feels the need to submerge that experience in the relatively impersonal style of the historian.

In contrast, Bergoffen is already working in a much more personal way in philosophy, making what she considers risky arguments and choosing to write in an alternative style to enact her feminist and postmodernist philosophical positions. While she sees this kind of work as increasingly important to the discipline, she also mentioned a number of times the nervousness she felt about her choices. Her nervousness and sense of risk, as we recount here and in more detail in the next section, illustrate, we think, the dilemma many scholars feel when they are somehow caught in a transitional moment in a discipline. Though they may feel that the discipline endorses such work, at least in theory, there are few models to help them understand allowed variations and, further, those models might be the subject of intense debate.

Feminism has "permitted" the "I" in philosophy and the personal pronoun is now almost "expected," Bergoffen told us. "It's understood that everyone speaks from a certain perspective and that perspective needs to be identified"; even so, she said she occasionally finds herself slipping back into the more traditional "we" when she writes. Bergoffen also sees "more and more personal, autobiographical material" being included in scholarly philosophical work. Still, that fact did not assuage the nervousness she felt in writing about herself for the collection *Portraits of American Continental Philosophers*, for which all the contributors were asked to reflect on "how their lives had led them to do the work they do." That she was asked to write for this collection demonstrates philosophy's recognition of the phenomenological and feminist work Bergoffen does. "Given what phenomenology was doing," Bergoffen said, "feminism just had to happen. If you have a philosophy that's starting to talk about the importance of the body, that talks about your body as your access to the world and different bodies have different access, you've got to hit the sexual difference." Illustrating the change Bergoffen has perceived is her story about a colleague who took "phenomenology and 'writing the body' seriously" by using her perspective as a gay woman, along with autobiographical details, to frame her analysis of Foucault. Even though the book "provided an analysis that is lucid and clear," the colleague worried that she would be perceived as sensationalist. Nevertheless, the book, according to Bergoffen, was "very well received."

We've used Bergoffen as a transitional figure between this section and the next on "Allowed Alternatives" because her observations illustrate that no matter how fluid the discipline is perceived to be, how firmly new theories and genres may seem to have taken hold, nor how thoughtfully reasoned the work may be, scholarly writers are still likely to feel that there is some risk involved in choosing to express themselves in alternative ways, even when the alternative is perceived to be allowed as a roughly equal option to the standard discourses.

Allowed Alternatives

As with Bergoffen, many of our other informants, when we asked them whether they had written in alternative ways, responded by explaining how shifts in theory had opened up the discipline to different ways of thinking and writing. We were not surprised to hear them describe how new theoretical perspectives not only shaped ideas and content in the discipline but also, for several, necessitated new methods, forms, and even language for articulating work that could not be adequately reflected in conventional manners. To go back to Carolyn Miller's formulation of genre as social action, we can say that the "exigence" of a new theory motivated a different kind of discourse, a discourse which could relay the values of some of its members and which, in the process, was gradually reshaping the mainstream discourse.

However, as we will show in this section, there is often considerable tension around this process even in disciplines perceived to be fluid and evolving. The degree of contentiousness around alternative methods and genres, our informants' descriptions suggest, might be related to how heterogeneous its members perceive the discipline to be.

"My discipline is history," Copelman told us, "but the truth is that's not really an adequate description. History is a very fluid category and, at least in the way I was trained, really quite open to new influences." For Copelman, this means that she has had the freedom to do feminist work, which she described as "a kind of alternative discourse created within the standards of historical discourse." Her work is feminist in its focus on women, their status as teachers at a particular historical moment, and on the examination of records, however tangential, that might be relevant to understanding this status.

Somewhat more controversial, though still allowed in her discipline, according to Copelman, is her current work for which she is "using an individual as a sort of launching pad into a variety of different issues that are all interrelated. It's not a biography and it's not something that is linear. It's more of an alternative discourse—I don't even know yet if it's an article or a book."

Similar to Copelman, Clark has also been experimenting with strategies that will allow him to show the larger cultural moments in which/by which black male bodies are interpreted. While Clark said he may be an "anachronism" because he prefers the standard critical voice in which he was trained, he noted that English and African American Studies allow for a diversity of content and styles, particularly given the theoretical frames of gender, queer, and cultural studies. Clark admires the "iconoclastic" work of Gerald Early, who "does fascinating things, blending politics, sports, Mike Tyson/boxing, literature, all these wonderful things, just seamlessly." Still, Clark sees a "literary hegemony" based on the standards he himself has followed and says he admires Early more for his content than his stylistics.

In contrast to Copelman's and Clark's qualified confidence that their disciplines would accept work that proceeds in a nonlinear, postmodern way from the "cultural moment to the text," Bergoffen described the "huge argument among philosophers about whether the alternatives [postmodernism and deconstructionism] are even philosophy." Even given this climate, however,

Bergoffen was somewhat surprised when a paper she had presented at a Derrida seminar, and which she was invited to submit to a mainstream journal, was rejected for being "disorganized" and "skewed." She described the style as being "sensitive to the fact that every piece of writing is gapped and when you make declarative statements you're hiding the gaps—and so for me that means I won't be hiding the gaps; I'll be putting them out there for exploration. Which also means I'm not going to be drawing conclusions. I'm going to be asking questions. I'm not going to be moving in this linear way. It all fits together but you have to work a little bit to put the pieces together. I'm just not going to map it straight out for you."

Without alluding to specific theories, Struppa also saw in mathematics standards the influence of change. He explained, for example, that "the template is era-dependent, not really language-dependent, because the notion of what is rigorously proved changes with time. In 1915, 1920, people had a different notion; what seemed fully proved then might not be fully proved now." Struppa's remark about mathematics corroborates a broader statement he made in a recent article from his perspective as Dean of the College of Arts and Sciences: "Thus, even very traditional disciplines constantly evolve towards a breaking of boundaries, towards an enlargement of their objects and, essentially, towards a more interdisciplinary view" (99).

We can see this process in Sorrell's description of how nursing opened up to admit a phenomenological approach, which it borrowed from philosophy. Sorrell told us that, at the time she began her research career, in the 1980s, nursing was dominated by a quantitative approach, with qualitative work becoming more accepted. But neither of these paradigms fits with the work she wanted to do, which was to value nurses' intuitions and the stories they told about their practice and commonly shared with other nurses. Nurses always talk among themselves, she noted, about "their feelings, say, that a patient is going bad, but they didn't want the docs, mostly men, thinking that they were crazy to go on intuitions about a patient." She knew that these data would be useful toward improving patient care, but would this type of analysis be accepted in the scholarly community? When Sorrell heard nursing scholar Patricia Benner describe using nurses' stories as data to analyze phenomenologically how they develop nursing skills, she thought she could use the same approach to analyze nurses' intuitions, which "had been downplayed because there were too many gender stereotypes to contend with." To learn how to do phenomenological analysis, Sorrell attended the Advanced Nursing Institute for Heideggerian Hermeneutical Studies. That there is such an institute in nursing studies indicates the degree to which this analytical approach and the objects of analysis have become allowed by the discipline.

Lancaster provided a very different view of standards and allowed alternatives in his field, anthropology. "For a big chunk of the nineties, it was almost mainstream to be alternative in anthropology," Lancaster told us. Since the 1920s, he said, ethnographic writing has always had a certain tendency to be "literary in quality, often experimental, inviting to be read." Following from Malinowski, the point has been "to take on the received wisdom, to dislodge the idea of clear universals, to problematize conceptions of what human beings are like," so experimentation in method and style were—and are—acceptable. Also central to anthropology, according to Lancaster, is its "fundamental check according to empirical everyday experience." To illustrate, he contrasted the methods of anthropology with those of formalist literary criticism. While someone doing a formalist literary analysis of Freud, for example, "would invoke the integrity of the text," the anthropologist would be centrally concerned with the "integrity of the social practice" Freud was describing. "What field experience did Freud base his work on?"

Given the paradoxical call for experimentation within an established framework, it is easy to see why a writer like Lancaster would feel ambivalence about what constitutes an alternative text. "I suppose a text could be aesthetically and compositionally alternative, but politically and socially quite mainstream. Or it could be the opposite, politically and socially alternative and still quite mainstream in terms of composition and aesthetics." At the time he was writing his book *Life Is Hard*, an ethnography about the Sandinista revolution in Nicaragua, he saw it as both politically and compositionally alternative. In the preface, he asserts that the book is deliberately written "against the grain," that "it misbehaves," and that it is "better to see the ethnographer in the ethnography." Better because, he argues, "Partisan analysis is the only resistance to power that a writer, as writer, can effectively offer" (xvii–xviii). To make his text "mirror the discombulation of a failed revolution," Lancaster created a kind of postmodern collage, composed of journalistic and impressionistic passages, raw fieldnotes, chapter-length interviews and life histories, newspaper articles, and letters. Though he thought at the time that he was "gambling with [his] career," the book is now mainstream reading in many anthropology classes. Labels such as "risky, alternative, avant garde" are tricky because "those things are always changing," Lancaster noted.

Thus far we have attempted to illustrate the range of views that our informants have about standards, conventions, and expectations in their academic disciplines. We have seen how many of our informants describe changes in their disciplines that allow scholars to work in alternative ways— ways that might formerly have been closed to them. For several of our informants, the terrain is unstable and ambiguous in troubling ways. They see alternative ways of thinking and writing that colleagues are pursuing and that they might wish to pursue, but they are unsure of the standing of those methods in the scholarly community. We now turn to a group of our informants who for various reasons have chosen to work extensively outside what they see as the clear boundaries of their disciplines.

Working Outside Disciplinary Boundaries

"What happened as I was working on *Signal Through the Flames* was that Mitch Snyder required me to jump in and get involved with the homelessness movement, and that changed my life," sociologist Victoria Rader told us when we asked how she happened to write her first book for a wider audience than just her colleagues—when she was still untenured. We also wondered why she has continued to pursue writing projects that take her well outside the boundaries of traditional sociological analysis. As a committed advocate for the homeless, Rader said she was determined that she would not make the same mistake as "those well-meaning and very well intentioned sociologists" whose initial response had been to count the homeless as a way to quantify the problem. As Rader explained, counting risks undercounting, which, in turn, can make people believe that the need is not as pressing. Rader's main goal was to educate the general public, so she "made sure there were a lot of quotes and stories about homeless people, even though that strategy may not have really furthered my argument among sociologists."[1]

We begin this section with Rader's comments because they capture the desire, expressed by many of our informants, to say something significant about their scholarly work to audiences other than their colleagues in the academy. For the five faculty we focus on in this section, choosing to write for different audiences meant that they might have had to break disciplinary conventions in many ways, such as by shifting assumptions about audience knowledge and attitude; changing vocabulary, sentence structure, and format; becoming more personal both in voice and content; allowing themselves to write with greater emotional intensity and with a clearer political bias. Yet, as

---

[1] She acknowledged that there were some models for writing about social change that combined quantitative and qualitative data. She mentioned Doug McAdam's work on the civil rights movement, which included a survey to determine how many people went into socially conscious areas after their Mississippi Freedom Summer experience and follow-up interviews with many of those people. "So he had a count of how many people went into socially conscious areas but he also had this wonderful rich qualitative data. What he did was he even had a control group, which were the people who applied for Freedom summer but didn't end up going." McAdam included himself by making evaluative comments, e.g., "in this exceptional person's life," but, Rader said, "You would never hear how moved he was by his experience of interviewing all these people."

we will show, each of the five we discuss is unique in the audiences they want to address, their motives for addressing these audiences, and thus in the kinds of rhetorical changes that are demanded.

While we find these scholar-writers interesting for the choices they have made and the motives behind their choices, we also think there are important implications for us as writing teachers. As we will discuss in the next chapter, most of our informants, while they may themselves write within the conventions of their disciplines, do not necessarily want undergraduates to learn to write within these conventions. Rather, for many, it is important for students to connect what they are learning in school with either their outside experience and/or ideas in the popular media and to write about these connections in a variety of forms.

While our discussions of the first four informants in this section are roughly similar in length, the fifth, focused on Lesley Smith, a tenure-line faculty member in the field of hypermedia, is much longer. We've devoted a large part of the section to Smith because she illustrates the degree to which new media shape both academic and personal exigencies, which, in turn, lead to new genres. Though Smith is in the technological vanguard, her career signals the thoroughgoing impact that technology will have on the methods and rhetorics of all disciplines. All academic writers will be affected, as they consider what qualifies as knowledge and the ways in which that knowledge can be communicated. Therefore, we need to study closely how Smith is negotiating these changes—for herself and with her students—and helping to bring them about.

The Persona Is Political

While Rader's primary goal in *Signal Through the Flames* was to put a human face on the homelessness movement in order to educate the general public, she felt constrained enough by her disciplinary training to avoid showing, in a sense, her own human face, other than in the introduction to the book. However, the success of *Signal,* which is often assigned as a textbook in undergraduate courses, convinced her that she wanted to include her own story of personal growth through social activism in her current book on accompaniment theory; that is, the theory of how "you walk with people who are struggling for their freedom without trying to take over." The book, which she has been working on for more than seven years, is an attempt "to offer support" for people like herself—white, privileged, middle-class—who are "socially concerned and don't know how to get involved, or they've gotten involved and gotten burned and need help going through emotionally difficult changes." But she also wanted to write a book her students and colleagues would read.

These overlapping goals and senses of audience have meant that she's having a great deal of difficulty characterizing her book in progress—to herself and to others. "So it's not a textbook, it's not a self-help book, it's not sociology exactly." Because of this unorthodox combination of motives, she has had trouble finding the right voice to make her central argument, which is that "our healing and our growth lie in reconnecting with the world, reducing our distance, and learning to give up control." At first, Rader said, she was "just going to tell these success stories, like people do make a difference, like privileged people can be allies, my own story." But, as she realized that the strength of the book would depend upon the story of her own growth ("Why else would anyone be doing this work?"), she committed herself to "going the full distance, at least as far as I'm able, emotionally and spiritually, in terms of the risk taking." Yet, because she's always mindful of the academic context within which she is working, she says that she tries to integrate sociological analysis in each chapter by referring to authors who have been helpful in putting the issues in perspective. "It's been hard," Rader said, to find the right voice and "to hold everything together in the sociological frame." Given these competing exigencies, we can see why it has been hard for her; she's struggling to find a form for a genre she's creating even as she writes.

Perhaps even harder has been finding a publisher, since she is trying to straddle several popular markets—how-to, self-help, self-actualization—while still maintaining credibility as a scholar in her discipline. For an academic publisher, she recognizes that "the spirituality stuff would have to go" and "there would need to be lots more references and footnotes." While "there isn't a lot of respect for a popularizer," Rader did see applied sociology as a possible niche for a book like hers because "you're writing to professionals—psychologists, social workers—to teach them how to use, for example, self-help groups." Still, she noted, even in applied sociology, she would have to leave herself out of the story, something she is not willing to do. In the end, what she cares most about, she said, is the response from her activist friends, not her sociology colleagues. "If my activist friends hate this book, that would be heartbreaking. If my sociology friends hate this book, I'll consider what they say, but it won't feel like so much is at risk. Maybe that's the privilege of tenure."

Putting on a Public Face

Unlike Rader, physicist James Trefil has for many years drawn a sharp line between his popular science writing and his scholarly work. His writing for a broader public moved over the years from a hobby to a second writing career to a commitment to scientific literacy. In addition to regular articles for *The Smithsonian,* he has written or coauthored seven books and serves as general editor of *The Encyclopedia of Science and Technology* (2002). Early in his career, Trefil did what he calls "the standard academic stuff": "I was in high energy theory and also worked with some people from cancer therapy; I was publishing about three or four papers a year, doing talks at conferences and so on." He achieved tenure and promotion to full professor through his research, and so it was without significant risk to his career when his writing for a popular audience "just started to take over, because there was then, and still is, such a need for it and so few people were willing or able to do it."

His popular science writing began with a lecture on quarks that he was asked to give at a University of Virginia event for parents and students. He was encouraged to submit the talk as an article to *The Smithsonian.* "So I sent it there and that's how I got started doing that kind of writing." For some time, he continued writing for both his physics colleagues and for the more general reader. The scientific community regarded the popular writing as a "hobby," he says. But he also noted a very different attitude elsewhere in the university to his growing popular audience: "Deans kind of liked it, provosts loved it, and presidents just ate it up, because that's great PR for the university."

The differences between scholarly writing in the sciences and popular forms he ascribes to specific exigencies. He describes scholarly scientific writing— "never using the first person, putting things as often as you can into the subjunctive, into a very formalized style"—as fulfilling "a real function in the community." The formality and the impersonality he sees as a means to contain the hostility that can arise during the "sharp debate" over conflicting results, "where each experiment costs a million dollars, and people's careers and reputations are at stake. A person might want to say, 'I think you're a real jerk,' but instead you say, 'I don't understand how you got to that result.'" He sees the same exigency across all the sciences. "The nomenclature changes, but not the very formal style."

As Trefil began to understand the stylistic requirements of science journalism—"I kept telling myself, 'No footnotes!'"—he continued to honor in his prose the science community's respect for other scientists. "I won't call a scientist for a comment and then do a hatchet job on the guy. Good reporters often delve into the personal conflicts, but I try to stay away from them." Trefil also has tried to maintain the third-person objectivity of the scientist. Unlike Rader, whose personal story is essential to the alternative goals she tries to fulfill, Trefil told us that he almost never writes about himself in his journalism. Although Trefil is careful to maintain an objective stance in his popular prose, he has developed a distinctive voice, as we pointed out to him. "I'm not conscious of having developed a voice; when I'm writing I don't think about that. I have a person in mind (a banker, a stockbroker), somebody who is very smart in a demanding profession but who doesn't know much about science; I talk to this person. One of the hardest things in learning how to do this kind of writing is to get rid of the formal scientific style; it took a while. My main goal is to get across a picture; I supply people with these mental videocassettes they can put on—'so the Big Bang…oh there it goes!'—so they can see it."

Economist Walter Williams explained his now 20-year alternative career as a syndicated columnist by quoting his colleague, Nobel laureate James Buchanan: "Economists are 'intellectual imperialists'—we feel entitled to get into anyone's field and comment on it." An "economic way of thinking, the analysis of costs and benefits," can be applied to any issue and can be translated for the nonacademic reader, Williams noted. That Williams has enthusiastically applied this credo is clear from his prolific writing career: a weekly column appearing in 160 newspapers, frequent radio and TV commentaries, and six books. Unlike Trefil, Williams began to write for a broad public audience—the *Philadelphia Tribune*, one of the oldest black newspapers—while still an untenured assistant professor at Temple University. He told us that the seeds of his ability to write for newspapers had actually been nurtured a few years before by his "tenacious mentor" in the Ph.D. program at UCLA, who had convinced him that the true test of one's knowledge of a subject is the ability to explain it to an ordinary person. He does not regard the writing he does for the broader public as a particularly difficult alternative to scholarly writing.

Indeed, he has similar standards for both. The scholar should be "terse.... The language might not be as beautiful or colorful as it could be; the point is to make the analysis logical and clear. Graphs and equations can do much of the work; written explanations should be brief. Footnotes should be used judiciously." He emphasizes brevity and clarity in his newspaper columns as well. "I'm given 600 words, so I write defensively. This means that I like to come in under 600 words, so the editor has no reason to mess with my prose." When we asked him for an example of how he'd write differently for the two audiences, he offered "airline fares" as a topic. "For economists, I'd talk about the principle of elasticity, but for my column I'd talk about the differing needs of business travelers."

In a sense, writing about dance is always writing for the public, Linda Miller, professor of dance, told us, because one "just can't use the kind of terminology that people in other disciplines can use and be understood. If you try to use pure dance terminology, most readers won't know what you're talking about. So our writing, I would say, is probably closest to making a translation from one language to another." Interestingly, Trefil and Williams both said that one of their goals for writing outside the academy is to translate their discipline to nonacademic audiences. For dance, however, as Miller sees it, there is no such distinction between academic and nonacademic writing.

Whether dance writers are academics or dance critics, she said, they are trying to describe "the intellectual process that is being manifested physically" and that process is not conveyed by "the vocabulary of dance technique. You can't say, for example, 'they did three jetés and two pique turns' and expect anyone, even dancers, to understand your thinking."

Miller talked about her own writing as a "kind of missionary work," with one of her major responsibilities being to "articulate a nonverbal discipline to people who know nothing about dance in order to make a case for funding." Faculty in other fields, she said, don't have to explain why they need a lab or more resources, because people understand these fields. "Dance scares some people. We don't have standardized tests for assessment that people can relate to; most everything we do in the academy has to be explained to someone not in our discipline."

While Miller talked at length about the challenges of writing in the academy, we could also hear her enthusiasm for writing and her sense of growth, both as a writer and as a teacher of writing. Part of this growth, she said, entailed gaining the confidence to talk back, in writing, to people inside and outside the dance community who "thought dancers can't think, let alone write." Then, too, there were the gender dynamics, which, for a long time, prevented her from being able to assert herself in writing. "Women in dance used to grow up taking direction most often from male dance teachers; it was engrained in me to curtsy—'thank you for the class.'" Through years of working with faculty from a wide array of departments, especially on committees, she learned to appreciate her intellectual and communicative talents, among them "to attend to details and to follow through." By developing her writing ability in this context, she gained respect from academic colleagues not usually accorded dancers.

Multimedia and the Intergeneric

"I don't think that I can define my discipline," Lesley Smith said in response to our question about her interdisciplinary study of multimedia and innovative technologies. With her Ph.D. in history, she noted that she feels she is always in some sense "teaching history no matter what I teach in that I'm always looking for context and connections, which is a kind of historical methodology." If she had to name a discipline, she said it would probably be writing. Immediately, however, she wondered if writing could be counted as a discipline. "Because I've got such a traditional academic background, I suppose I never think of writing as a discipline. I always think of writing as something that happens in lots of different disciplines." Still, she acknowledged, "Writing is what I've done for most of my life—writing for history, writing scripts for television, writing when I did my M.F.A., when I'm teaching, or the kind of writing I do now."

It's the kind of writing Smith does now—writing (in) new media—that made us want to include her as one of our informants. We see this writing as "intergeneric," a term we'll explain later in this section when we describe her current scholarly output. We want to begin, however, by describing the uneasiness Smith feels about expectations for her scholarly work as she moves toward tenure in an interdisciplinary technology-rich college. We believe that her confusion vividly illustrates both the difficulties of working between and across disciplinary traditions, and the particular challenges of working in media that are so fluid and subject to so many artistic influences. "I think that I'm being put in the academic and not the creative box," she said. "Maybe it's because I'm seen as having an academic background, with degrees in history and in poetry, which to most academics seems like an academic degree."

Still, she brings to her position a background that makes it difficult for her or any observer to categorize. Following her history degree, she worked for 14 years in British television, writing and producing documentaries, including a 60-part series on the history of Britain. After marriage to an American historian, she moved to the United States and entered the M.F.A. program at Mason. While completing her creative writing degree and teaching English composition, she began to experiment with applying new computer technologies to teaching, an interest that became over several years her forte in the university. The tenure-line position in New Century College, which she began five years ago, gave her the opportunity to develop these talents in a curriculum that prizes experimentation, builds interdisciplinary "learning communities," and balances conventional academics with service learning and preparation for the postmodern workplace.

The rub for Smith is that achieving tenure means not only winning the approval of the tenured faculty of New Century, but also that of the more traditionally academic faculty of the College of Arts and Sciences in which it is housed. Although her third-year review produced strong endorsement of her teaching and program development, it also produced the judgment that her scholarly agenda was too broad; she was urged to focus her writing on articles about her creative experiments with technology and teaching for such journals as *Computers and Composition* or *Kairos*. Certainly, few observers would consider such advice conservatively academic, at least not in terms of the journals named nor in its acknowledgment of the scholarship of teaching; nevertheless, Smith's response to the advice pinpoints a basic distinction, perhaps almost a dichotomy, between the nature of academic discourse and that of discourses in which Smith is more experienced and which she much prefers. Moreover, it also pinpoints a conceptual distinction between most academic fields and the discipline in which she now works: hypermedia.

If dance, as we noted in the previous section on Linda Miller, is a tremendously fluid discipline that "scares some people" because of the difficulty of pinning down conventions, standards, and even a vocabulary for academic writing, what might be said about the discipline of hypermedia? To address that question, it is useful to compare hypermedia, as a field, with dance. While Miller, like Smith, is uncertain about the role of scholarly writing in dance, she has no doubts about the measurability of a dance performance. After all, there are models in dance, some going back thousands of years, which performers work within or against. The same can be said about other artistic academic fields. Toulmin, whom we discussed in Chapter One, makes a similar judgment about the fine arts, calling them "quasi-disciplines" because, while there has been a traceable "historical evolution of [their] collective techniques" (a characteristic of "fully disciplined" fields), individual artists enjoy a "creative autonomy and independence [that] gives every artist the liberty to employ the collective techniques of his profession in the pursuit of essentially individual goals" (398–99).

In contrast, hypermedia is a field that is still too new to have the evolution of its techniques historically documented, at least in the definitive sense in which Toulmin means it; moreover, its standards, methods, and materials are constantly—almost frenetically—evolving as technology evolves. The models for "good" hypermedia exist only until the next generation of tools; the critical theory that would help people understand, analyze, and evaluate hypermedia cannot keep up, the many efforts of scholars notwithstanding. Indeed, while understanding and analysis are typically thought to be much the same intellectual operation in most academic fields, in hypermedia they are not. Similar to the way in which a reviewer responds to a dance or a musical performance in the moment and through many senses, so the user or reviewer of a hypermedia creation must understand its multisensory complexity from moment to moment. But the models in dance provide a critical lens for the reviewer, a way of putting the performance in context. Moreover, from performance to performance the dance will remain essentially the same, though reviewers may receive it differently. By contrast, a good hypermedia work will change from use to use because the user is actively participating in the "performance." In addition, the software and hardware on which hypermedia is based are constantly changing, so the context of any performance is also always changing.

Given the volatile nature of this new discipline, it is easy to understand why Smith feels uneasy about her niche. Indeed, the idea of "niche"—a comfortable place—may be antithetical to the field. In her responses to our questions, Smith consistently expressed an impatience with stasis, which she illustrated through her distaste for the demand on academic analysts to dissect and write about, often over years, what has already occurred or has been created earlier. With her doctorate in history, her impatience is ironic, to say the least. But Smith, as a hypermedia specialist, feels pressure not to get behind when the models and tools (i.e., methods) are constantly changing. Moreover, she knows that if you treat the hypertext object as static, which you have to do in order to be able to analyze it, you are, in a sense, losing ground.

So Smith is torn between the demands of academic writing, even liberally defined, which the academic hierarchy has committed her to meeting in order to achieve tenure, and her two writing loves in the new field: (1) critical writing about—*and for*—mass media and (2) hypermedia composition, much of it to support her teaching in New Century. She knows what the academy expects of her, but she finds it uninteresting. Smith chafes at what she sees as the redundancy and belatedness of this act: "When I've created something new for the classroom and then used it, I'd much rather just think and write about what I've learned as part of the process of building that learning into what happens the next semester, rather than sit down and write about it for academic readers once it's dead and gone."

Moreover, she sees the analytic academic model as deadly for understanding hypermedia—not to mention producing it. "Despite all the work that people are doing now in visual literacy and visual storytelling, in fact writing about hypertext still follows a very strong literary paradigm," she noted. She makes a sharp distinction, however, between "actively working with a relatively fixed text," as one does with literary analysis, and moving into hypertext, hypermedia, and multimedia where one is being "active with a dynamic text." Further, she said, unlike the dynamic texts of film or television, which move along in time, hypermedia not only passes in time, but "every time it passes in time it could be different. And, if it's a complex piece of hypertext, or hypermedia, or multimedia, it should be different every time." For Smith, it's "a sign of failure if a piece of multimedia is the same every time you look at it." Not only does the literary paradigm not work, she said, but there's the danger that hypermedia creators will try to produce work that can be analyzed more traditionally, "and you end up not necessarily getting great theory and you get horrible multimedia."[2]

---

[2] See Wysocki and Hocks, among others, on visual literacy changing the face of composition studies.

Adding to Smith's conflict as a scholar and writer is that this new discipline also privileges a rhetoric, in particular a sense of audience, that goes against the academic grain. In Chapter One, we stressed that academic writing continually shows other scholars that the writer is a careful student of the subject by demonstrating knowledge of the prior literature. This performance is formalized in style manuals and in journal after journal. We also stressed that while academic writing may appeal to some extent to the senses and the emotions, the intellectual, analytic persona is primary. In this sense, academic writing is highly self-conscious: even if the "I" is only implicit in the piece, as is most frequently the case, the presence of the scholar's consciousness is everywhere. In contrast, hypermedia, as Smith defines it, succeeds only when it hides its intellectual processes and background—its careful study—and presents to the user/reader an array of facades that appeal to the eye (and perhaps other senses) and that draw attention to the subject and away from the designer. When we asked Smith, as we did all our informants, about the presence of the "the personal" in her work, she likened her ideal presence in her work to that of the "auteur" in film—"you can often tell who the director is by the style of the work, but there is no 'I' in the film and we never see or hear the director. Yes, there are ways of saying 'I' and having my view, my signature," but if she has to use the explicit "I" in some way in her hypermedia creations, she feels that she has "somehow failed."

Further, even though the skilled designer of hypermedia is a dedicated student of the work of other designers, successful hypermedia—in order to be useful to its users—never is explicit about these influences. To be useful, hypermedia strives for simplicity—i.e., "user-friendliness"—and the irony in this elegance is that those who use the materials rarely appreciate the depth and intricacy of the work that goes into them. One of Smith's worries about the academic readers she must please for tenure is that their inexperience with the technical, production side of hypermedia will keep them from appreciating the sophistication of analysis and judgment—not to mention the sheer volume of hours it takes to learn and apply new software—that goes into well-crafted hypermedia. "Unless the person doing the evaluating is a person who also does this work, it's not seen as research. Somehow people think that I've been touched by the finger of God and so just know all these new programs."

To better understand ourselves what is involved in writing (in) new media for the academy, we asked Smith to describe her writing process(es). Currently, she said, her main work has been in course development, specifically designing new curricula to "flesh out" the multimedia concentration in New Century College. Since she tends to write extensive online syllabi for all her courses, she talked about the ongoing experimentation this entails.

There's finding the right tone, for example. "It's easy to sound very stuffy on the Web if you use the same style you use on a paper syllabus." More complex than stylistic choices, however, are decisions about navigational structures. She described one unsuccessful experiment with a "very playful hypertextual syllabus." She said, "I know from experience that even though students are sophisticated in their uses of technology, they are still highly critical of a website that isn't absolutely crystal clear. They want it to have flash and look wonderful, but they also want to be able to read all the links wherever they are and get to the key piece of information they need."

In the 10 percent of the time she estimates she has available for her own "pleasurable" multimedia writing, she's been experimenting with "the ways abstract visual images trigger moods or words"; these experiments, which she calls poems, started when she wanted to learn better ways of using Adobe® Photoshop®. "So I began playing around with images and then I found that the images started crying out for words, so I added words to them. Next I'd like to pull the poems together into a big series." Because she wants to make these poems interactive, she's also become interested in "programming in the interactivity, so that the programming is one kind of creative writing and the text that appears with, under, through, and by the programming is another kind of creative writing." Also squeezed into this 10 percent are the film, television, and DVD reviews she writes for *PopMatters*, an ejournal that "tends to be very strict about not having 'jargony' language or getting too cultural studies-ish, but, at the same time, wants things to be set in an intellectual and cultural context."

The conflict for Smith, as we suggested earlier, is that she thrives on the dynamism of new media, which doesn't sit still for the kind of disciplined analysis and reflection characteristic of academic writing. Perhaps more significant to our discussion of alternative disciplinary discourses is that her work, more than that of any of our other informants, is "intergeneric" in that she crosses many genres and invokes multiple audiences. So, for example, when she talks about multimedia and hypertext, she invokes audiences ranging from the end user of a piece of software, typically the student, to people who have to produce parts of the software, to readers of hypertext journals and creative writing (e.g., her poetry experiments), and, always in the back of her mind, the academic audience who wants her to step back and reflect on the scholarship of teaching with/on/about the Web.

So what is a scholar like Smith supposed to do, when working in a discipline whose genres—the "typified recurrent actions," exigencies, and audiences, as Carolyn Miller identified them—are still being defined and may be indefinable, yet who works within academic culture, which presupposes rational and deliberate principles of scholarship?

To think about this question, we want to come back to Toulmin's discussion of quasi-disciplines, e.g., the fine arts, which are "quasi" in that they can be characterized by a certain continuity over time but also by the "nondisciplinable" personal goals of the individual artist. Yet, Toulmin says, the idea of the "unconstrained individualist" is relatively new. Until the late nineteenth century, there was little distinction made between artists and craftspeople, i.e., those who put their art to practical use, as denoted in the terms "artisan," "industrial arts," and the "Royal Society of the Arts," which was devoted to technological innovation. Thus the "arts" originally described "repertories of practical skills" and "developing sets of technical methods" transmitted by an apprenticeship in a particular school. As the distinction between arts and crafts evolved, however, the "artist" was set apart from the "run of the mill 'artisan,'" who emphasized "mass market" production—the "not so–fine arts" (397–98).

How does Smith's creative hypermedia work fit into this historical trajectory? Because of its newness and its connection to popular technology, hypermedia lacks the prestige of other fine arts, perhaps most so because of its mass-market accessibility. Hypermedia is public in a way that most other fine art production is not; the audiences are enormously varied, which potentially multiplies the exigencies that any hypermedia design could possibly serve. So, for example, when Smith is given instructions for writing reviews for *PopMatters*, it's implied that she's writing for a nonacademic intellectual audience *and* a popular audience any place at any time. Moreover, these audiences, as we've noted, read/write new texts according to their own goals, whims, and motives; they are very unlike the disciplined, linear, deliberate readers imagined by academic scholars as they lay out their carefully reasoned arguments. Nor are they like the historically adept, critical, deliberate readers of the academic poetry that Smith wrote for her M.F.A. Make no mistake: those academic audiences are included in the vast group of users of hypermedia, but even academics, trained as they are, most often expect from Web-based materials—unlike scholarly prose—the same visual and other-sensory sophistication, plus ease of navigability, that nonacademic users expect.

If she chose, Smith could jump the academic hurdles that her committee has recommended. She already has among her credits a few analytical, even theoretical conference presentations and a couple of articles of that nature. Moreover, if she did choose, as her committee has recommended, to define herself as a "computers and composition" specialist, she could request to be evaluated within the guidelines approved by the Conference on College Composition and Communication (CCCC) for scholars who "work with technology" (http://www.ncte.org/about/over/positions/level/coll/107658.htm). Among the several recognitions in this statement are the following:

. . . the rapid pace of technological change means that each case will need to be decided on its own merits, and each case is in a sense precedent-setting.

CMC [computer-mediated composing] technology, particularly the World Wide Web, is blurring the distinctions between traditional areas of evaluation for promotion and tenure; i.e., research, teaching, and service. For example, developing web pages for class, department, university, or global use might fit all three categories.

The CCCC statement implies that faculty such as Lesley Smith should not have to choose between scholarship that appears to be "more academic" and work that does justice to the full range of the candidate's scholarly and creative talents. In Smith's case, it suggests that she could see her creativity as all of a piece, a coherent 100 percent productive work, rather than the bifurcated 90 percent/10 percent she worries about now. The statement sets aside the standard boxes and advocates a flexibility that may be foreign to the academy but that is the essence of the new technologies that the academy claims to embrace.

The five cases presented in this last section show academics who have chosen, for very different reasons and in different situations, to pursue what they view as distinct alternatives to the academic paradigm described in Chapter One. Unlike their colleagues in the first two sections of this chapter, who have either found workable accommodations in the conventions of their disciplines or who see their disciplines changing to accommodate them, these five have chosen to work outside academic convention to meet exigencies important to them and the readers whom they most want to reach. Nevertheless, as in the case of Lesley Smith, the academy can move, albeit with deliberate speed, to adapt to the vision and energy of its members who are willing to cross borders, whether disciplinary, technological, or rhetorical.

In Chapter Three, we turn from our focus on the faculty as writers to them as teachers. Does our informants' thoughtful, often bold endeavor in their research and writing carry over into their work with students? How do these writers' struggles with subject matter, with academic strictures, with their senses of integrity and personality affect how they teach? In particular, how are their own sometimes circuitous and multiple paths as writers reflected in how they teach their students to write: in the assignment they give, the criteria they espouse, the responses they give? Do they, by and large, preach conformity to academic principles? Do they tolerate, even encourage, alternatives, and how far from the conventional will they allow students to venture?

Chapter Three

How Our Informants Teach Students to Write

How do you like this for a chutzpa answer—teaching students to think philosophically is teaching them to think? I want students to cut through the crap and get to the issue and then to understand whether or not the issue has been presented in a way that makes sense, that's trustworthy, that's convincing, that's arguable.

—DEBRA BERGOFFEN, PHILOSOPHY

Chutzpa or no, Bergoffen's response to our question about the conventions students need to know to be successful writers in the discipline was typical of many of our informants, who suggested that good writing is good writing and hence good thinking, no matter the discipline. Even those informants who saw standards for good writing varying with the discipline usually began their descriptions of the qualities of writing they wanted their students to learn by giving us a similar group of imprecise terms: "clear," "logical," "well-reasoned," "grammatically correct," and so forth, just as they had when they described their expectations for writing in the field. As we pointed out, it was only with more questioning that we were able to uncover the nuances and often major differences not only among fields but also from one writer to another.

This repetition of similar terms is, we feel, easily explained by reference to the principles of academic writing elaborated in Chapter One:

- Clear evidence in writing that the writer(s) have been persistent, open-minded, and disciplined in study

- The dominance of reason over emotion or sensual perception
- An imagined reader who is coolly rational, reading for information, and intending to formulate a reasoned response

This paradigm was confirmed over and over in our informants' responses, some doing so more strenuously than others. That their first responses tended to follow from the academic paradigm, rather than bespeak rhetorical and epistemological difference, also confirms what David Russell has called the "myth of transparency" in academic rhetoric:

> Because apprentices in a discipline very gradually learn its written conventions as an active and integral part of their socialization in a community, the process of learning to write seems transparent. Scholars and researchers come to view the particular genres that the disciplinary community has evolved (and each member of it has internalized) not as rhetorical strategies, conventional—but gradually changing—means of persuasion; instead, the community's genres and conventions appear to be unproblematic renderings of the fruits of research. (*Writing* 16–17).

The problem for us as researchers, then, is that when our informants use similar terms to refer to their goals and expectations for student writing, we can't be sure that they share the same values or are actually talking about very different things. As we will show in this chapter, our data confirm that there is an academic way of conceptualizing writer, reader, and task, and that these follow the academic principles we've laid out. But, as we will also show, the common terminology that faculty use often hides basic differences in rhetoric, exigency, epistemology, style, form, and formatting—differences that are revealed when faculty elaborate on their assignments. When very real differences are cloaked in the language of similarity, it's understandable that students would find it hard to decode what teachers want and come to see their assignments and expectations as esoteric to the teacher's disciplines, if not just idiosyncratic.

Indeed, this confusion by students may result from teachers' own misperceptions of just how representative their expectations for students are. Every WAC/WID workshop leader has encountered faculty who are surprised when their assessment of a piece of student writing differs greatly from the assessment by a colleague. We recall in a recent workshop a faculty member from a technical discipline who wondered how faculty could benefit from a group analysis of sample student papers in their discipline—"after all, we all think alike"—only to discover in the workshop major differences. A common composition teacher's nightmare is embodied in Susan McLeod's story of the historian at her institution who berated her and "the entire discipline of English" for not teaching "these people how to write." When the two teachers looked at the same student's work from each of their courses, they saw that the student had merely and wrongly assumed that the second teacher would expect the same voice and argumentation technique as the first, each teacher working squarely—as each perceived it—within the convention of the field (Tate et al). Within the ever more specialized compartments of the modern academy it's no wonder that such misperceptions of uniformity exist. Indeed, we might posit that, when teachers think about their own expectations, they most likely do not know to what extent their standards for "good writing" conform to

- The academic (pertaining to the broad principles described in Chapter One)
- The disciplinary (pertaining to the methods and conventions of the teacher's broad "field")
- The subdisciplinary (pertaining to the teacher's area of interest, with its own methods and conventions, within the broader discipline)
- The local or institutional (pertaining to the policies and practices of the local community or school)
- The idiosyncratic or personal (pertaining to the teacher's unique vision and combination of interests)

Russell and Yanez use Engestrom's (2001) version of "cultural historical activity theory" to explain and illustrate how this confusion leads to mutual misunderstanding by teachers and students, with the typical result being the teacher's misjudging of student ability and the student's "alienation." They illustrate this process through a case study of an Irish history course used to fulfill a general education requirement for students across fields. They see in the concept of general education, as it is practiced in most American colleges, confusion between nonspecialist goals for all students and goals for specialists. Since the teacher in the study intends the writing assignments to lead to students' improvement in generic academic rhetorical and thinking skills, yet assumes that his epistemology and rhetoric as a historian are synonymous with these, there is inevitable conflict between the nonspecialist students' understanding of the assignments and the teacher's expectations. Using activity theory's focus on goals and motives to understand the success or failure of "tool-mediated social activity systems," such as a student's attempts to fulfill a teacher's assignment through writing, the authors perceive that only further negotiation between student and teacher, in which their differing motives and understandings can be elucidated, can overcome the alienation of the students.

Based on our research with faculty and students, we want to extend Russell and Yanez's thesis. The confusion for both faculty and students stems not only from differences in expectations based on unacknowledged disciplinary preferences but also from subdisciplinary and idiosyncratic preferences, both also unacknowledged and frequently unexamined by faculty. Our research suggests that any time a teacher evaluates student writing (or writing by colleagues) the expectations for that writing are an ambiguous mix of all these preferences. As we show in this chapter, faculty differ substantially in their awareness of these distinctions in their judgments. Understandably, then, as we discuss in the next chapter, students see the idiosyncratic as dominating the academic in teacher's expectations, and have the same difficulties that teachers do in understanding the various influences on expectations for writing. Further, when the students in our focus groups perceived that teachers were being idiosyncratic in their evaluative criteria, they may actually have been perceiving this mix of academic, disciplinary, subdisciplinary, local, and individual preferences.

To enact our inquiry into the similarities and differences of expectations from teacher to teacher, we spent a good portion of our interviews asking our informants about their uses of writing in teaching. We wanted to know their goals for student writers, what they assigned student writers to do, how they responded to what students produced, and how open they were to student attempts that fell outside of what they perceived to be disciplinary convention, attempts that might, for example, fit into the taxonomy of alternatives we described in Chapter One.

Further, we were curious about the degree of match between who these faculty were as writers and who they were as teachers of writing. We wondered whether and how their own writing practices, based on the ways they constructed the expectations of their discipline for themselves, would be translated in the assignments they give to students. If Roger Lancaster, for example, saw his own books as taking risks in anthropological subject matter and style, would his assignments permit his students to be equally daring? If Debra Bergoffen wrestled with the legitimacy and fullness of the "I" in her philosophical prose, would her assignments push students toward the same inquiry? If Chris Jones saw himself as both environmental research scientist and public policy advocate, would his assignments ask students to play both roles? How would Jeanne Sorrell's commitment to phenomenology play out in her undergraduate and graduate course designs? In other words, would our informants, in their assignments and course designs, encourage students to be as "alternative" in their treatment of the subject matter as they themselves have been? We gleaned the answers to these many questions primarily from our interviews with the informants and follow-up queries with several; we also analyzed course materials that they sent us or that we searched online. In addition, we analyzed the significance of criteria rubrics created by teams of faculty in individual departments as part of a state-mandated assessment of the writing proficiency of university students (to which we alluded in Chapter One).

Three Perspectives

We've organized this chapter into three large sections that illustrate differing perspectives by faculty. The first group of informants we'll discuss is those who are very aware that what they want students to do is discipline-based rather than generically academic. The second group is those who perceive that what they are asking for is a nonspecific academic essay, but, upon examining their goals and assignments, we see that their expectations are solidly rooted in their disciplinary traditions. The third group is those we consider to be the most alternative within a disciplinary framework (and thus very difficult to group) in that they want students to write prose in a surprising array of forms that bear an ambiguous relationship to disciplinary expectations. In a brief fourth section, we discuss the teaching of a multimedia specialist in an interdisciplinary college, specifically how her expectations for writing are inevitably alternative to any disciplinary framework given the convergence of so many influences in this emerging field. Although we are making distinctions among these groups, our analysis will show that even within the groups there is such a range of goals and assignments distinguishing one teacher from another that students will find it impossible to assume that what one teacher wants is what another teacher will want.

"How to Think Like a Scientist": Teaching the Tools of the Discipline

> My purpose in general is to link the class with the world and to try and get them to see that the material that we're trying to put in front of them has some usefulness and some relevance in the world at large.
>
> —*Chris Jones, Environmental Science, on his goals in 100-level classes*

We begin this section with Jones because he recognizes the specific relevance of the forms of writing he requires of students and the limited relevance of the ways of thinking those forms embody to those outside the discipline. The faculty we describe here do not imagine that their assignments replicate the general goals of faculty in other subject areas, except in the vaguest way. For them, "good writing" in any assigned format differs in clear ways from "good writing" in others.

For Jones, his differing goals for students determine the quite different things he asks them to do and how he expects them to present their work.

Jones's primary rhetorical concern for undergraduate majors in biology and environmental science is that they learn the genre of the experimental lab report—according with his primary epistemological goal that they learn the methods of scientific observation and analysis. Jones's majors are expected to read journal articles and write full reports "as if" to be submitted to a journal. When we asked him if he would accept a report from an environmental science major that did not conform to conventional arrangement, he said, "I'd ask them to rewrite it in the proper format, as most of my colleagues would. I try not to be negative to people, but even our general education students should toe the line in that way."

Unlike the biology and environmental science majors, Jones's general education students learn the methods of the laboratory and the format of the report only to the extent that they can fill in blanks and answer multiple-choice questions. His primary goal in the freshman-level course for nonmajors is expressed in the quote that begins the chapter; one assignment he gives to help students achieve this goal is a poster presentation that requires them to select, summarize, and critique several recent newspaper articles that bear on a topic that they have studied in the course. His objectives behind the assignment include (1) showing students what it means to think like a scientist by comparing textbooks and labs with popular representations of scientific discoveries; (2) increasing students' motivation to study science by showing its relevance to their everyday lives and (3) making them more critical of the "world according to newspapers" and other popular media.

Note that while the poster presentation is a familiar form used by scientists to convey information about research at conferences, Jones has adapted it for a very different exigency—hence, the questions he asks, the sources to be used, and the format of the poster are specific to the writer, the audience, and the purpose, each different from those of the poster of the scientific researcher. We see how misleading it could be to an outsider to Jones's teaching to be told that his gen ed students are creating "poster presentations." Again, the familiar term masks the complexity of genre in this situation.

Corroborating Jones's emphasis on teaching scientific method to majors, Robert Smith says, "We teach people how to write in standard scientific reporting formulas. We also teach people how to think in that way because we're very much a database discipline." The core course for psychology majors (a "writing intensive" course in the GMU program) teaches students the structure and exigencies of the APA reporting form, regardless of the branch of the discipline in which they will later specialize. Yet, he acknowledges, "How they use that training is going to vary a lot. About 30 percent of our undergraduate majors go on for some form of graduate study, the rest of them do not. Nevertheless, the data-based mode of thought and the ability to communicate factual information clearly is our overriding goal."

When we asked him about rhetorical options in the psychology curriculum, he immediately noted the use of journals in some undergraduate and graduate courses, including his own use of a several-entries-per-week journal assignment in his mentoring of Ph.D. students teaching their first undergraduate courses. Consistent with his emphasis on "data-base thinking" was his rationale for the journal, as an "efficient way for me to know what's going on in their heads when they're not in the class." Rather than dichotomizing the journal as "personal" and the APA report as "impersonal," he saw the journal as "a different way of collecting information about what's going on in these students' classes," more efficient, hence more informative, in this context than would be the standard report.

Neither Jones nor Smith enacts a one-size-fits-all pedagogy in his applications of writing in classes at different levels. Yes, both are explicitly guided by the scientific paradigm most conventionally embodied in the experimental report, and this form they are committed to teaching to their majors. Nevertheless, they adapt, often significantly, the standard format of the scientific report to the purposes of the given course (the "exigencies" of the genre) and to the nature and needs of the learners. We can't emphasize enough the possible disjunction between *format* and *genre* that outside observers, such as composition teachers and their students, should be aware of when they hear assignments identified by teachers across disciplines. In the hands of a Chris Jones or a Bob Smith, the "poster presentation" and the "journal" are tools that are refined for particular exigencies and that must be understood within those contexts.

Perhaps none of our informants so starkly represents the precise linking of assignment, form, and teaching method to rhetorical exigency and course objectives as does physicist Trefil, whose own writing career, as we described in the previous chapter, has enacted a dramatic divergence between academic science and scientific journalism. Trefil's writing career has to a significant extent paralleled his teaching emphases. Since coming to George Mason in the late 1980s after having built reputations as both theoretical physicist and popular science writer, his teaching has had twin foci: on the one hand, he teaches undergraduate general education and honors science courses; on the other, he has taught science journalism courses for English and communication majors. When he speaks about each type of teaching and the writing he assigns students in each venue, he firmly states the distinctions between the environments and the nontransferability of the rhetorics. To Trefil, "good writing" in one context is not good writing in another.

The most important teaching contexts for Trefil are (1) the general education courses he teaches (Great Ideas in Science), (2) first-year courses for physics majors, and (3) the course in science writing he gives to majors in English and communication. The Great Ideas course crosses a range of disciplines and presents Trefil's "scientific worldview." Not a lab course, it's Trefil's opportunity to make the world of science meaningful to all students, much as his book *Science Matters* has. Although it is a lecture class for upwards of 80 students, he uses writing "to get them thinking about science outside of the classroom, either by watching television, or reading the newspaper, or going on the Web, or however they get their news, to see the scientific component." In his most recent iteration of an assignment, he asks students about five times a semester to choose several different, recent articles in popular media that touch on a scientific topic of interest, summarize them, and then state their own critical reaction to the coverage, all in 2–3 pages (with the articles attached). As a variation on the learning journal, these summaries and reactions are primarily exercises that reinforce course objectives, not "papers" in a scientific sense.

By contrast, his assignments in first-year courses for physics majors teach skills working scientists will need. However, unlike Jones's emphasis on the correct format and rhetoric of the scientific article, Trefil has prioritized writing for oral presentation—and the oral skills themselves. He assigns each student to research an important experiment in the history of physics, then summarize it in a written report, then present the results orally to the entire class. "It forces them to do the talking about experiments rather than have me lecture on them, and it gives them practice in finding the information. The writing and speaking they will need to do persistently as scientists."

For these new science majors, Trefil's concern for scientific method corroborates that of Smith and Jones. But Trefil has his own take on how writing can teach this epistemology. He is critical of what he calls "cookbook" labs with preconceived right answers; these, he says, encourage students to "work backwards from the answers to their data. So not only are they not learning science, they learn antilearning—it has nothing to do with the real world. When I design labs, I never have labs done in a room. For example, I'll have them go out and measure the position of the sun at nine o'clock every day, all through the semester, plot the results, then speculate in writing—hypothesize—why the points fall as they do."

In sharper contrast still is the writing that makes up Trefil's course Science Writing, which he offers occasionally through the English department. The juniors and seniors who take this course are preparing for careers in nonfiction writing and journalism; he intends this course "to get students to where they can write about a complicated subject on which they have limited background; craft an article that a wide range of readers would want to read *all the way through*, that will capture the main ideas, and that will not get derailed into side issues." He does not believe that these students need to be scientists in order to write engagingly and accurately about scientific matters; his students have written well enough to convince him of that. But they do need to be serious writers: in his course they write to weekly article deadlines and they build to a 3000-word article by semester's end. His feedback is intense, too, and stresses technique: "My comments are fully detailed—I can get down to the choice of a particular word. I spend a whole week on opening sentences; it doesn't make any difference if everything is beautifully written if somebody stops reading after the first sentence."

"Engagement" is also a critical criterion to Clark from English and African American Studies; however, he differs from Trefil in his emphasis on engaging with the field itself. Clark "assumes" that the literary and historical texts his students read are engaging—and that the students will be engaged in the study. "I'm sort of a dinosaur. I assume the subject is engaging. I want them to read and write carefully and critically." Similar to the way in which Jones and Smith prioritize undergraduate science majors' learning of the format and rationale of the experimental research report, Clark strives to commit his English and African American Studies majors to close reading of texts and to critical analyses that employ the range of "interpretive stances" he teaches them. True to his background in literary studies and to the expectations for scholarship he learned and has practiced, as we described them in Chapter Two, Clark focuses his students' energies on the analysis of text, to the point that he often limits the number of secondary sources that they might use. "I'm almost harshly critical—I want students to see that they have to look much more critically and carefully at some minute facet of the text."

Much like Trefil when he teaches the English and communication majors in his Science Writing course, Clark pays intense attention to the words and sentences of his upper-division students. Whereas Trefil's purpose is to make his proto-journalists and popular essayists readable to a nonacademic audience, Clark's is focused on the academic readership. He related his own epiphany as a college student to the need for such care for correctness in standard English, as he recalled a teacher in an advanced writing course who had shown the same attentiveness to student academic prose that he shows in his own detailed comments. Hence, it is not surprising that Clark does not encourage students to experiment in their essays with nonstandard dialects. "Sometimes students are hostile, but I say I'm grading in this way and it will behoove you to listen to me. I feel I have to toe the line. Too often people in the university don't."

To this point in the chapter, each informant whose teaching we have portrayed evinced a definite sense of the most conventional form and exigency of writing in her or his discipline. While Jones, Smith, and Trefil vary at times, often significantly, from convention in specific assignments for specific groups of students, all three share a standard picture of the scientific article. Clark is similarly unwavering in regard to critical analysis in literary study. For these faculty, the standard is that of fellow professionals in their fields, and they expect graduate students, and in some cases undergraduates, to learn it and write it.

By contrast, as we pointed out in Chapter Two, there is no scholarly tradition of writing in dance. The writing of dance professionals and dance educators is primarily a "translation" for nondancer readers: performance audiences, funding sources, college administrators, and so forth. Miller described in that chapter various translations she must make in her own prose as dancer, teacher, and administrator. When she assigns writing to her undergraduate students, her emphases parallel the priorities in her own prose. In dance, as we've noted, there is no standard that dictates convention that teachers either strive for or work against in their assignments. Nevertheless, we include Miller in this section of the chapter because she, like the others, knows that good writing in her field is not the same as good writing elsewhere and tailors her writing curriculum to the rhetorical contexts her students will encounter when they leave college.

Even if her undergraduates are not yet having to write proposals, reports, and reviews, she finds it critical that they develop the ability to see their performances as audiences would, rather than as a sequence of technical moves. She is particularly concerned that they develop an overall idea of the performance and communicate this idea through appropriate metaphors. She pushes students to avoid the typical extremes: on the one hand, mere exclamation ("beautiful" and "graceful" she forbids her students to use) and on the other, mere technical jargon ("two jetés and a pique turn"). "Again, it's translating: you have to talk about ideas, images, metaphors. It's like reading authors in whose work you can smell where you are. It's more than just saying 'gray tights and a gray leotard' and 'I thought it was a cool dance.' Better to say, for example, 'they looked like naked bodies covered in ash.'"

"Good Writing Is Good Writing": Perceiving the Universal in the Disciplinary

Economics is a way of thinking. It's deductive and rigorous. My goal in undergraduate writing is to have them see that you can apply an economic way of thought to just about anything.

—*Walter Williams, Economics*

If undergraduates can write clearly, logically and reasonably, I'm happy. I'd rather awaken in them a sense of how to essay an experience logically in a little five-page paper than to have them execute an ethnographic study.

—*Roger Lancaster, Anthropology*

I'm not trying to make undergraduates into political scientists. I want them to be clear and logical writers. But, to tell you the truth, I'm not sure what the difference is. I think good political science writing is good scholarly writing in terms of clarity, organization, and use of evidence.

—*Priscilla Regan, Political Science*

The informants we've placed in this second group—Williams, Regan, Lancaster, and Bergoffen—all observed that their rhetorical expectations for undergraduate writers are synonymous with general principles of good academic writing. Unlike the informants in the first group, who articulated these principles in the context of discipline-based exigencies, those in the second group talked in much more general terms about the forms they assign, such as the "essay" or simply "papers" to help students write analytically and persuasively. As we will show in this section, however, their expectations for what it means to "essay" a topic logically as well as what constitutes appropriate evidence and a readable style are actually quite different, revealing how firmly rooted these informants are in their own disciplinary traditions even as they profess otherwise. To be successful writers for these teachers, students need to be attuned not only to the explicit instructions they may be given but also to the disciplinary nuances implicit in the assignments.

Possibly more than any of our other informants, Williams's assignments and expectations for student writing seem to reflect his own writing outside of the academy. As we mentioned earlier, Williams has never forgotten his mentor's advice that, if a writer truly knows his subject, he can explain it to anyone, and he regularly enacts that advice in his syndicated columns, which apply economic principles to social problems. Not surprisingly, then, his assignments for both undergraduates and graduate students entail writing brief essay responses to everyday questions, like the following based on a biblical passage: "'A man shall not worry about what pertains to a woman and a woman shall not worry about what pertains to a man.' What's the economic interpretation of that passage? I don't have the answers to this question, but the thing that I look for is how they reason through to an answer." When we probed for more details, Williams talked about features of usage and syntax rather than forms, formats, or other rhetorical elements, i.e., contexts, audiences, purposes, that writers might face. He was particularly adamant about the need for students to learn to "economize with words" and, no matter their language backgrounds, to write in standard edited English. Further, he has no patience with discussions of alternative dialects—for example, Ebonics—regardless of their political intent. As an African American himself, he believes it "cruel to talk about alternatives. There is a culture here and we're born into it. To accept some of the nonsense, and I see it as nonsense, I think that's crushing."

Williams seemed surprised when we asked him what advice he gives to students to help them fulfill his expectations for clear, economical writing and analysis. "I don't really give them instructions," he explained. "I'll ask a question and then, when a student answers, I say 'I think I understand the answer, but I don't like your answer.' Then I tell them how a typical question should be answered. So I somewhat model the answer for them, but this is all oral." Even though Williams sees his expectations as generic to good writing, his modeling process presumably points students to specific rhetorical strategies, even exact wordings, they should use in their papers. Interestingly, Williams's modeling process, as we discuss more fully in the next chapter, points to one of the ways students in our focus groups said they learn to write for different teachers; that is, by listening to lecture styles and to teacher's answers to student questions they can figure out what the teacher might want, especially when the assignment instructions are vague or nonexistent.

Like Williams, Regan said that the skills students learn to employ when they write in political science are the same as those they need to write well in college in general. "I'll always emphasize the need to be clear and logical and organized regardless of what the purpose of the writing is or the form that it takes," she explained. Typical forms in political science, she said, are "compare/contrast" and "opinion" papers. While this general description may sound very much like the modes-based assignments used by many composition teachers, the purposes for writing and the rhetorical tasks she assigns, along with the readers she asks students to envision, have everything to do with a political science epistemology and the disciplinary exigencies that shape them: such exigencies, for example, as the need to explain political events to constituencies, to understand and address competing interests, and to inform or persuade individuals to take specific actions.

Regan's language in describing one of her "opinion paper" assignments is telling in this regard. She routinely asks both undergraduate and graduate students to write a memo to a member of Congress—as a "device" for teaching them how "to give an opinion and argue for that opinion." She asks them "to picture the member of Congress they're arguing to so that they have a sense of the importance of the argument." Writing for "an applied audience," she said, helps students write at a more sophisticated level. While Regan sees the memo format as a useful device for teaching argument, it might be more accurate to say that the applied audience is the device that helps students to write for a political science teacher. Sophistication, for Regan, may entail students' understanding that they must react to people and to specific situations, not only to ideas, theories, and/or other texts. Their arguments, then, have practical consequences. They must learn to draw on the kinds of evidence that will be persuasive in other political contexts besides that of the class. Types of evidence may include, depending upon the issue, data from surveys and polls, authoritative testimony, legal precedents and cases, and so on, as well as secondary research and analysis of primary data.

Similarly, Regan's comparison-contrast assignments, one of which she gave to us, speak to the disciplinary exigency to understand the competing interests that motivate individuals to take political action. Students in her upper-division government course, then, are asked to analyze a current political debate in terms of theoretical controversies they've been studying in the class. They are expected to include "some quotations" from the text and explain their significance. Finally, they must provide their own analysis of the issue and "make sense of the conflicting views." Their paper must be "well organized and logically developed." When we read between the lines of this assignment, we can see Regan's expectation that students, by their close reading of the assigned texts, will understand what constitutes a logical argument and appropriate quoting in political science. Further, if political decisions and the theories that attempt to explain them are made based on the interests of individuals who make up the polis, then the exigencies for writing and the writing itself are necessarily quite different from that in, say, psychology, philosophy, or literature.

They are not so different, however, from economics. Like Williams, Regan believes that in college and in their careers after college, students need the ability "to distill information, form an opinion, and present it in a way that's concise, brief, and to the point." In their emphasis on concise style, both Regan and Williams reveal the similar natures of their disciplinary concerns; that is, both are concerned with the self-interests of individuals acting within political and economic systems. Both envision nonacademic audiences who must be informed and/or persuaded to act within those systems. And, for both, that entails prose that is "precise, logical, and clear," meaning prose that will speak effectively to these audiences. The emphasis on conciseness in both disciplines might be compared to the standard emphasis on conciseness in business writing that, likewise, imagines a nonacademic reader and is action-oriented.

For anthropologist Lancaster, such a prose style is anathema. Student writing, according to his "pretty basic and conservative" standards, "should be clear, it should be logical, and it should be readable." While Lancaster is using almost exactly the same terms that Williams and Regan are using, he means something very different by them. Readable prose, for Lancaster, is prose fashioned after the classic literary texts of anthropology, like those by Mead,

Turnbull, and Pritchard, who appealed both to academic and nonacademic readers who enjoy—and expect—belletristic writing. "I hate that scientific paradigm that prose is supposed to be transparent," he said. "I think most Americans tend to think of writing as something that gets you to the point rather than something you live with." He described an anthropology major he once worked with who had been trained to translate scientific texts into short digests. "You'd look at her writing and it was all bullet style writing, close small sentences, active verbs. I couldn't help saying 'This is not how you write. Don't bring that to this class. You cannot get traction on ideas that way.' She got better, and, if I'd had another semester, I could have done more."

"More," for Lancaster, starts at the sentence level:

> A good sentence should be alive. It may be Ernest Hemingway style, lean and sparse, or George Orwell style, very rational, logical, with no excess anywhere, or Jean Paul Sartre, roundabout and elusive with a fine structure. Like Brechtian *geste*, there's an order in which you write the sentence so that when you reach the end it comes as a surprise, or it comes to you that there's a sense of completion, or a sense that the sentence is incomplete and leaves you wanting more. Sentences have to behave differently.

While others in anthropology may not "obsess over style" the way he does, he notes that the books people assign in their courses, particularly in introductory courses, tend to be those that are "well styled" and written "the good way."

It's this good way that Lancaster wants his students to learn; however, as he sees it, the standard ethnographic report is not the best form for teaching "basic good writing." Nor, he said, is it standard practice to assign ethnographic reports to undergraduates, at least until their senior year. In his classes, he teaches students to write what he called "standard academic essays"—essays "composed out of other essays"—in which they refine their ideas and arguments and, most emphatically, their prose through a process of careful revision. Sometimes, Lancaster said, he lets his undergraduates—both majors and nonmajors—do ethnographic research for their essays because, when students use ethnographic techniques, they learn "to form reasonably informed opinions supported by primary data from participant-observation research." Further, Lancaster said, students can "very quickly develop an array of critical thinking skills about how they interact with other people, how they draw conclusions about everyday life, and how they mobilize evidence to work up an argument. In other words, they're not just constructing an argument out of a book, they're trying to work up an argument out of the stuff of everyday life, and this is not a bad little thing to include in the bag of tricks that you teach undergraduates." Though he may characterize his bag of tricks as basic good writing, Lancaster, like Regan and Williams, is working from a disciplinary paradigm, from his preference for the literary style of classic anthropological texts to his view that valid evidence comes either from other empirical studies or from systematic observations of everyday life.

Bergoffen, too, clearly works from a disciplinary paradigm even though, in her view, when she teaches students to think philosophically, she is teaching them "to think." For Bergoffen, this entails helping them to reflect critically on philosophical arguments and to write "straightforward papers: here's the thesis, here's the development, here's the conclusion." Straightforward papers, as her reflection paper assignment reveals, can be written in creative forms. Sometimes, she said, she sets up an "imaginative situation: Socrates is in the Eternity McDonald's and he meets John Stuart Mill and Locke, and they find themselves at the same table because it's crowded and they start arguing about human nature. What would they have said? What is this conversation about?" She encourages students to write in dialogue form and delights in the way some of them set up introductory stories about how the philosophers got to McDonald's, what the McDonald's looks like, and so on. If students "don't enjoy that kind of creativity," they can write in an "essay" form. Whatever the form, the expectation is that students will engage in a dialectic as they work through the philosophical arguments; that is, they must "take a position, state their opinion, and make clear that their evaluation is not going to be about opinions but about arguments." The reflection assignments, she said, are generally set up as "compare/contrast questions," similar, it seems, to those Regan asks, although the exigency, the form, and the imagined audiences are quite different.

The general term "reflection paper" is interesting to think about in a philosophical context where the questions that drive the discipline have to do with how one lives a rational and reflective life. In this paper, Bergoffen is not interested in how students "feel" about these questions nor is she asking them to reflect on their own lives; in fact, she gets "distressed" when she discovers, as she so often does, that students who might have done a good job of "analyzing, dissecting, and critiquing the readings" tend to "fall apart" when she asks them to give their own opinion. "I get this statement that they don't back up, that just tells me how they feel, and it's like a total disconnect." When she asks students, "'What do you think?'" she expects "the same kind of attentiveness"—the careful analytical critique—that they have applied to their readings. Instead, students seem to see the question as "an invitation to be lazy." It's "discouraging," she said, to think that they may walk out of the classroom and, when they're "having conversations among themselves or reading the newspapers, just go right back into these sloppy ways of thinking." While Bergoffen has used standard academic terminology such as "argument" and "essay" to describe her assignments and sees them as a general corrective to students' lazy thinking, she too is privileging a disciplinary approach, one that assumes close reading, a dialectical structure, and a reasoned ethos. Moreover, even the act of close reading itself differs considerably from close reading in, say, history or literary studies, where the meanings of primary sources or imaginative texts are interpreted within those disciplinary frameworks, as our discussions of Copelman and Clark illustrated.

To help students be better prepared for the reflection paper and to be sure that they are keeping up with the reading, Bergoffen also assigns journals. Again, however, her use of the journal is quite discipline specific, very different from the purposes behind Bob Smith's use of the "journal" in psychology, for example, as described earlier. For her, journals offer students a more informal place to engage in a dialectic, as they connect the texts they've been reading, raise questions, and reflect on answers. "I'm trying to have them ask questions in these two pages," she explained. "They can't just drop a question, they have to show how a text provokes the question, so I'm tying them to the text." When she first began using journals, she tried having students free write, but found that approach unworkable. Next she gave students short prompts for their weekly two-page entries. She intended their responses to inform the reflection papers—"My theory was they'd have all these little pieces ready to cut and paste into the bigger paper"—but found that students "didn't translate" the assignment in the same way. Instead they saw the journal as a discrete form with little connection to their papers, so it always seemed that they were "starting their papers from scratch." Now, Bergoffen explained with enthusiasm, she seems to have hit on the right formula. Instead of weekly journal entries, each student has to do only six, which can be spread out across the semester as the student wishes. In addition, each student must choose one reading on which to lead a class discussion. So, she said, "I'm looking at these logs as a classroom discussion tool and I'm not expecting anything else."

What Bergoffen was not translating to students initially, as we see it, is her construction of the journal as a place to practice a philosophical ethos and way of arguing that could then be formalized in their papers. It's understandable, then, that her first approach—free writing—would fail since most students will have a dramatically different conception of what it means to free write, just as they will of the journal as an "informal" writing space. Now that her expectations have changed, she is much more "excited" about the work that the journals seem to be accomplishing. Bergoffen continues to see the journal as a place for risk taking, but again her definition of "risk," as we saw when we asked her to clarify, is bound up with disciplinary concerns. For her, taking a risk means making a provocative argument, such as the one a student made when he wrote, "Job didn't change, God did." Just as she no longer expects that students can easily cut and paste a journal entry into their formal papers, she also does not expect them to take the same kinds of risks in their reflection papers that she wants to see in the journal. This would be "a little too scary" for them, she noted, given that a larger percentage of their grade is at stake.

A risk Bergoffen did ask students in one of her upper-division courses to take, however, involved writing personally about aspects of their identity related to their philosophical engagement in a particular topic. Bergoffen had told us earlier that one of the biggest—and scariest—risks she had taken in her own work was writing about herself in an essay published in a collection on how philosophers' lives have informed their philosophical outlooks. She wrote about her academic path into philosophy, her identity as a woman and a Jew, and her feminism. When her students expressed discomfort about disclosing personal information in the assigment she'd given them, she put her own essay on reserve in the library for them to read and explained how uncomfortable she too felt sharing personal details with readers, perhaps even more so when those readers are students she sees face to face in class. While one might argue that this kind of personal writing represents an alternative to the impersonal discourses of philosophy, we see it, as does Bergoffen, as a response to the turn in philosophy to feminist and postmodern arguments that acknowledge the identity of the thinker as central to what is thought.

Similarly, we can see the experimental tradition in anthropology reflected in an alternative assignment Lancaster sometimes gives to his upper-division students. In sharp contrast to his insistence on lower-division students mastering "the standard essay form" and his impatience with the "impressionistic bullshit they often get away with writing in some of their other courses," Lancaster told us he sometimes tries to "liberate" his anthropology students from the "disciplinary police" by telling them to "do anything they want other than a standard essay" as long as they convey the course material and demonstrate a "serious engagement" with the ideas. "Some students have written epic poems; some have written plays. One group of students staged a Punch and Judy show on Bakhtin, which is very appropriate. Another group wrote a soap opera and acted it out. I don't allow belly dancing. I don't allow bizarre rituals. And nothing dangerous. But pretty much anything else," he said, adding that it's the newness of the experience that seems to "click in" and enables students to have "a much deeper engagement with the texts" than when they write in standard forms. He suspects this is the case because they are "drawing on other forms of learning than just sitting down and producing a linear paper." He grades these alternative assignments on "the content and not the aesthetics or performance value," he explained. "Even if they've done a video, or a play, or a montage of photos with text, they're still writing. It's just a different kind of writing." Further, he has a "strong impression" that "the content is actually better, richer, and shows more seriousness of thought" than the content in their more linear papers. In many ways, Lancaster's description of this assignment reminds us of his description of the "montage" approach he used in *Life Is Hard*, which he initially believed to be quite daring and subsequently came to see as "standard ethnography." Further, his emphasis on student engagement, like Copelman's, represents an attitude he feels is essential for students learning the discipline. The unorthodox assignments that each gives are ways to achieve that goal. Thus a student product need not follow a standard format in the field to achieve the discipline's goals.

Neither This Nor That: Alternative Exigencies, Alternative Forms

As Chapter Two shows, a number of our informants regularly write or have experimented with writing in ways they consider to be alternative within their disciplines, including, for example, Trefil and Williams, who currently write predominately for popular media, and Bergoffen and Lancaster, who have "risked" writing in postmodern voices and styles. Both Bergoffen and Lancaster also recognized, however, that their disciplines were at least somewhat open to texts that engaged with alternative discussions already occurring in the discipline. In turn, while both described, as we showed in the preceding section, their generally traditional expectations for student writing, each also occasionally experimented with giving assignments that mirrored their own theoretical preoccupations. The informants who are our main focus in this section, however, are those who are most firmly committed, in their own academic work and in the assignments they give to students, to exigencies, audiences, and forms that, as they see it, are truly alternative in their disciplines. These two informants spoke with conviction about their reasons for using unconventional assignments.

> And the students read these stories out loud in class, which can be really emotional. I've learned to bring a box of [tissues] to class.
>
> —*Jeanne Sorrell, Nursing*

What is perhaps most alternative about the assignments that both Jeanne Sorrell and Victoria Rader give is their expectation that students will experience a deep, emotional engagement with the topic and that they will, in turn, convey this feeling to readers as a way to motivate some kind of social change. Sorrell, for example, recognizes that the unequal relationship between doctors and nurses has meant that nurses are often afraid to trust their own intuitions about a patient's condition, sometimes with unfortunate consequences. Sorrell is also very concerned about the current shortage of nursing professionals. For her, then, it is almost more important to give assignments that address these concerns than to have students write yet one more abstract or experimental report although they do these assignments as well. Rader, who has always integrated her social activism with her academic work, requires her students to do "action projects," for which they identify some cause they want to work on. "What is it you care about?" she asks students. "What would you like to be more fair? How can you join with someone else to make a change?" While Sorrell's and Rader's assignments are alternative in different ways, as we will show, both ask students to write personally about people and events that have influenced who they are and/or what they believe. They do this writing as a way to get in touch with larger social goals, i.e., larger than the academy, that the course and assignments promote.

We'll begin with a discussion of two of Sorrell's alternative assignments, which seem to share with Lancaster's and Bergoffen's assignments an overall goal of deepening students' engagement with the discipline. However, Sorrell's assignment goals extend, perhaps inevitably given the preprofessional status of nursing, beyond the academy to the field itself, where one of the most pressing concerns is the critical shortage of qualified nurses. Contributing to this shortage is the sense that nursing work is undervalued and underpaid. To address the first of these concerns, Sorrell has asked students in her upper-division Nurses as Writers course to write stories for children about what it's like to be a nurse. "I believe this kind of alternative writing," she said, "is more needed now than scholarly articles written for ourselves." The inspiration for the project came from her memory of becoming attracted to nursing as a preteen when she read the *Candy Stripers* and *Cherry Ames, RN* series. Sorrell thought young people—both boys and girls—might be similarly drawn in by "fictional accounts of some of the exciting and satisfying things that occur daily in areas such as neonatal nursing, oncology, E.R., for example." So she asked her students to write stories using "themselves as characters but also using characters not as often featured in nursing publications, like males and minority nurses." This project culminated in *The Magic Stethoscope*, a small soft-cover book authored by her students under the pseudonym R. N. Hope.

If the underlying motive for the children's book is to recruit nurses to the profession, the exigency for another of Sorrell's assignments—"paradigm cases"—is to help students get in touch with the realities of nursing work and, since most are already practicing or interning, to gain confidence in their abilities and intuitions. For this assignment, students write two stories, one about themselves and one about a patient. This is where the tissues come out, according to Sorrell, as students read their stories aloud in a kind of "read-around," a standard activity of the Northern Virginia Writing Project, in which she participated. She also contributes a story to the read-around. "The reading aloud seems to serve a purpose, as the student's voice really comes through," she notes.

> And it is always a very powerful experience for the students and for me. Maybe it's the intensity of reading them; maybe we store stories differently in our memory. We usually don't analyze the story. I try to make it stand alone, and we go from one student to the next. But sometimes the story really hits home, and it seems best to stop and talk about it. In a way, the spontaneous discussion is a kind of phenomenological analysis, though we don't do a formal analysis.

The stories students tell, she said, reveal students' joys, their fears, their sometimes reluctance to contradict doctors, their sense of having made errors in judgment by not acting on their intuitions. "We need to write about our mistakes," Sorrell insists, "because that's what forwards our practice."

Sorrell uses the paradigm case assignment in her Advanced Clinical Nursing courses, and it is also a staple of the upper-division Nurses as Writers course and a required piece in students' capstone portfolios. In addition, faculty sometimes use the assignment in other undergraduate courses. However, Sorrell told us, some of the undergraduate faculty are uncomfortable with "the unstructured nature of the story" and so will substitute a more traditional case study. Some students too, Sorrell said, express discomfort with the assignment, thinking that it is not "the kind of sophisticated work that they expected to do in college." Some "will write the story with all of the details typical of lab study values, like they've learned to do in experimental reports." When this happens, she suggests they write to "a nonnursing professional to see how to alter that voice and eliminate details they don't need."

The emotional power of the stories and the discomfort that some faculty and students feel points to the inherently nonacademic nature of the assignment. In Chapter One, we said that, in academic writing, reasoned analysis always takes precedent over emotion or sensation. Yet here is an instance where emotion through story is allowed to exist without analysis or with what Sorrell characterized as a kind of spontaneous phenomenological analysis. Nevertheless, Sorrell obviously feels that an exercise of this kind plays an important role in the curriculum. While these assignments are clearly the ones Sorrell feels most passionate about, and which she described to us in detail, we don't want to give the impression that her students are not also doing more traditional academic work. As her syllabus for the Nurses as Writers course reveals, the culminating portfolio includes abstracts and executive summaries, a "persuasive paper," and a critique of a professional article, as well as other short, reflective writings, and a resume.

While Sorrell believes that her alternative assignments are central and necessary to the nursing profession—and hence the discipline—if structural changes are to occur, Rader notes that "the overwhelming number of students in my classes are not sociology majors nor are they are going to be sociologists, so I'm training them to think about the world and to develop a social consciousness." As part of this process, students must necessarily learn and practice some of the principles of sociology, including, for example, careful observation, analysis, and reflection. Yet, unlike the discipline of nursing, which, as we discussed in Chapter Two, has opened up to accommodate a phenomenological methodology, Rader does not see the discipline of sociology accommodating social activism among its methodological concerns. Her description of the "action project" she assigns in both upper-division and introductory courses illustrates the weight she places on what might be called alternative methods—an insistence on practicing activism with "the goal" being "not just to get the action but to practice the process." The "analysis-reflection-action" process is a cycle, she said, that "actually comes from radical Catholic activism" and includes "analyzing the problem you want to commit yourself to, reflecting on the ethical, political, moral, and personal dimensions, and then acting on that analysis and reflection. Then you analyze your action and take the next action."

To prepare her students for the action project, Rader often gives them chapters from her book in progress. As noted in Chapter Two, her book discloses some very personal details about her life, such as stories about her alcoholic family and fights with her brother and father. The chapters seemed to make some students uncomfortable, she said, as she could tell not by what they said but by how "their eyes looked down when I asked for feedback." Still, she said, it's important to talk about these things because "it is part of who I am. Lots of families experience difficulties and disconnection, so I wanted to be honest." She wanted feedback from students because she thinks of them as a "major audience" for her book. (She acknowledged that part of their discomfort may have come from being asked to critique a professor's work.) Perhaps more important than getting their feedback, however, was her desire to model a reflective process for them.

To reinforce why we think of Rader's teaching as alternative, we want to compare her use of personal story to Bergoffen's. As we mentioned earlier, Bergoffen also shared her autobiographical writing with students, a published essay about her educational path into philosophy. In the essay, Bergoffen maintains an analytical distance, it seems to us, relying on a reader's familiarity with "woman" and "Jew" as categories of identity that influenced her educational and scholarly choices (that of a girl growing up in the 1950s who has to come to terms with having different academic interests from other girls, a woman philosopher who embraces Simone de Beauvoir as someone who helps her formulate a feminist response to the Holocaust). In contrast, Rader seems to step outside of an academic persona to reveal the nitty-gritty, often painful, details of her dysfunctional family even as she also relates these experiences to alcoholism in families, racism in schools, social class, and so on. Her intention in giving readers this personal glimpse into her family life is not only to show how these experiences led her to become a social activist, but also to argue for the necessity of confronting and examining our personal pasts in order to understand why we feel the way we do about a particular social injustice. She asks her students to follow a similar process in her action project assignment.

Disciplines, Alternatives, and Perceptions of Risk

In its insistence on the particulars of a writer's lived experiences, Rader's action project is similar to Sorrell's paradigm case assignment. Both assignments, whether accompanied by analysis or not, unabashedly allow students to revel in their felt experience as a means for getting in touch with that reality. In this way, both assignments reveal, we think, a belief in the power of the personal to testify, to give witness to, experiences that cry out for social change. To understand the risks that writers—both faculty and students—might feel they are taking when they write in such personal ways, we think it is useful to look again at the exigencies motivating personal disclosures and how these relate to disciplinary epistemologies. It's not unusual in sociology, for example, to study and write about dysfunction and social deviance. And, while Rader described her action project as something apart from "sociology," the assignment requires students to use many of the analytical skills used by sociologists. Further, she told us that even her more traditional assignments "have a reflexive component built in" and students are encouraged to use first person: "So I might ask something like, 'Do you think people can make a difference? What's your understanding of that? What's your experience with that?'"

So what are the perceived risks for Rader and her students, we wonder, compared to the risks Bergoffen perceives she is taking—and asking her students to take—when they write about how they have come to feel connected to a philosophical position. Perhaps for a philosopher any personal disclosure might feel risky in a discipline that prizes objective, rational inquiry. When we ask students to write personally, then, we need to think about our reasons for doing so, the kinds of revelations we're expecting, the ways students might be asked to use the personal in their disciplinary endeavors, and the degree of risk they might feel related to their own disciplinary inclinations.

We also think it's important to consider the criteria by which these kinds of assignments will be evaluated. When they described their alternative assignments to us, Lancaster, Sorrell, and Rader all observed that it can be hard to put a grade on this kind of work. "Students can get mad," Rader said, "like 'My story is my story, how can you evaluate it?'" Sorrell said she also struggles with how to put a grade on the paradigm cases and generally gives them all high marks for fulfilling the assignment. Lancaster does not mark students on the artistic merit, originality, or creativity of their alternative presentations; rather, he judges them on whether they have adequately conveyed an understanding of the course content. While these teachers may have come to terms with the pitfalls inherent in evaluating assignments that fall outside of disciplinary expectations, students are quite likely to be suspicious of such assignments and their teachers' motives in giving and grading them, as we will discuss in the next chapter on students' perceptions of writing and writing assignments in their majors.

New Media, Hypermedia, Multimedia

We've put Lesley Smith, new media specialist, into a separate section because we see her assignments as part and parcel of a field that is itself a little-understood alternative within the academy. Further, she is tenure-line faculty in a relatively young interdisciplinary, integrative college. Given the convergence in "new media" of so many disciplinary perspectives accompanied by the dynamic development of technology, it can be difficult, if not impossible, to predict the framework for assignments and expectations for writing in this emerging field.

Students in Smith's classes can expect an ever-new mix of assignments that blend academic standards with rhetorical versatility and a flair for the avant-garde. With her historian's devotion to accuracy and thorough research and her poet's devotion to precision in language, she expects all student writing to "make every word count" and she expects "enough high-quality research so that they're not reinventing the real." Similarly, her years as a TV producer have given her deep respect for "professional standards" in the workplace as well as in academia; thus, she expects student work "that would convince me that if I were someone employing this person, or commissioning them to do this particular project, they were able to do what they said they were going to do."

At the same time, she gives students tasks that they are not likely to see in other courses, and the range of genres in even one course can be daunting, to say the least. In her most recent version of Writing for Multimedia, for example, students wrote (1) a news story "as if" for the university student paper or a major daily, (2) an audio script meant for National Public Radio or the network news, (3) a "sparkling" 6–7 minute video script, (4) a script for an informational multimedia production, (5) a narrative script, nonfiction or fiction, and (6) a collaborative proposal, treatment, and script for a production in one of the media studied earlier—this project is meant to be done in concert with a media production course in which some are enrolled. Smith says she wants all this writing to be "clear, dynamic, and precise"; the instructions for every assignment caution students to think creatively and clearly about audience and purpose and to tailor the work accordingly.

While Writing for Multimedia shows students writing a wide variety of scripts in different forms for different audiences, the team-taught courses Information in the Digital Age and The Social World require students to create multimedia web-based projects even as they maintain the precision of language that she expects in all her courses. Her learning goals for Information in the Digital Age demonstrate the breadth of new media skills the students must learn in order to fulfill their writing assignments; they include learning to write hypertext, demonstrating an understanding of basic design principles, incorporating graphics, posting coursework for peer review, and publishing high-quality digital products. Smith sees the products created in this course as giving each student a place to create a "digital identity." "Who do you want people to perceive you to be?" she asks in the course overview. One assignment in this course requires students to research how "digital information is transforming the way we conduct our social, cultural, business, educational, political and economic affairs" and to publish a "multilevel website, which includes appropriate design and graphics and the ethical citation of sources."

This concern for the links between technology and culture is shown even more emphatically in The Social World, an integrative course that caps the freshman year experience for students in the interdisciplinary New Century College. In this course, the final project is a collaborative website that analyzes "how our location in a particular country at a particular time influences our writing of history and our ability to interpret and understand the histories and contemporary experiences in other regions of the world." Not only does Smith expect from these first-year students a multifaceted cultural critique, but she expects a multimedia presentation that tests the technical acumen they have been developing during this first year in NCC. Each group creates a "formal website that demonstrates intellectual rigor, narrative fluency, navigational coherence, and grammatical correctness. The site should also demonstrate attention to visual rhetoric: consider your layout, choice of colors, and use of graphics and photographs carefully. . . ."

Certainly Smith's "alternativeness," unlike Sorrell's or Rader's, does not consist of a departure from the academic stress on research-based analysis, nor does it emphasize expression of emotion or sensation. The hypothetical "subject" of the capstone project in The Social World is a "self" only in the context-laden analysis by the reasoning student. When, in Information in the Digital Age, Smith asks students, "Who do you want people to perceive you to be?" she's not asking for emotion or even introspection, but for a carefully calculated digital identity, as image-conscious, if not so cynical, as anything on Madison Avenue or in Hollywood. In that regard, her perspective among our informants is perhaps closest to that of Miller or Regan, but even more multi-faceted and intense: though in an academic environment, she is ever aware of the rhetorical demands of the world outside, of the student's future tasks of influencing employers, potential clients, the "public" at large. (This recurring focus on audiences outside the academy was corroborated by the students from New Century College whom we interviewed, as we describe in the next chapter.)

Like our informants in the first section of this chapter, Smith does not imagine any innate transferability of what students learn in these writing-intense courses to the environments in which they'll write later. Nevertheless, what sets her apart from all our other informants is her commitment to "teach transferability" to her students. She has learned from teaching, she says, that students assume no transferability from one course to another, or from the academy to the workplace or citizenship—that students need to be convinced that what they learn in one context will be useful in another, and teachers have to show them how:

> I realized that I took transferability for granted because I went from doing a highly academic Ph.D. in a very academic environment, to working for the British government, to working in television. I had to work out why my degree made me equipped to do these things. Then I went into an M.F.A. in creative writing and, from there, to teaching with technology. I'm very lucky that I can always pull out these experiences for students. I can say to students that I'm not just talking theory when I talk about transferability, I'm showing them, "This is what's going to happen to you."

Indeed, Smith's assignments demand that students become both academics and business professionals. They need to explore a range of nuanced analytic/synthetic questions and cite sources accurately. They need also to present their work with visual panache and a crafted "digital identity." By framing the visual qualities of their Web designs and navigation schemes as "you," she is pushing the students toward an examination of self that forces students to be risk-takers. They must leave the relatively familiar confines of literacy—in which many of them do not feel all that comfortable—in order to probe and then express their "identity" in visual and logical electronic structures that are unfamiliar, maybe wholly new to them. Risk is everywhere in the enterprise. In stark contrast to Bob Smith, Jones, and Trefil, whose students work more or less in proximity to the conventions of the scientific article, Lesley Smith's students, like Smith herself, are using the ever more flexible tools of electronic technology to craft "interfaces"—much more complex than anything implied by a writer's "format"—that are simultaneously an "identity" and a rhetorical transaction. There may or may not be contradiction in the requirements to conform to "grammatical correctness"—the logic of academic print—and also to "create" a "coherent, user-friendly navigation scheme"—the logic of hypertext—but clearly the student is being pulled in different, if not opposite, directions. Such is life in the academy's new digital age, as led by scholars like Lesley Smith, and it is certainly alternative to what's gone before.

Faculty Expectations in Department Assessment Rubrics

In addition to what we have learned about faculty's expectations for student writers and writing in their disciplines, we have gathered a rich set of data from the writing assessment workshops we have been conducting with faculty in departments for several years. In this section, we'll discuss how these data—the workshop process and the rubrics faculty developed—augment what we have learned from our faculty informants. At the same time, we are also aware that these data provide a much more limited picture of expectations for writing in the disciplines than do our interviews, since all the papers being assessed in each workshop were written in response to one assignment given in a writing-intensive course in that major. In the workshops and the rubrics they produced we don't get the range of exigencies that our informants covered when they spoke about first-year students, undergraduate majors, graduate students, and so forth. Nevertheless, the data are valuable because the discussion of sample papers and the rubrics that emerged from that discussion highlight each department's sense of the genres students in their major need to learn in an upper-division writing-intensive course. The assignment they selected, for assessment purposes, represents one of those genres.

    The initial impetus for our assessment initiative was a state mandate to assess students' writing competence. Because faculty often have very different ideas about what makes writing good based on their own disciplinary expectations, as we have been arguing here, we were committed to a process that put responsibility for this assessment into the hands of departments. Our first step was to invite the departmental liaisons who would be in charge of the writing assessment effort in their departments to a "training the trainers" workshop. In that workshop, we modeled a process that showed how criteria for assessment could be derived from careful consideration of a range of student sample papers. For workshop purposes, we chose papers written in response to a "Review of the Literature" assignment in an advanced composition course. The next step required the departmental liaisons to run their own workshops, using sample papers from their upper-division, writing-intensive courses. In these workshops, participating faculty produced rubrics that could be used for assessing writing competence in the major. As might be expected, the evaluations of papers in the "training the trainers" workshop showed more starkly the differences in personal and disciplinary preferences than did the similar exercise in the departmental workshops.

The first "training the trainers" workshop we conducted consisted of faculty liaisons from the humanities, the social and natural sciences, and business. As we described briefly in our first chapter, we had anticipated that faculty would prioritize adherence to conventions of form and style when they evaluated and ranked the sample literature review papers, though we knew they might differ somewhat based on disciplinary traditions. We were surprised, then, at seeing major disagreements about what constituted a "good" paper; that is, many faculty ranked what we had considered to be the most poorly written paper in the sample higher than what we considered the most competent one, saying that they valued its fresh voice and perceived risk-taking, while the more proficiently written paper was deemed to "say nothing new."

Although we didn't see such stark differences of opinion in the departmental workshops, at which one or the other of us assisted, the scoring process always yielded a rich and nuanced discussion of what constitutes "good" writing in the major. Most of this talk is not captured in the scoring rubrics that were subsequently developed to assess and report on student writing competence. Invisible behind each rubric, with its succinct list of briefly explained criteria, is a chalkboard full of qualities that faculty articulated as characteristics of good writing based on the sample papers they read. Also invisible are the lengthy discussions that occur as faculty—in the same department—strive to come to consensus about what each of the criteria might mean in practice.

Discussions in the Public and International Affairs workshop about the criterion "clear thesis" offer a good case in point. After reading the sample papers and developing a rubric, the fifteen or so faculty present discovered that about half of them told their students to state their argument in a thesis early in the essay; the other half strongly objected, saying that writers should not give away their "conclusion" before they had presented reasoned evidence in support of their argument. Who, they asked, expected which kind of thesis? And what were students supposed to do, they asked, when they went from one person's class, where they were taught one way, to the class of another, who said that it was terribly bad form to do it that way. In the end, they realized that the best thing they could do for students was to share with them these differences of opinion. On the rubric, under the criterion "Structure of Argument," they include, along with other specifying details, this parenthetical statement: "(Note: Some would like a thesis paragraph to lay out a framework for the argument to follow; others noted that the 'conclusion' should not come in the first paragraph.)"

Because so many of the rubrics we helped to develop in departmental workshops included criteria related to thesis statements (or the appropriate place for an hypothesis), Terry was curious when dance faculty in the workshop she was helping to lead made no mention of a thesis statement. When she questioned them about whether that was something they wanted to include when they looked at papers "reacting to" a performance, they explained that they were very tired of students making opening generalizations about the meaning of the overall performance when, instead, they should be considering each dance on its own terms and, if appropriate, explaining how it fits into the larger performance. A thesis statement in this case, they argued, only seemed to encourage students in their bad habit of making unwarranted and unwanted generalizations.

In addition to discussions about structure and organization, faculty frequently mentioned appropriate prose style as a criterion. And, as with the thesis discussions, unshared assumptions sometimes surfaced. For example, in a workshop with nursing faculty, led by Terry, to assess portfolios from the capstone course, the 19 faculty present disagreed over what constituted "good" prose style in the field of nursing. Readers were sharply divided about whether one student's portfolio was, at one extreme, "excellent" or, at the other, "unsatisfactory," based on whether the complex sentence style employed by the writer (incorrectly labeled by some as "run-on's") was appropriate in a discipline where precise, clear communication to doctors, patients, administrators, and the public was the chief goal. The discussion turned to the value of an "interesting" style, depending upon the purpose of the writing and the intended audience. The resulting assessment rubric, which is also now circulated to the capstone course teachers and students as both a feedback and evaluation rubric, takes care to note that appropriate style may vary depending upon the rhetorical situation.

Departmental Rubrics

While the departmental assessment process has yielded useful data for our analysis of expectations, the rubrics produced by this process are useful in a different way. The assessment initiative has thus far produced rubrics of criteria from 15 (at this writing) undergraduate degree programs. More will be forth-coming as the university-wide assessment proceeds, but what we have thus far ranges across the arts and humanities, the social sciences, the experimental sci-ences, technological fields, and professions. We have found that the rubrics demonstrate clearly the replication of the "generic academic" terminology that our faculty informants tended to use, with the nuances that contrast the dis-ciplines much less evident, though visible in most cases upon closer reading. All rubrics are available on the GMU WAC website at http://wac.gmu.edu/program/assessing/phase4.html#part3.

To compare the rubrics, we carried out four procedures. First, we looked for the terms that were repeated from rubric to rubric and observed the fre-quency of explicit use of a term across all. Second, we also looked for use of similar terms (e.g., "diction" and "usage") that implied the same concept and observed frequency based on these observations. Third, we noted what seemed to be criteria exclusive to one or just a few fields. Fourth, we attended to the emphases or priorities in the lists of criteria, as suggested by the order of items and the amount of coverage given to a specific concept. These meth-ods enabled us to observe not only the presence or absence of a criterion in a rubric, but also how faculty in that discipline might prioritize or define a con-cept differently from another.

To exemplify how this comparison worked, one of the more detailed rubrics, that for the Department of Public and International Affairs (PIA), contained 23 terms that were replicated in at least several other rubrics, ordered as follows:

> argument, clear, engagement, original, balanced, thesis, supporting evi-dence, logical, sources, development, well-organized, flow, appropriate voice, audience, purpose, transitions, consistent documentation style, quo-tations, active voice, grammar, spelling, punctuation, format

These were arranged in five categories, in this order: "content of argument," "form of argument," "structure of argument," "documentation and citation," and "style and mechanics."

Comparing this rubric with another—for example, psychology's—shows a notable reiteration of terms—15 of the 23—but how these are elaborated shows important distinctions between the fields. For example, where the PIA rubric requires consistency in the documentation style chosen by the student ("one style of documentation used adequately and correctly"), psychology specifies "APA style and format." Psychology is the only unit in the sample of rubrics to specify one style, and, indeed, the designation of APA (American Psychological Association) style signals the emphasis in this rubric on all things APA. Thus, where "content" in the PIA rubric includes such criteria as "engagement with topic" and "original ideas"—terms reiterated in several other rubrics—psychology's "content" section prioritizes "justification of hypotheses," "reasoned/logical presentation of research," and criteria specific to the APA report sections "literature review" and "methods." Where PIA writes of "audience" in a situated way—"appropriate voice/tone for audience and purpose"—psychology says categorically, "Paper is written for the appropriate audience; namely, individuals who read research articles." Both rubrics share the academic priority of evidence used to support an arguable position, but the rubrics vary significantly in ethos and flexibility.

Certainly, the rubrics vary in the amount of detail; nevertheless, even the least detailed rubric (School of Management), which is notably sparer than any other, overlaps remarkably with the rest. Its mere seven key terms are "audiences," "purposes," "evidence to support," "argument," "organize," "grammar," and "mechanics"—terms and ordering repeated in most of and sometimes all the other rubrics.

The most common terms among the rubrics are "evidence," "organized," and "grammar" (90+ percent in each case). "Audience," "thesis," "consistent documentation style," "sources," "appropriate voice," "punctuation," and "clear" are each mentioned by at least 70 percent of the rubrics. "Argument" is explicitly used by more than half, but the ubiquity of "evidence" implies that each program expects writing that makes and supports some sort of claim. The dance rubric, for example, asks for "opinions/ideas that are well supported using specific examples from the dance."

The repetition of important terms and concepts certainly supports the common academic criteria we defined in Chapter One, and it corroborates our contention based on the interviews and assignment descriptions that students are likely to hear many of the same terms from course to course, discipline to discipline. But the student will need to keep in mind that the recurrence of terminology and of such broad concepts as "evidence," "grammar," and "appropriate voice" mask distinctions that begin to come out in some of the rubrics—and that would be far more evident if faculty, like those in our assessment workshops, were to look at samples of what passes for "good student writing" in another field. These rubrics were developed by faculty working *only* with colleagues and *only* assessing sample essays of kinds they were used to seeing from their undergraduate majors. The terms may be to a significant extent "generic" to academia, but the meaning and application of the terms in any of the departmental norming sessions was common only to those colleagues. In other words, the terms represent "insider" talk, and so each term, such as "evidence," covers a wide range of inferred connotations for that group of readers. Thus, what might appear to be "transparent" criteria are in fact to a great degree impenetrable to those outside the discourse.

A blatant example of the impenetrable comes from the minimalist School of Management (SOM) rubric, which, in addition to the few criteria noted above, contains the category "discipline-specific criteria." The SOM faculty evaluating the sample essays recognize that there will be local criteria pertaining to assignments and subdisciplines within management, and they have chosen to leave these criteria undefined. A student reading this rubric will know quickly that there are more expectations than meet the eye—and the rubric does nothing to relieve the anxiety that the student will feel as a result. The SOM rubric, as it stands, thus appears to give students a touchstone by using familiar academic language, then takes away that touchstone through the cryptic "discipline-specific criteria." Other rubrics, like the PIA example already described, show faculty struggling to make the subtle differences in individual teachers' expectations clearer to students and colleagues, but all the rubrics share to a greater or lesser degree the paradox of difference masked by the illusion of similar terminology.

Conclusion: The Standard vs. the Alternative

At the beginning of the chapter we asked two main questions, which we paraphrase as follows:

1. To what extent does the remarkable similarity of terms that faculty use to define "good writing" in their fields show shared values? Is it more accurate to say that the similarity hides differences in meaning and application that trap the unwary neophyte and that mislead the composition teacher trying to prepare students for writing in disciplines?

2. To what extent do faculty teach as they write? Specifically, we wondered whether and how the writing practices of our informants, as well as the ways they constructed the expectations of their discipline for themselves, would be corroborated by the assignments and instruction they give to students.

The answer to both questions under (1) is a paradoxical yes. The overwhelming commonness of an array of terms such as "evidence," "organized," and "grammar," as shown in our informants' responses and in the departmental assessment rubrics, demonstrates a community of values. As vague and abstract as such terms may be, we heard and read very little that would contradict the three general principles of academic writing outlined in Chapter One. Indeed, the number of common terms in the rubrics seems to suggest an even more detailed sharing of beliefs.

At the same time, as we heard our informants and witnessed faculties arguing criteria, and as we read assignments and rubrics, we were more and more impressed by the variety of meanings and significances of these common terms. Not only did we uncover major differences in how faculty from different disciplines understood the common terms, but also we saw time and again faculty redefining "evidence," "audience," "purpose," "style," and other terms for first-year students, undergraduate majors, graduate students, and other constituencies. In no way does our evidence suggest any transparency of the terminology of "good writing," even though some of our informant data would suggest a belief in transparency.

In regard to Question 2, we were pleased to see in most cases consistency between informants' values as writers and the values that they preached to students and enacted in assignments. For example, looking at the teaching of the four faculty mentioned at the start of the chapter, we have seen how this consistency is shown. Anthropologist Lancaster, who values teaching undergraduate majors the methods of the ethnographic essay, also prizes the inventiveness with form and style that he values in his own writing by encouraging undergraduate majors' formal experiments (e.g., the Punch and Judy show about Bakhtin). His own care for the literary variety of his sentences is carried through in his comments on student essays. Environmental scientist Jones, both researcher and public policy advocate, emphasizes in his guidance of both graduate students and undergraduate majors adherence to methodological rigor and to conventional scientific rhetoric. Nevertheless, the doctoral program he teaches in requires students to regard both the scholarly and public policy audiences, while his "poster" assignment for first-year undergraduates calls for careful comparison of the ways scientific topics are discussed in science texts and the popular media. Philosopher Bergoffen honors the dialectic of philosophical argument in her own prose and that of her students. Still, her own ventures to write personally for the philosophical audience about her life and the uneasy path of her coming into the profession are reflected in her asking philosophy majors to write about their own lives in relation to their choice of a discipline. Nursing professor Sorrell embodies her belief in the phenomenological approach to the discipline by assigning classes to tell their most profound stories, "paradigm cases," that depart from the quantitative convention of the field to validate emotion and intuition.

We also saw in the informants' data, amid the many, many items that confirm the conventions of academic and discipline-based rhetoric, a validation of alternative discourses. These we would like to place in the taxonomy of alternatives presented in Chapter One.

- *Alternative formats,* as exemplified in Lancaster's *Life Is Hard,* with its use of journalism, field notes, interviews, letters, autobiographical detail, etc.; these may also include unconventional formats and typography; shifting margins; overlapping text and text boxes; creative use of sentence and paragraph structure

If we were to look only at the rubrics generated by the assessment committees in each department, we would be convinced both of the apparent similarity of the criteria espoused by these groups of academics and of the firm endorsement of the typical format of scholarly work in each field. But as we talked with our informants and analyzed assignments, we saw examples of departures from the typical, most often in response to the ways teachers tailored expectations to the different learning goals for different groups of students. Certainly, Lesley Smith's multimedia assignments in several of her courses represent this strand of the alternative vividly (more on "alternative media" follows); but Sorrell's paradigm cases and children's book, *The Magic Stethoscope*, and Trefil's greatly shifting formal applications of scientific rhetoric from course to course show openness to diverse, purposeful rearrangements and representations.

• *Alternative ways of conceptualizing and arranging academic arguments*

In Chapter One, we summarized work of contrastive rhetoricians (e.g., Helen Fox) on cultural differences in methods of argument, conceptualization of evidence, and arrangement of information. We wondered how responsive our informants would be to such differences that students might display in their academic papers. For the most part, as comments throughout the current chapter reveal, our informants, who are used to working in a university with great cultural and linguistic diversity of students, would encourage students to revise their work to conform to their expectations. They would not reject it outright—the specter of failure that scholars such as Fox consider all too common in American academe. Nevertheless, bespeaking their care in explaining the reasons for their expectations, none were inclined to accept such difference in discourse as is.

It may seem paradoxical that teachers who, in most cases, are so inventive in assignment design, so willing to tailor expectations to the level of the course, would be relatively unwilling to accept students' own variations from those expectations. But the paradox can be explained in a couple of ways. First, their very care in planning and tailoring shows that they have already considered a range of differing student responses that fall within their objectives for the discrete course. Their concern for having those careful objectives met results in their expectation that students will revise their work to meet them. Thus, Jeanne Sorrell will not accept in a "paradigm case" a student's falling back on reporting "lab values" in what she means to be a deeply felt personal story. Second, the assignments themselves often already anticipate and implicitly accept a wide range of idiosyncratic student responses. Hence, the range of stories Sorrell has learned to expect may be great. Likewise, when Jim Trefil or Chris Jones assigns first-year students to choose current issues in science, select items from popular media that address them, and analyze for themselves the connections and disjunctions between those versions and what they've learned in class, the teachers expect a wide range of subjects and views. Similarly, when Vickie Rader asks students to write about the life experiences that provide motivation for the causes they espouse, she expects multiple approaches and perspectives.

- *Alternative syntaxes (language and dialect differences),* which we have characterized as varying in their acceptance by academic readers

Because of the linguistic diversity of our students (25–30 percent are nonnative speakers of English), faculty are accustomed to seeing nonstandard English constructions in student prose. Nevertheless, the departmental rubrics all mention grammatical and mechanical correctness, as well as "appropriate" usage and voice, among expectations. By and large, our faculty informants treat nonstandard constructions as they do the alternative conceptions and arrangements discussed just above—as prompting revision and editing. As shown in this chapter, several of the informants regard themselves as "sticklers" in this regard (e.g., Miller, Clark, and Williams, with his particular emphasis on "the King's English"). Trefil, when interviewed, revealed relaxed expectations for the syntax of nonnative speakers in the first-year courses, where he was concerned not with syntax but with students' engaging with science issues. Conversely, in his courses in popular science writing for English and journalism majors, he closely marked syntax and usage. Perhaps because of their working in a linguistically diverse environment, and therefore their seeing many nonstandard constructions in essays, none of our informants made a simplistic connection between the ability to use standard academic English and to do competent academic thinking. Nevertheless, all saw it as an essential of publishable work for the discipline, hence necessary for students to learn.

- *Alternative methodologies,* which, as we discuss in a later chapter, entail experimenting with methods and ways of thinking outside a particular disciplinary tradition

The alternative formats described at points throughout this chapter most often reflect alternative ways of thinking that faculty want students to probe toward learning aspects of their disciplines. That is, the "alternative methodologies" we've seen in our informants' practices are not "outside" the discipline, but rather enact their deeply felt senses of how their disciplines are, or should be, evolving. So, for example, Jeanne Sorrell's commitment to the phenomenological approach to nursing is enacted in her emotion-focused "paradigm cases" by students; Walter Williams's merging of the scholarly and public audiences in his goals for students, as in his own writing, enact his conviction that economic ideas should always be widely intelligible, not esoteric; Debra Bergoffen's privileging of the "I" in some of her students' assignments parallels her desire for the merging, at least to some extent, of the impersonal standard of philosophic reasoning and the honoring of the subject in feminist thought. The alternative, looked at this way, enables our informants, and by extension their students, to perform intellectual work that cannot be accomplished in ways conventional to the field.

Similarly, alternative methodologies help our informants achieve objectives for certain courses and groups of students. Frequently, as we've shown, our informants define undergraduate objectives differently from those for graduate students, and objectives for general education students differently from those for majors. "Engagement" is an explicit or implicit motive for many in the general education and/or undergraduate major contexts. As political scientist Priscilla Regan said, "I don't want to make my students into little political scientists"; i.e., she doesn't want undergraduates to imitate the exigencies of professional scholars, even as she wants them to learn the more basic exigency of reasoned persuasion of various constituencies. She therefore "engages" their imaginations by having them write editorials and letters to members of Congress. Similarly, mathematician Daniele Struppa does not expect undergraduates to perform the standard scholarly literature reviews, but he does want to engage their desires to hypothesize mathematically and to argue propositions. Jones and Trefil attempt to excite their first-year students about ideas in science and scientific method by having them explore the representation—and misrepresentation—of science in popular media. Lancaster largely avoids standard ethnographies in teaching anthropology to undergraduates; rather, he encourages through the diverse projects described earlier their thinking about how they interact with other people and how they draw conclusions about everyday life.

Ironically, as we show among many other findings in the next chapter, the undergraduate students we interviewed and surveyed from across majors showed much less desire to experiment with format and method in their disciplinary classes than to conform to their professors' expectations. Thus, the "alternative discourses" in student work in the various disciplines we observed were much more often born of professors' desires to broaden students' thinking than sparked by students themselves. We explore details, causes, and consequences in the next chapter.

- *Alternative media* (email, hypertext, digitized text and images, video), which we recognize have the potential to change utterly the way "academic writing" gets written and read

Had we chosen to focus on new media in this research, we could no doubt have found at our university (one of the "most wired" in annual surveys of that phenomenon) many examples of the alternative influence of these tools on how "writing" is carried out by students and faculty. Indeed, we did not dissuade our faculty informants from talking about email, multimedia, hypertext, the Internet, etc., in their examination of their own writing and that of students. That we did not hear frequent mention of these media tells us not that our informants by and large lack media savvy; rather, we infer that, like we ourselves and most other faculty, they have incorporated digital media—e.g., email, word processing, file transfer, Web browsing, etc.—in ways that don't radically change their concepts of academic scholarship and writing. In describing changes in their disciplines and their own partnership in change, they did not, as a rule, cite technology as reason for change. In specific regard to written rhetoric, all our informants, except Lesley Smith, regarded writing as literate, not significantly pictorial or aural, and discursive, not hypertextual. They may use websites in their scholarship or as sources for students, but, except for Smith, don't require students to construct emphatically visual, hypertextual documents.

Nevertheless, Smith, as we've already said, does represent the technological vanguard, and in so doing offers a disconcerting alternative to traditional ideas of "discipline" and "discourse." Her assignments, as described earlier, call on students to develop visual as well as verbal sophistication; they must build a versatile rhetorical sensibility, as they build sites to reach the teacher, fellow students, and, at least hypothetically, diverse publics. "Navigational design" is a requirement only in her assignment instructions. However, as online scholarship proliferates in all fields, so that multimedia become an ever more prominent part of how research is presented, we expect that future studies of disciplinary rhetoric, including student writing and departmental rubrics, will feature "navigational design," "integration of images," "appropriateness and quality of sound," plus a wide range of other multimedia expectations for student and professional discourse. But that time is not here yet.

What is certain, based on our data, is that faculty who prepare students to write in college can't just say, "Here's what you're going to be expected to do in writing in your major," and present simple formulas—not to mention such blanket misinformation as "avoid the first person." There is too much variation dependent on the level of the course and the exigencies seen by the professor to warrant such generalizations. Consensus documents such as the rubrics we analyzed mask some of these differences, but even they, in the vagueness of their similar language, suggest an openness to options that their overall tone does not. Moreover, the frequency with which even the rubrics expect student "originality"—an expectation confirmed in the assessment workshops we observed—shows that academic writing, across all disciplinary contexts, is definitely not an exercise in filling in intellectual blanks. Finally, given the readiness of our informants to work with undergraduates to revise prose to meet conventions and expectations, it may be "safer" for faculty to encourage student risk-taking with ideas than to emphasize adherence to formatting rules.

In the concluding chapter, we present strategies and techniques for teaching that come out of our research. In the next chapter, we offer counterpoint to our faculty voices by hearing from students.

Chapter Four

Students Talk About Expectations, Confidence, and How They Learn

The writing itself is important, but it's also important that my teachers understand the person who's writing the material. For everything that's written, there's the story of the person behind the writing. But does the teacher see that person? I'm always aware I'm being graded by someone who could have 500 other things going on in their life.

—MELANIE, STUDENT

As we've argued in previous chapters, when teachers talk about their own professional writing and their expectations for student writing, they are never simply representing their disciplines nor, conversely, are they reproducing generic standards for "good writing." Rather, their writing practices, products, and often-unacknowledged preferences derive from a complex mix of variables, including:

- Generalized standards for academic writing
- Disciplinary conventions
- "Subdisciplinary" conventions
- Institutional and departmental cultures and policies
- Personal goals and idiosyncratic likes and dislikes

These are some of the "500 things" going on in teachers' lives—to echo Melanie—that make her and so many other of our student informants suspect that teachers aren't telling them the full story when they assign and grade writing in the disciplines. In previous chapters we presented that fuller story behind the writing in regard to our faculty; in this chapter we'll focus on the stories students tell about their goals as writers and how these coincide with perceived conventions for writing in their disciplines. We wanted to know the degree to which they feel bound by these perceived conventions and how they come to understand—if they do—what it means to have their own voice when they write in or outside of their chosen discipline.

Based on these concerns and the students' responses on surveys, in focus groups, and proficiency exams, we've organized our findings into the following four clusters:

- *Expectations:* What students say about expectations for writing in their disciplines
- *Passion and the disciplines:* How they understand what it means to be original within the context of their discipline, thereby gaining the confidence to write with passion and voice
- *Learning disciplinary writing:* What they say about how they learn to write in their disciplines
- *Students and alternatives:* How the student data relate to the taxonomy of alternatives discussed in preceding chapters

Our Sources of Data

As noted in greater detail in Chapter One, the findings in this chapter derive from three sources:

1. A 19-question survey completed by 183 upper-division students representing a total of 40 majors; all were enrolled in sections of English 302, an advanced writing course
2. Focus-group interviews of 36 undergraduate students from a range of majors
3. Timed (2-hour) essays by 40 upper-division students from 22 majors, written as part of a portfolio process for English 302 proficiency credit

While all the informants are George Mason undergraduates who had completed at least 45 credit hours by the time of their participation, the three populations differ sufficiently from one another so that we need briefly to point out these differences and suggest how they might affect the significance of the data derived.

The Survey

The 19-question "Survey on Writing in the Majors" (see Figure 4–1) was distributed by teachers of sections of English 302 to their students in the fall

Survey on Writing in the Majors

1. What is your major?

2. Approximately how many courses have you taken with the prefix of your major, e.g., HIST, ENGL, PSYC, GOV?

3. Within your major do you have a particular area of interest or concentration? If so, what is it?

4. Are you aware of some specialties or concentrations within your major? If so, name some.

5. How aware are you of characteristics of good writing in your major? Circle one.

   Very aware   Somewhat aware   Unaware   Never thought about it

6. List some characteristics of good writing in your major:

7. How have you learned characteristics of good writing in your discipline? Rank (1=most important):
   _____ teachers
   _____ reading
   _____ fieldwork
   _____ published writing guides
   _____ other students
   _____ articles on websites

8. How confident do you feel about your writing in your major? Circle one:

   Very confident   Somewhat confident   Not confident   Scared to death

9. From the following list, check those writing assignments you've been given in your major courses (those with the prefix of your major, e.g. HIST, DMIS, ITEU, CS):
   _____ Researched paper
   _____ Journal, reflection paper, or narrative
   _____ Collaborative project
   _____ Lab report
   _____ Impromptu in-class writing
   _____ Critique, review or reaction paper
   _____ Position/issue paper
   _____ Summary, abstract or outline
   _____ Letter (e.g. to an editor, a public official, a family member, etc.)
   _____ Other _____

   From those you circled above, which have you done most often?

10. Have you ever been given writing assignments in your major courses that surprised you? If so, describe briefly.

11. Have you ever been asked to write about yourself in an academic paper in courses in your major? If so, describe briefly.

(continues)

Figure 4–1.

12. Have any teachers in major courses allowed you or asked you to write in ways you thought were not typical of the major? If so, describe the assignment and how you approached it.

13. Have you ever been discouraged from using a style you thought would be a more original and/or individual way to respond to a writing assignment in your major? If so, describe briefly.

14. To what degree do your teachers in your major courses expect you to conform to strict guidelines for writing in your discipline? Circle:

    1 (not strict at all)   2   3   4   5 (very strict)   Don't know

15. Do you find that your teachers' expectations for writing in their courses are generally similar? If not, describe briefly a time you felt a teacher's expectations were atypical.

16. Have you ever read any of your professors' writing? Check all that apply:
    _____ book
    _____ professional article
    _____ conference paper
    _____ website article
    _____ assignments

17. If you have not read any of your professors' writing, how aware are you of what they might be writing?

    Very aware   Somewhat aware   Not at all aware   Never entered my mind

18. Is English your first language? If not, for how many years have you been educated in an English-speaking culture?

19. If English is not your first language, do you recall any time(s) teachers in your major were dissatisfied with your writing because of something other than grammar or content—for example, organization? If so, describe briefly.

Figure 4–1. *(Cont.)*

semester of 2002. Some 70 sections per semester of this course are offered to GMU students, who must have completed first-year composition and at least 45 credit hours at the time of their enrollment. The required course is subdivided into groups of sections tailored to the needs of students in five areas of the curriculum: arts and humanities, social sciences, natural science, business, and technology. We selected for the survey a roughly equal distribution of sections (12 total) from all versions of the course. All students who completed the surveys did so during a class period. We chose sections of English 302 for the survey because they were more likely than any other venue to produce an overall picture of student awareness of disciplinary standards in writing from an array of undergraduate majors. Moreover, because English 302 is a required course, it was likely to produce responses from a broad range of student performance levels.

The Focus Groups

Focus group interviews began in winter 2003. We planned them as an essential extension of the data-gathering of student perspectives begun with the survey, as we'd anticipated that the survey results would leave us with questions that we could pursue in conversation with groups of students. This indeed turned out to be the case. Most of the focus group participants were English 302 students at the time of the interviews, and all formally agreed to participate (see Figure 4–2). Not all participants were English 302 students. In addition, three master's candidates (with recent B.A.s) also took part, as did a group of three undergraduate students from New Century College, an interdisciplinary degree program.

Our method in the sessions themselves was to cover the same issues that the survey had, often to ask the same questions, and then to follow up as appropriate to a response. For example, a theme that emerged in the groups was the students' sense of the relationship between writing in school and writing at work, and the looser framework of the groups allowed us to pursue this line of questioning as appropriate in a given conversation. All the group conversations were taped, although the two of us also took notes as the interviews progressed. In general, we stayed with a line of inquiry until everyone had had a chance to speak; this procedure meant that if a response took us off on a tangent, we would come back, when appropriate, to the original question to be sure that several points of view had been represented.

The difference in method from the surveys meant that responses by focus group members were richer than those on the surveys. Whereas survey responses gave us trends and impressions, focus groups gave us examples, explanations, and comparisons. As the analyses of responses in this chapter will show, the focus group responses tended to reinforce the trends revealed by the surveys, but the focus groups gave us the reasoning and experiences behind the trends—plus a fairly keen sense of the diverse lives and voices that the numbers dull and obscure.

The Proficiency Exam Essays

This third source of data derives from a course exemption procedure that has been in place since the late 1980s, but that was modified for the purposes of this research in fall 2003. GMU undergraduates who desire exemption with credit from ENGL 302 may submit a portfolio of course papers that represent work from the sophomore year and beyond.[1] The reflective essays we analyzed for this research are submitted as part of the proficiency process.

[1] In 1997, we wrote about this portfolio proficiency option as a vehicle for gathering data on the effectiveness of our WAC program. The essay appears in the Yancey and Huot collection *Assessing Writing Across the Curriculum: Diverse Approaches and Practices.*

Informed Consent Form

Professors Christopher Thaiss and Terry Myers Zawacki of the Department of English are conducting research on students' perceptions of writing in their major courses. The research results will be used toward preparing books (scholarly book and textbook) on writing in the disciplines. They are seeking informal input from students to questions in the following areas:

- What students see as the characteristics and standards of "good writing" in the disciplines in which they are majoring
- The experiences, courses, and written materials that have helped them learn how to write successfully in major courses
- The students' favorite types of writing, in school and otherwise
- How they have been encouraged as writers
- How they would advise younger writers

If you agree to participate in this focus group, you will be joining a small group of students who will be asked to respond informally to the questions listed above. The discussion will last about one hour. The group discussion will be audiotaped and portions may be transcribed. You will be identified by your first name only; you are free to give a pseudonym should you choose. You will also be asked to identify your major area of study.

Participation is completely voluntary. Refusal to participate will not involve penalties or loss of benefits to which you are otherwise entitled. You may discontinue participation at any time without penalty or loss of benefits to which you are otherwise entitled. There are no foreseeable risks or discomforts involved in participating nor any costs to you or any other party. There are no direct benefits for participating. However, your participation may help contribute to knowledge on students' perceptions of writing in their disciplines.

All data in this study will be confidential. Should specific information be quoted in the research write-up, all names will be changed.

If you have any questions about the research project, you may contact Professor Thaiss at 703-993-1273 and/or Professor Zawacki at 703-993-1187. You may also contact the George Mason University Office of Sponsored Programs at 703-993-2295 if you have questions regarding your rights as a participant in this research. This research has been reviewed according to George Mason University procedures governing your participation in this research.

Date:_____

Signature:_____

Major:_____

Figure 4–2.

The proficiency exam prompt asks students (1) to define and explain "the distinctive features of writing in your major"; (2) for one or two courses in the major, to "describe specifically the writing lessons (e.g., research methods, techniques, style) you had to learn in order to succeed as a writer"; (3) to "describe in detail how [one or two pieces from the portfolio] illustrate the distinctive features of writing in your major."

In any given year, fewer than 100 students (compared to 4000 who take the course) attempt the exemption process, and roughly 75 percent are asked to write the two-hour essay. Of these, it is rare for a student to be unable to successfully complete the essay and earn credit with exemption. From September 2003 through March 2004, 64 students attempted the process; 55 (86 percent) were invited to write the essay; all did so successfully.

Although all the essays showed at least minimal understanding of distinctions between writing in the student's major and writing in other course contexts, we have chosen to use for our analysis only those (40) that offer what we regard as especially articulate insights that help to clarify and illustrate findings from the survey responses and focus group interviews. We are well aware, and wish the reader to keep in mind, that the group of 40 proficiency exam writers we are analyzing are both demonstrably proficient as writers in their majors and also highly reflective about their process of writing in different contexts, for different courses, and for different teachers.

Student Expectations for Writing in Their Disciplines

When George Mason upper-division students reported on writing in their majors on the survey, in focus groups, and in their ENGL 302 proficiency essays, their generalizations for the most part paralleled those of our faculty informants, both those we'd interviewed and those who developed rubrics in departmental assessment teams. The good news for faculty is that at least in broad terms the students are "getting it": they clearly understand, even if they cannot always enact, the characteristics of academic writing, as we've defined them and as they've been confirmed in the rubrics.

Less certain is the degree to which they've internalized the more esoteric standards in their major fields, not to mention the "ecologies" and exigencies of the subdisciplines and concentrations that most of our student respondents have already defined for themselves. Less clear still is how they see their own developing senses of "style"—as well as what they perceive to be the idiosyncrasies of their teachers—as either meshing or in conflict with their ideas of the discipline. Nevertheless, our focus group and essay informants provide a range of nuanced perspectives that illuminate these issues.

We can generalize as follows from our three sources of data:

1. Only a few respondents to the surveys reported that they had done little or no writing in major courses, and these students tended to be those who had taken few major courses as yet.

2. Almost all, even in a brief survey, can delineate a few expectations for writing in their majors, and students who share the same major are remarkably consistent in the terms they choose. By and large, all three groups of informants express confidence in their understanding of disciplinary expectations.

3. In the survey and focus groups, these expectations for the most part echo those of our faculty informants, especially the terms we saw repeated in the rubrics (see Chapter Three), but also those that our primary informants gave us in their first responses during the interviews. These are the terms we refer to as "generic academic" in Chapter Three.

4. Students reveal a wide array of assignment types across majors, with research-based writing dominant.

5. When students are given more time to talk or write about writing expectations and the assignments that embody them in their majors, they achieve significantly greater specificity and insight, as particularly illustrated by the ENGL 302 proficiency essays.

6. When students regard writing expectations in a comparative framework— if, for example, they have a double major or have done considerable writing in more than one major—they are usually more articulate about expectations and how majors differ therein.

7. While formal standards (e.g, formatting, documentation styles, and argumentative structure) are seen by the great majority of students as defining their stylistic options, only a small minority feel hampered by these guidelines. Indeed, many of our informants clearly prefer assignment guidelines to freedom of choice.

8. While stylistic freedom is limited, most students see their teachers and courses as giving them freedom in choice of subject for writing.

9. Depending on their frame of reference, respondents can see teachers' expectations for writing as either remarkably unvarying or unpredictable. Our most varied responses were in this category, with, for example, most of the survey respondents seeing their teachers consistent from one to another in their expectations, while the focus groups saw their teachers' expectations as varying—necessitating the students' reliance on teacher feedback for guidance.

10. Although neither the survey nor the proficiency essay prompt asked students to focus on audience, our informants by and large do see a sharp distinction between writing for teachers and writing for other audiences, including audiences that they imagine as part of their writing goals in the discipline.

1. The Prevalence of Writing (and Feedback) in Majors

The less than 5 percent of our 183 survey respondents who reported not having written "as yet" in their major courses all had fewer than 9 credits in such courses. George Mason has had an active writing culture across disciplines for at least 20 years[2]; in the latest (2003) survey of graduating seniors conducted by the Office of Assessment, 72 percent said that they had been *required* to revise papers or projects in at least three of their major courses, and 86 percent said that writing in major courses had improved their ability to write. In addition to required English composition courses in the first and third years, all students must complete at least one "writing intensive"(WI) course in the major at the junior level or higher, and many departments designate two or more courses WI. Moreover, our interviews with faculty and the proficiency portfolios demonstrate that substantial writing is being assigned in many courses besides those listed as WI. We were not surprised that almost all survey respondents from the 39 major programs could identify characteristics of writing in their major fields.

Indeed, a finding from the focus groups that surprised and gratified us was that students had come to expect that major faculty would give them commentary on their writing early as well as later in a semester (more on the significance of this finding later in the chapter). When we pointed out to two groups that before the advent of writing-across-the-curriculum programs, a student could not have expected to receive "feedback" on their papers in courses across disciplines, their response was puzzlement. As one student said, "Then how would you know how to improve?"

2. Students' Awareness of Disciplinary Writing Characteristics

On the survey, 93 percent said they felt "very aware" (73/183) or "somewhat aware" (95/183) of "characteristics of good writing" in their majors. The students in the focus groups showed no less eagerness than our faculty informants to describe such characteristics. The 40 students whose ENGL 302 proficiency essays we read went into great detail to describe such traits and explain their rationale in the disciplinary context.

Corroborating our survey respondents' confidence that they are "aware" of disciplinary writing characteristics was the consistency of traits observed by students representing the same major. All but one psychology major emphasized "adherence to APA format"; "precise observation" was frequently mentioned. Business majors, from management to accounting to finance to management information systems to marketing, mentioned "getting to the

---

[2] Starting in 2002, Mason has been ranked among the top universities in *U.S. News and World Report*'s "America's Best Colleges" edition for its program in "writing in the disciplines."

point," "avoiding repetition," "being organized," and "writing for the intended audience." Government and politics majors stressed research, analysis, persuasive argumentation, and convincing rhetoric. This consistency within majors was also displayed in the focus groups and the proficiency essays, though, as we describe below, the greater detail of these data sources gives us a richer, more nuanced picture of disciplinary writing than does the survey.

3. The Prevalence of "Generic Academic" Characteristics in Survey Responses

In the survey responses, in some of the focus group remarks, and in a few of the proficiency essays, we were struck by how similar to our faculty responses the students' were. When we'd interviewed faculty, one of our first questions had been, "How would you characterize good writing in your field?" Their first responses were most often drawn from what we came to see as a short list of common academic criteria. Only as interviews went on, and we probed our informants' individual histories and visions as writers, did we get differentiating detail. As we reported in Chapter Three, a similar short list of items appeared on rubric after rubric as departments debated the expectations for student writing in the major. Some of the common terms from the student surveys include:

> conciseness, clarity, looks/sounds professional, gets to the point; efficient, organized, cohesive; research; accurate facts; reliable sources; thoroughness of argument; good supporting points; sentence structure, good grammar, correct terms; adherence to correct style (MLA or APA usually); directed toward intended audience

No academic could ask for better evidence that our students had understood—even if they imperfectly enacted—the principles of academic writing, as we outlined them in Chapter One. Even if our informants, as noted in Chapter Three, did not see their undergraduates as needing to learn and display the more esoteric rhetoric demanded of graduate students, the faculty's assignments and feedback were clearly getting across the less fine characteristics not only of writing in the academy, but also of writing in disciplines, broadly defined. In points 5 and 6 below, we show examples of how some of these undergraduate writers can express sophisticated awareness of varying disciplinary exigencies and rhetorical strategies.

4. Most Frequent Types of Writing Across Majors

"Research, research, research," said one of our focus group informants when we asked about the most prevalent writing tasks in their college experience. Certainly, the emphasis on research-based writing comes out in the lists of common characteristics on the survey and in the stories of the essay writers, as well as in focus group transcripts. On the survey, students checked most frequently that they'd had assignments clearly based on research processes: "researched paper" (167/183), "critique, review, or reaction paper" (139), "summary, abstract, or outline" (135). When asked which type of assignment they'd written most often, the "research paper" (90/183) was the clear first choice, with "critique, review, or reaction paper" (50) and "lab report" (30) distant but still clear second and third choices.

But research-based writing is not the whole story of student writing in majors, and the term itself, like the other "generic academic" terms that reappeared, masks a wide range of source types, methods, and purposes. "Journal, reflection paper, or narrative" was marked by 114 of our respondents as a type of assignment they'd been given in a major course, and 11 percent chose it as their most frequent assignment category. Of course, "journal," "reflection," and "narrative" may reveal merely different aspects of or approaches to a research process, but at the very least they show teachers expecting students to use diverse methods, formats, and cognitive structures to think about materials and ideas. In the same regard, just over half the respondents had worked on "collaborative projects" (95/183) and 6 percent noted it as their most frequent type of assignment.

Some insight into the nature of "journal" and "reflective" assignments that survey students reported having received is gained from noting that 30 percent of respondents said that they had been asked in at least one major course to "write about themselves." In the section on "Passion and the Discipline" later in this chapter, we elaborate on the complex relationships that exist for our students between their sense of personal goals and the perceived expectations of disciplines and teachers. As we will explore later, the research demands of disciplines and the opportunity for personal expression coalesce for many of our students, as exemplified in this statement on her proficiency essay by Thuy, an anthropology major: "the expansive theories, techniques, and styles inherent in anthropological research provide the discipline with the potential to make worthwhile statements about everyday existence while also allowing room for personal reflection and experience."

5. Student Insights into Nuances and Complexities of Disciplinary Writing

However, just as our faculty informants revealed a significant diversity of methods, audiences, and acceptable rhetorics, so too did the students in both the focus groups and, particularly, the proficiency essays cohort. Karinna, a government and international politics major, illustrates through her description of the "scenario response," an assignment she'd received in an early course in her major, the "practical" exigency for government majors of writing quickly for decision-making audiences. "I was required to act as if I were the foreign policy advisor to Crown Prince Abdullah of Saudi Arabia. Whereas with most papers enough time is given to do sufficient research and produce a well-written and informed paper, this particular assignment required me to do thorough and comprehensive research in order to brief the Prince in only three days."

Richard, a sociology major, differentiates in his essay three methodological and rhetorical strands of the discipline and how they have intertwined in his writing: "For me, the distinctive features of writing in sociology are threefold: explaining complex ideas in terms of social theory; report writing while conducting applied sociology; and writing ethnography for field work. While these three tasks require very different styles, none is more important than the others and all three contribute equally to the discipline." Indeed, as he details specific assignments that combine "qualitative research through ethnography and quantitative research through statistical analysis and reporting," he comes to a recommendation for the department: he sees ethnography as so integral to the field that he believes that a course in ethnographic method should be required for all majors.

6. The Richer Specificity of Those with Double or Interdisciplinary Majors

We also found that when students could knowledgeably compare one discipline with another, *because of their experience of having done a significant amount of reading and writing in those fields,* they were more quickly able to describe differences and convergences; they could pinpoint how the methods of one field might be useful in meeting the exigencies of another.

For example, Cary, a double major in history and religious studies, focuses in his proficiency essay on the interdisciplinarity of his studies, describing a final research paper he wrote for a religious studies course on "Zealots and Their Time in Roman Judea." Students who focused only on rabbinic Judaism, he argued, would not be able to fully grasp the topic without some knowledge of the historical events surrounding the rabbis' rise to prominence within Judaism "due to the Roman destruction of Jewish Jerusalem in CE 70 and the resulting decline of the Sadducees/high priestly class."

7. Student Attitudes Toward Strictness of Disciplinary Expectations

Survey respondents definitely saw the teachers in their majors as "strict" (76/183) to "very strict" (34/183) in adhering to formal expectations for their writing. Nevertheless, when we asked them if they'd ever been "discouraged" from writing in a way that they preferred, the great majority (133/183) said "no." less than 20 percent wrote comments or gave examples; these indicated that the "no" votes were based on a range of reasons, from preference for the strictness—"I'm more comfortable using an objective style" (government major)—to resignation—"No, I conformed a long time ago" (systems engineering major)—to what we might call "flexibility"—"I just wait until prof tells me what style to use" (communications major). The small minority of "yes" responses varied in the tone of the student's dissatisfaction: from the resistant "I like a conversational voice, but am always being told to be more formal" (English major) to the pragmatic "yes, so that's why I go to the Writing Center to get help" (nursing major).

The cryptic survey responses made us wonder how students would respond if given more time and encouragement. Hence, we made a main theme of the focus group discussions this issue of students' perceived autonomy as writers. The responses reveal a wide range of attitudes and rationales, which we explore in the section on "Passion and the Discipline" later in the chapter. The writers of proficiency essays were not specifically asked about the freedom they felt in such choices, but the essays reveal spontaneously again and again that students care deeply about how they can find room for their "own ideas" and ways of expression within the intellectual and formal framework of a discipline. "Passion and the Discipline" includes some of these writers' perspectives also, as we try to understand the complex of reasons behind an academic writer's feelings of freedom or restriction.

8. Freedom of Choice in Topic

Related to the writer's sense of self and to the options available to academic writers were the responses to our survey question about freedom of choice in topic and style in major courses. The great majority of students answered "yes" (130/183), but when students gave examples, in almost all cases they said that they had freedom in choice of topic on research assignments, but not any freedom in style. A systems engineering student's comment was typical: "Yes, we get to pick our own projects. This involves a lot of writing of documents in a specific format." The proficiency essays and focus groups corroborate the survey in showing that students have significant choice of topic in major assignments but little flexibility in stylistic and other formal elements.

This response trend, coupled with the prevalence of "no" responses to the "discouragement" question, suggests several possible explanations, which may be overlapping. (1) Perhaps most students feel comfortable complying with formal and methodological demands, as long as they can exercise choice in what they write about (and in the conclusions they reach?). (2) Students give higher priority to other factors, such as the grade in a course, than to their stylistic autonomy as writers. (3) Some undergraduate students have not yet developed a sense of their own style or voice, and so are open to conforming to disciplinary restrictions as part of their learning. (4) At least some undergraduate students have reached the point of understanding how their own goals, preferred ways of knowing, and voices can move comfortably within the structure of the discipline. The focus groups and the proficiency essay writers provided us insights into these possibilities, and these we explore in the following paragraphs and in "Passion and the Discipline."

9. Teachers' Expectations: Consistent or Unpredictable?

Survey responses, focus group comments, and proficiency essays agreed that teachers were the most important sources of knowledge about disciplinary writing characteristics. According to informant comments and survey responses, this knowledge from teachers came through their written assignments, their lectures, their comments on student drafts and papers, and students' inferences from the teachers' own writings. That the great majority of survey respondents (85 percent) thought their teachers in major courses largely consistent in their expectations for student writing helps to explain why there was such a large degree of confidence by students that they knew the characteristics of good writing in their majors. On the other hand, we've already noted (in 3, above) that the characteristics of writing mentioned in the survey responses tended toward the "generic academic" rather than the discipline-specific. So it's reasonable to speculate that the "consistency" agreed on by most survey respondents had to do with the broader aspects of writing in a field, e.g., the devotion to APA documentation and formatting in psychology, rather than with the students' experience of finer discriminations from course to course or teacher to teacher.

As with students' sense of freedom in their writing, we used the focus groups to pursue the issue of teacher consistency in expectations. Here we saw a different picture from that painted by the survey, with more shading. Courtney, an international politics major, noted that "Probably 50% of the time in a research paper you're just meant to report on an issue and the other 50% to use the information that you learned from history to make predictions for the future. So in a Comparative Politics class we would take for example "'China and the European Union, which is going to be more powerful in 20 years?'" For Courtney, then, expectations are predictable in general, but unpredictable in any given class until the student learns more about specific assignments.

For Huan, a psychology major now in graduate school, there was surprise in certain assignments: "We were twice asked to do personal writing in psychology and both occurred in the senior year. It was weird that the papers weren't supposed to be scientific—a total break from the type of paper that we had written up until then." Again, the difference is a surprise only because it breaks an established pattern, but there is still an element of the unpredictable in any class.

It is not really an inconsistency for students to see regularity in the broad expectations of their teachers across the major and at the same time difference in teachers' emphases on papers. For example, common in surveys was the note that some teachers care more about "grammar" than others. "Good grammar" is a generic academic expectation that students regard as independent of the conventions of the discipline, but differences in this expectation can make a big difference in how students write for a given teacher.

Moreover, students may see "surprise" or inconsistency at a point in their progress through a major when they have not yet encountered the array of exigencies and therefore genres that typify it. In other words, the mature writer in a field has encountered a sufficient range of course environments to develop an overall sense of disciplinary goals and methods—and comes to see the differences from class to class within that overall idea of the field. Of our informants, the proficiency essay writers reveal clearly this sense of pattern within difference. For example, Pamela, a studio artist with a double major in art history, describes the particular need of art historians to "convey an image in words, and care must be taken not to supplant image with description." This understanding relates, she has learned, to the overall goal of historians to "study events in their historical context: events are contrasted and compared with earlier events; other influences are discovered." As she is now an experienced writer in her majors, any sense of "surprise" about disciplinary strictures Pamela might have felt in early art history courses has long since given way to her understanding of those strictures in the merged contexts of history and visual art.

Thus, we might posit three rough stages in the development of a disciplinary writer[3]:

1. A first stage in which the writer bases a sense of disciplinary consistency on writing experience in very few courses with criteria in these courses generalized into "rules."

[3] These stages are reminiscent of William Perry's analysis in *Forms of Ethical and Intellectual Development in the College Years: A Scheme*. He posits nine "positions" through which students may develop as they move from either/or thinking to relativism to commitment that recognizes possibilities within an array of perspectives.

2. A second stage in which the writer encounters different exigencies in different courses, and the sense of inconsistency, sometimes interpreted as teacher idiosyncrasy, supplants the perception of consistency

3. A third stage, described above, in which the writer understands the differences as components of an articulated, nuanced idea of the discipline.

Interestingly, on a blunt instrument like our survey, a response of "yes" on our consistency question could mean that the writer is at either the first or third stage. Only a more sensitive instrument like the proficiency essay can reveal a "yes" as evidence of either naivete or maturity.

Some students, at least as undergraduates, may not reach the third stage. The most troubling explanation is that some students don't get enough writing experiences in their majors to enable them to develop this nuanced view. Our proficiency writers are able to show the sophistication of their perspectives because they've written substantially in a number of upper-level courses. In addition, some students may not reach the third stage because they do not become sufficiently invested in the discipline's academic discourses, developing instead a greater connection to nonacademic audiences and exigencies. These students may reveal impatience with academic conventions ("all these big long research papers") and see differences among teachers not as varied aspects of the discipline but merely as ineluctable differences. For example, Kelsey, a government major, spoke in praise of a professor who eschewed the research paper in favor of "lots of those short little things [one-page memos] throughout the class." She added, "That was helpful—it felt more realistic as far as getting out into your field. But I haven't had a lot of professors like that." Clearly Kelsey identifies with that aspect of the government major that emphasizes results in the polis and does not yet appreciate what motivates the scholarship nor its connection with the practical. In contrast, Samantha, also a government major, appreciates that the demand of most of the research assignments in her classes to "break down every argument into claims and warrants" has helped her "better connect with her audience, be more persuasive, and create concrete ties to real world concepts," all skills which are critical to her chosen career path with progressive nonprofit organizations.

10. Writing for Different Audiences

Although questions about audiences besides the teacher were not on the survey nor in the proficiency essay prompt, our informants in focus groups and the essay writers commented on the subject, as Kelsey's and Samantha's comments illustrate. The comments showed sensitivity to differences between readers inside and outside the academy, as well as the impact of audience on the goals of writing in disciplines.

For example, Rhonda, a criminal justice major, in her essay, distinguishes sharply between the writing she did, as a salon owner, for periodicals on dog grooming ("mostly based on my personal experience and opinion") and the writing she does now for classes: "analysis based on research." But this academic writing is varied based on the demands of the particular class and teacher. Thus, her analysis of police work on a famous criminal case demanded an evaluation of the "facts of the case within the context of the available legal and social norms of the era," while her analysis of criminal motives in a recent high-profile case delved into the "psychological theories that best explain the investigation." Her description of a third paper noted specifically the importance the professor's perspective played in determining the appropriate blend of personal opinion and documented sources.

By and large, students in the focus groups distinguished between academic and workplace readers, much as Kelsey, quoted earlier, did. Typically, they contrasted the professor's demand for detailed analysis based on documented research with the demand of bosses and customers for succinct, action-oriented prose. But the stereotypes don't always hold. Eric, a double major in economics and management information systems (MIS), characterized his MIS writing as business-like ("you write a proposal where you go technically in depth into what each system can provide and you match the client with what they're looking for"). In economics, he said, "there is any number of things you can do, from straight research papers to opinion pieces." He distinguished further between these varied environments and a lesson he learned about audience in an early accounting class. "I modeled my paper on some accounting reports that I had read—my dad's been in the business for 25 years—so I tell him I have this assignment and he gets excited and wants to help me with it. I just got a little beyond the scope of this assignment and so I got this negative feedback from the teacher, even after having worked so hard on it."

Rather than seeing a disjunction between academic and other readers, a number of our informants saw that the writing they were learning in their disciplines was intended to reach both academic and nonacademic readers. In particular, our informants from government and politics, such as Steven and Courtney, whom we'll talk about in more detail later, emphasized how their courses often required them to visualize policy makers and voting constituencies as their readers in order to learn how to explain political theories, policies, and events to the people who act and react within political systems. A significant awareness of audiences was perhaps most advanced in the focus group consisting of students in the interdisciplinary New Century College, about which we've written in Chapters Two and Three in relation to the work of faculty informant Lesley Smith. The NCC curriculum makes students highly conscious of rhetorical differences through complex projects that demand both documented analysis and "real world" succinctness and ease of use. (See our descriptions in Chapter Three of Smith's syllabi for the courses Writing for Multimedia and The Social World.) For example, students engage in service-learning and other community-focused projects that require writing for nonacademic readers, but they also write analytical and theoretical essays for professors.

Our findings regarding "what students say about writing in majors," which we've summarized in the preceding ten categories, show a student population whose considerable experience in writing in disciplines has given them confidence and knowledge. The differences in responses from our many informants have led us to project a three-stage developmental process that produces many students whose sense of "writing in the discipline" acknowledges the variety of exigencies and hence forms that characterize any field. These writers' nuanced understanding takes them beyond the "generic academic" conventions that the first-stage academic writer perceives and makes them, even as undergraduates, able to appreciate and begin to participate in the shaping of disciplinary rhetorics that our faculty informants have undertaken in their own careers.

What we see in these third-stage students is not only knowledge of disciplinary forms and purposes, but what we think is best called "passion" for their fields. We first explored this term in Chapter One, when we noted the ambiguous relationship between "reason," "feeling," and "sensation" in constructions of "discipline" and "academic writing." We returned to this relationship in Chapters Two and Three; we saw it manifest in diverse and exciting ways in the scholarship and the teaching of our faculty informants. In the next section, we describes its characteristics using what our student informants say about themselves and their writing.

Passion and the Discipline

> Through this course and with the guidance of my professor, I realize what I am destined to do in academia.
>
> *—Luz, music major talking about an ethnomusicology course*

As we read the essays students had written in response to the proficiency exam prompts, we were struck again and again by these students' level of engagement in their chosen field(s), their sense that, like Luz, they were destined to be doing this work. In contrast to many of the focus group respondents (though certainly not all), these students seemed to have a clear sense of what it means to be an original writer, one who is passionate—even as their passion is disciplined by the academic conventions they've learned—and personal even though their "I" may never appear in the text. Their voices resonated with confidence.

In this section, we want to highlight some of the themes and contributing factors we saw recurring in these students' explanations of how they learned to be confident, engaged writers and scholars. In particular, these students exhibited a passion for the topic along with a belief that they could be original, disciplined thinkers. Interestingly, a strong subtext in many of their responses on the essay exams and in the focus groups was the role of a teacher's passion for his or her subject as a powerful model for engaged scholarship, a point we discuss in more detail at the end of the section.

Passion and Reason

We begin with Luz, the music major, who gradually became aware that "someone who is passionate about her topic [the history, culture, and musical traditions of her native Puerto Rico] and naturally creative can produce a paper that is clean, neat, and sometimes even dry." Luz writes that she found it difficult to control her feelings, especially when writing about the effects of colonialism. She tended to write in Spanish, which allowed her to be "poetic" and metaphorical, unlike the "bluntness" of English, and then translate her writing into English. She learned, however, with her teacher's patient guidance, that, though she was trying to be "proper and scholarly," her strong adjectives, when translated from Spanish, revealed her biased perspective. She understood that she had to change those adjectives. Her story illustrates the preference for reason over passion in academic writing, a topic introduced in Chapter One and explored in Chapters Two and Three. Another important factor in learning scholarly control, Luz writes, is understanding that a documentation guide, like the *Chicago Manual of Style*, can force a writer to be disciplined, "orderly," and clear. While Luz may have some misconceptions about the power of documentation to impose order, we're interested in the lessons she seems to have internalized: her "definitive" opinion that the format rules she learned from Chicago style kept her from "drowning in her material," allowing her to focus on her rich primary and secondary research; and also that she can "effectively translate" what she learned from research in a "prudent" and persuasive style because the footnotes allow her to voice her additional concerns.

In contrast, Steven, a government major, writes that with the guidance of two of his professors he was "able to regain the emotion and individuality" he'd lost with the emphasis in high school on standardized tests. When one of his professors explained that a person majors in government "not because you want to know how government works but because you want to change it," he felt freed to "dive" into topics that allowed him to explore a range of cross-disciplinary sources—a "multicultural" paper, for example, in which he looked at anthropological definitions of culture, histories of American cultural identity, theories of multiculturalism, and so on. Two important lessons have guided him in his work: "Only through making waves can you tell what direction the ship is moving" and, once the ship is moving, you need to find "the perfect combination of emotion, logic, historical evidence, and vision." He found that combination once he became "a student of the topic" instead of "just amassing a pile of research and cramming it all in." Critical to his understanding of how to be this kind of student were ongoing discussions with his teachers, who gave him the latitude to explore the topics, told him to anticipate contradictions, and, when writing, to make his arguments "relatable" to a public as well as the academic audience. "You can't win by confusing the public," he learned.

Kathleen, an English major, shows this symbiotic relationship between reason and passion in another way. She describes a teacher in an African-American literature course who told her to quit playing it safe and to "go with your gut." What that advice meant to her was that she should risk making an argument she believed in rather than relying on plot summaries. In describing one of her papers for that class, she said she could be "freer in expressing" herself when she wrote about the "horrors of slavery" and the "emotional tales" she wanted to analyze. To do that, she read other sources' views and then drafted until she'd generated a strong thesis for her argument. Finally, she let the authors' words "wash over me" so that "I could reflect clearly on their meanings."

We found this emphasis on passion through reason and reason through passion in many of the students' essay responses to the proficiency exam prompts and, to some degree, in the focus group responses. We see in these responses an understanding not only of the exigencies—disciplinary and personal—that shape writing in a discipline but also a belief in the individual writer's ability to move his or her readers. They have learned, in other words, that the academic readers they describe as their audience are persuaded not only by carefully reasoned arguments but also by a rhetorical stance that conveys their deeply felt intellectual passion(s). Therefore, the principle of control of passion by reason really implies a vital interconnectedness of these principles, not the erasure of one by the other.

The confidence that these students exhibit when they describe their writing indicates that they view themselves as insiders in their disciplines, able to understand and negotiate the demands of individual teachers and courses. We see them being in the third of the three stages we suggested earlier, in that they typically see teachers as reliable guides rather than as idiosyncratic arbiters of style and taste, as so many of our focus group students did; likewise, they come to see genres in their major as examples of multiple and varied disciplinary concerns rather than as a confusing array of teacher preferences.

But these writers, as they explain, have gained this confidence over time and through experiences both inside and outside of the academy. One of the focus group students, John, a well-read history major and a community college transfer, is particularly intriguing to us because of his "lack of confidence in the structures" that teachers in upper-division courses might want. While he may have lacked confidence because he hadn't yet experienced upper-division courses, he was certain that history teachers would not be looking for the kind of writing he was doing in his advanced composition course, even though the composition course was focused on writing in history. More than most of our respondents, John had a keen awareness of the difference between an academic writer of history and a popularizer, and in this awareness he echoed our faculty informant from history who talked about an academic reader's "suspicion" of texts that are too "seductive," "gripping," or "easy." John dismissed the popular history "stuff we've been reading in English class" as "a wordy, good example of bad writing." The intention of that kind of writing, he thought, was to make the reader "get emotional" about the topic, and the teacher's intention in assigning it, he said, was to show that "if you feel strongly about a topic, you're going to write very passionately." Although he was clearly passionate about history, that was not the model he wanted to follow—"opinions and assumptions without enough verifying evidence"; rather, he saw himself writing for "Ph.D.s in history," for whom the writing has to be as clear and carefully researched as possible. Once he'd begun getting some feedback from his history professors, he noted he was beginning to feel more confident about his ability to write for the kind of readers he envisions and in the voice he wants to use.

Originality and Voice

If the more confident students learned how passion for a topic could be conveyed through disciplined research and "clear," "sometimes dry," prose, they also ultimately learned what their teachers intended by style, originality, and voice. In contrast, for many of our focus group and survey students, the question of what constitutes an original voice and style seemed particularly fraught, sometimes, as one survey student wrote, from the moment they entered college: "The teacher in my very first English course discouraged me from using my own style. She had to admit I was grammatically correct, but she simply didn't like my style and so critiqued it." A focus group member from communication lamented having to relinquish her ideas to please the teacher—"It's kind of sad, you want to have original ideas, but you know you'll get a good grade if you say what the teacher says." Others complained about vague or even "weird" criteria like "Be original" or "Be aggressive towards the topic." "I'd like to be original," one student said, "but I have no idea what my professor's ideas of originality are."

Many of the focus group respondents had figured out, however that originality and voice can inhere in even the most conventionalized disciplines. So, for example, Huan, a psychology major, noted that by the time he was a senior he understood how "all the rules you worry about following when you're just beginning to write sort of fade into the background and become the foundation from which you work. I guess that's how you feel like you have more freedom to say what you want to say." Lynn, an economics major, explained in her essay that a research review allows for original thinking because "by defining the current frontier of knowledge, economists can then go on to show the cutting edge nature of their work and why they are making an original contribution to the discipline."

Still, for many of these students, this understanding did not come without struggle. Some talked about the difficult process of finding their voice and authority in the midst of all the expert sources they'd been researching. For example, Courtney, a government major, said, "When I write an academic paper, I worry that I am not producing an original paper per se, that it is merely a thoughtful and organized submission of information I gathered and then properly cited." When one of her teachers told her that he couldn't hear her voice in the paper, she was confused. "That threw me off," she said, "I have been blatantly told by professors that as an undergraduate and an inexperienced scholar it was more important to learn how to research well and come up with information that's already present rather than try to develop an original voice." To find a solution to this seeming contradiction, she said she concentrated on developing her own set of criteria for evaluating political events, which she was able to do once she'd listened to the teacher's "interpretation," read widely on the topic, and also drew on her knowledge of democratic theory learned in other courses. "I use my experience as a student of political science to frame my essays as a whole," she observed. Through her experiences writing for many different government teachers, Courtney has learned that "professors don't want you to relate information that's already been discussed. You need to answer questions in a thoughtful way so it's obvious that it's you doing the thinking, drawing on all the things you've learned."

As we discuss in more detail in the next chapter (on the implications of our findings for pedagogy), Courtney's realization—that she could bring together knowledge she'd accumulated as a student of government even though she was still an "inexperienced scholar"—is important to consider in the context of many of our faculty informants' views that it is not their purpose in undergraduate courses to train little psychologists, mathematicians, biologists, and so on. Whether or not faculty intend to inculcate disciplinary ways of thinking and writing into their undergraduate students, they inevitably bring their disciplinary inclinations to their teaching, as we argued in Chapter Three. Further, while students in lower-division courses may resist assignments they perceive as too specialized to be useful to them (as Russell and Yanez found in their study of the conflict between the teacher's and students' motives and goals in an introductory history course), the more proficient upper-division students we've been discussing in this section understand that they are practicing discipline-based writing, even though their teachers may not be fully aware of the degree to which this is happening. Not only do they understand, but also many, like Huan and Courtney, have worked to internalize the motives and genres of the discipline while also finding ways to exercise an original voice and/or perspective. Moreover, as we've said, they tend to see differences in teachers' expectations as deriving from the array of disciplinary and subdisciplinary interests possible in the field. (What we're discovering is closely related to processes of enculturation Russell describes in "Rethinking Genre in School and Society: An Activity Theory Analysis.")

According to many of our focus group respondents and essay exam writers, a teacher's passion for his or her academic project or for the student's project was a significant contributing factor to the student's ability to internalize disciplinary motives, goals, and genres. With this ability come confidence and their own passion. "Reading my professor's book put me more in awe of her because it made me realize how passionate she was about her subject," a sociology student said. "It also gave me more of a sense of what she expected from me as a writer." Another student said that she learned to pick topics she felt passionate about after a teacher wrote on one of her papers, "Wow, you've taught me so much." The idea that they could teach a teacher was a powerful motivator for many of the students. Grace, a double major in music and nursing, described a teacher's positive response to a project she did on music and "everyday education": "My professor had never heard of my topic and she was extremely interested in it, so I took the extra steps of doing more research. And, by putting in the work, I was able to impress and enlighten her to the point that she has kept my project and considers me an expert in that subject."

Disciplining the Discourse to Meet Personal Goals

Most of the students we've been discussing in this section have learned, or are in the process of learning, that their chosen disciplines can accommodate their individual voices and academic interests. We also encountered in our focus groups and proficiency essays a number of students, not unlike our faculty informants, who were actively reshaping the rhetorics of their disciplines to meet their own individual needs and goals, whether these were academic or workplace, and thereby creating new forms. One of the most delightful was Melanie, an individualized studies major, whose expectation that the academy would accommodate her personal goals was striking to us. Both of us were thoroughly impressed by her clear sense that writing assignments should be made to serve her own well-defined career goals, as well as by her seeming success in persuading her teachers to the same view.

We quoted Melanie at the beginning of this chapter on the "500 things" that might be going on in a teacher's life to prevent him or her from hearing the individual voices of the writers in any given course. Melanie was determined that her teachers would hear her voice. And she had a lot to say in her chosen concentrations of sociology and communication. When she was not yet 21, Melanie started her own business doing beauty treatments, selling makeup, and, in a newsletter, promoting her products and counseling her "hundreds" of customers on "their cosmetic needs," while also addressing "fashion, relationship and family issues, and women's spiritual needs." She gathered information for her newsletter stories from the Internet, but also based them on "my grasp of what I knew my customers needed from me from our hours of conversation in my shop. So I included poetry, small articles, usually in connection with an approaching holiday, and short pieces that would be inspirational to people." Melanie returned to school to finish her degree when the economy faltered; however, she still has a small business and is also preparing to become an inspirational speaker.

When we asked Melanie how this kind of understanding of her readers translated into writing for her teachers, she explained that she has learned how to be persuasive, to use descriptive details, and to catch people's attention. She always strives to make her personality come through in her writing, and, she says, her teachers seem to like that. She might, for example, take an informative assignment "where I have to show that I know what I'm talking about, and I'll try to turn it into some kind of a narrative, maybe about my life or a situation with my clients. I'll compare that to the information I've learned in class. My teachers have been okay with that." One time, however, a sociology professor commented that "I had gone a little bit overboard. She knew some of my beliefs and where I'm coming from and she basically said 'this is sociology, this isn't a class about morals.' But I figured I was learning this information for my benefit so that I could use it to change some things in society that I believe need to be different." To her teacher's comment "'Well, that's not sociology,'" she replied, "I know it's not sociology, but I don't consider myself a sociologist. I want to learn more than just the facts. Like how society got to be the way it is and how it can be changed." Her teacher accepted that reasoning, she said. Melanie believes she is unlike most other students, who, she feels, are willing to write what teachers want to hear and aren't thinking about their own personal and career goals. She herself "cares more about how to make an assignment somehow fit it into what I'm trying to do with my future" than with getting a good grade—although she gets A's and B's.

While Melanie sees herself dissimilar to most students, we found a similar sense of empowerment in our New Century College focus group students; often, as with Melanie, this sense derived from a strong personal investment in shaping the curriculum and a conviction that their primary goal is to appeal to the audiences they will encounter outside the academy. However, whereas Melanie felt she had to persuade her teachers to consider her own personal learning and writing goals, the NCC program is based on that principle. When we asked the NCC students to describe the characteristics of good writing in integrative studies, they immediately responded, "a strong personal voice." While that voice should not "overpower the content or the message," it can, according to Lindsay, help the writer "explore [her] own knowledge and weave [her] own perspectives and opinions into the research." Lindsay talked about discovering her own voice as she experienced writing in the variety of styles and forms expected in an integrative program, in the range of audiences projected by her teachers, and in the collaborative writing situations that are typical in most NCC courses. Personal voice, then, is not something separate from all of these influences, nor is it just the product of them; rather it is a practical understanding of who she is as a writer and all the possibilities she has for self-expression. This point, we think, bears on and reconciles the distinctions made in the oft-cited debate between Peter Elbow and David Bartholomae on how best to teach students to write in the academy.

While we're both very familiar with the kinds of writing assignments teachers give in NCC pedagogy, we were struck, as we talked to these students, by their confident assurance that all their teachers would and should adapt themselves to the goals of writing in an integrative environment. In response to our question about whether they had ever been discouraged from experimenting with voice and style, two of the students mentioned an NCC professor trained as a biologist who "tends to lead his students across a very narrow bridge and doesn't allow them to stray far from the scientific format he expects." Yet, these students continued, in a "rare showing of nonscientific openness," the teacher has been "including students in the pedagogy of his constantly evolving courses" and has also been "relaxing some of his rules." One of those rules is that students cannot use "I" in their papers. "He's just recently let that rule out of his clutches," largely, they think, as a by-product of the reflective writing that is fundamental to NCC pedagogy, as we discuss shortly.

Within the NCC community, there is a high level of consciousness about teaching writing and the nature of assignments, almost all of which are multi-layered; that is, most ask students to think about audiences beyond the teacher(s), usually both within and outside of the academy; most require varied methods and formats, typically one of which is a Web document; and many are collaboratively written. Both faculty and students share in conversations about assignments and their purposes, so one would expect, in this kind of environment, more willingness to negotiate a sharing of activity systems.

The Importance of Reflective Writing

In the NCC focus group, the students talked at length about the requirement for reflection as a critical component of good writing. With the others nodding their heads in agreement, Matt defined reflection as "discovering the interconnections between areas of knowledge that you've explored and then exploring the significance of this knowledge." As an example, he described a "photo-journalistic essay" he wrote after traveling to Australia, which described not only what he saw and did but also included reflection: "What did nature have to do with the culture? What does the culture have to do with the history? How do these all come together? What are the implications? So the reflective writing becomes a lens for viewing these different areas of knowledge." The other NCC students agreed that reflection is an integral part of the research process because "you are incorporating and synthesizing all that you have learned and experienced and asking why it matters." Without reflection, Matt noted, both the research and the writing risk being "flat and unengaged." While reflective writing may be central to NCC pedagogy, the students understood that it is not necessarily a common feature in most disciplines, and, in fact, they said, NCC work is sometimes seen as being "elementary" because people seem to think that "we're sitting under a tree writing in our diary, whereas what we are doing is integrating all of our coursework, outside experiences, previous experiences, things we've read from different courses and so on."

While explicit reflection on their writing and thinking processes is not a typical requirement within most majors, many students are aware of how and why they have come to acquire a disciplinary way of thinking. We saw this point illustrated most strikingly in the proficiency exam essays when students were asked to describe distinctive features of writing in their major by referring to a piece of writing in the portfolio and also explaining their process of writing that piece. Although they did not indicate that they had ever been asked to reflect on their writing prior to this exam, most of the student writers were able to pinpoint specific courses and teachers that helped them learn how to be successful writers in the discipline. Perhaps not surprisingly those who were most articulate tended to be students with double majors or minors. Working within two disciplines enabled them to contrast features of writing in different disciplines and also to explain how they negotiated those differences in their own work.

Earlier in this chapter we posited three stages in the development of a disciplinary writer and suggested that students who are in the third stage understand that differences in teachers' expectations are indicative of the varied goals, interests, and concerns that motivate work in a discipline. Clearly, students need the experience of writing for many different teachers and courses within their majors to gain this understanding, which, in turn, helps them to become more proficient and efficient writers. But students also need, we think, many more opportunities than they currently have to articulate what it is they understand and why that knowledge matters to their growth as writers. For some students in our focus groups, particularly those in advanced composition for science and technology majors, the English class was the place where they encountered focused conversations *about* writing. Eric, a systems engineering major, noted, "It's kind of odd that in this [advanced writing] class, I feel like I've grown more as a writer because I've done more research and found out more things on my own, whereas in actual classes in my major it's more that they know what you need to write so they want to see if you can write or not." John, another engineering major, said, "What's been most valuable to me in this [advanced writing] course is that it has made me aware of the things that I'm doing when I write in my other courses."

How Students Learn to Write in Their Disciplines

We've described two important factors in students' gaining the confidence and ability to write proficiently in their majors: (1) frequent writing for a variety of teachers and courses and (2) opportunities for reflecting on their writing: reflecting on the rhetorical choices they've made based on purpose, content, and audience; on the connections they've discerned among topics, formats, and styles; and on their discovery that writing can be a means of realizing their own interests and desires as writers. As we've also noted, teachers play a significant role in a student writer's development. Indeed, when our survey respondents overwhelmingly listed teachers as the major factor in learning the characteristics of writing in the disciplines, we spent considerable time in the focus groups probing the ways in which teachers function as guides to disciplinary writing. We also looked for descriptions of interactions with teachers when we read the proficiency exam essays. In the preceding section, drawing on focus group and essay responses, we've shown how teachers have encouraged and inspired highly motivated writers to acquire disciplinary and personal knowledges through both verbal and written interactions. Now we want to focus more specifically on what our student informants say about the ways they have learned to "read" a teacher's expectations and thus write to fulfill those expectations. As we will discuss, while students pick up on a surprising number of cues from teachers before they ever begin writing for them, even the most confident writers rely heavily on feedback on the first paper as a guide to writing subsequent papers and/or revising their work. Many also noted the importance of having models for their writing, be they examples of successful papers, the teacher's own writing, the readings that have been assigned, and/or workplace documents they perceive (or misperceive) to be relevant to the course.

"Reading" What the Teacher Expects

"I'm an observer. I've learned to perceive other people's wishes," Karen, a psychology major, explained when she told us why she feels fairly confident the first time she is writing for a teacher. Although we are well aware that most students are adept readers of classroom environments, we were nevertheless fascinated by the range of verbal, nonverbal, and written cues they use to predict what a teacher might expect in response to the first writing assignment. Many of our informants noted that they discern teachers' expectations for writing from the syllabus, the textbook, and teacher's lecture and presentation style: "If a teacher presents him- or herself very formally, you know they expect a more formal response, whereas if they're personable and they joke around and digress, they might not have as rigid expectations," Chris, an information technology (IT) major, observed. A teacher who is "nitpicky" about his or her syllabus and grading methods, he said, "is going to be nitpicky about your writing as well." In economics, Eric noted, "It's just assumed that you go in there knowing how to write. The professors don't really touch on what they're looking for, so I find myself more often than not going through the textbook and looking for examples of what I'm trying to model." In Eric's case, the model he used was not helpful. "I'd basically looked at the quarterly reports I found and I modeled those. But it turned out not to be what the professor was looking for because I went beyond what the class was covering. But that's what I was seeing and assuming we had to present."

We find Eric's situation particularly interesting in light of the stages of a student's writing development we posited earlier. Just as teachers often "assume" that students should know how to write because they themselves see academic writing as generic rather than discipline-specific, students also "assume" (understandably so) that the genres and conventions they are learning will apply from course to course and teacher to teacher within the same discipline. When students in the first or second stage of their writing development encounter different expectations in different courses, they are often surprised and chalk this up to differences in teachers' personalities and preferences rather than seeing them as nuanced articulations of the discipline, a subdiscipline, or an area of interest. Andrew, a geology major, said, "I go by a teacher's personality. For example, one of my teachers is a big environmental freak, so if I write with a big environmental spin, I know he'll be happy with it." He also attributed some of the differences he saw to the regions his teachers came from: "One teacher grew up in England, and we've got people from out west and people from the Appalachian area, and all of them have different writing styles; they expect different things. It makes it really tough at times to give them what they want." Karen thought that her psychology teachers' expectations varied according to where they were in their careers. Mike, an information technology major, said, "To a degree it's like flipping a coin. I think a lot of teachers look at writing sort of based on their own writing, and so I get different impressions from teacher to teacher."

When students can't pick up cues from their teachers, they tend to fall back on prior experience and on stereotypes they have about what different disciplines will expect. Chris, in IT, noted, "I had a professor who didn't have any writing assignments all semester and then we had a nine-page term paper to do. It was weird because once again you didn't talk to him about writing in general, so you didn't know how he wanted it to be written. I didn't expect him to grade it like an English teacher. I just wanted him to see that I had found a lot of information and that I was able to get the word count. That's what I expect from those who aren't English teachers because it's not their job to critique my writing, it's their job to critique what I learn." In computer science, Poona said, "My experience is mostly that if you cover things they want you to write about, they're happy. They're not too concerned about your writing style." She added, however, that teachers often do not return papers, so she is not too sure whether her perceptions of their grading standards are correct.

Because students rely heavily on feedback they receive on their first papers in the course, as we will explain shortly, they found it particularly disconcerting when they had to write a second paper before getting the first paper back. Matt, an NCC student, recalled a time when he had to write a second paper for a large section of a "standard history class." "Obviously," he said, there was "no personal feedback and I certainly felt apprehensive about how I was going to approach the next paper." Yet he did well, he said, because he picked up cues from "the ways the teacher led discussions in class, thinking about his academic focus, the things that he would devote a whole class period to. These were the kinds of things that I made sure I included at the very least."

Other student informants apparently were not as successful as Matt in perceiving a teacher's expectations, and some seemed to sense that the teachers themselves were unsure about what they wanted. Grace told us she "failed" a music history course in her major because of the grades on her two papers, the second of which was submitted before she'd gotten the first one back. This was a problem, she said, because, "when he returned the first paper, he told the entire class that we had to redo it because he wasn't satisfied. When you get no feedback, you don't know what to do, and so we all did poorly in the class because he didn't give us the proper guidelines." Amanda, an IT major, described getting an unsatisfactory grade on a paper for which the teacher had "only vaguely touched upon what he wanted." When she queried the teacher about her grade, she said, "It was kind of like talking to a wall; you ask why you got the grade that you did and the response is 'I don't know' and now here I am bringing the assignment back to get some feedback and it's still 'I don't know.' It was submitted via email, so there was no hard copy and no remarks ever came back." While she didn't expect the teacher to remember all of the students' papers, Amanda noted that she preferred hard copy submissions so "at least you can discuss with the professor what it is that needs to be improved or clarified."

We were struck, as we listened to these students' complaints, by the anger they still seemed to feel about their teachers' lack of responsiveness to their work. Since we didn't look at graded papers by these students, we don't know whether their complaints are justified; clearly, however, these students think that feedback is important and they are looking for it to be specific. As Amanda noted, "Students are there to please and to get the grade and when they don't let us do that, that's what brings us down." Perhaps nothing shows the lack of transparency of writing in the disciplines more than these students' sensitivity to the rhetorical situatedness of the classroom. While many, like Matt, may have learned to read the rhetorical contexts in which a writing assignment is located, even he experienced some unease as he approached writing the second paper when he hadn't received feedback on the first.

Students' Reliance on First-Paper Feedback

In focus groups and, to some degree in the essay exam responses, our informants, no matter how confident they felt about their writing, stressed the need for feedback on the first assigned paper. Robyn, a psychology major, explained, "Sometimes professors vary so much in what they expect that getting that first paper back is a sigh of relief. It's done, and I'll have the feedback and I'll learn whether I'm meeting the professor's expectations and how to improve. I feel confident that I can do well when I write for my classes. It's just getting those parameters set."

In their need for "parameters," students reveal their understanding that academic writing is transactional writing and, as with any transactional situation, a writer needs to know what the reader wants, perhaps even more so when there is a grade at stake. Prior to the writing itself, teachers can effectively convey parameters, according to a number of our informants, when they give detailed guidelines and criteria, often on a syllabus, so that students can see "ahead of time how rigorous they are and what they are going to look at when they read the paper," as Kelsey, a government major, said. While all four of Jess's sociology professors included "exactly what they were looking for" in the syllabus, one professor, she said, also "listed five things an 'A' paper and a 'B' paper would include, which made it very clear what her expectations are."

Students found models particularly helpful. Some communication professors write "an example paper" for the assignment, Laura said. She liked this because "you see how they write and obviously they would like you to write it similar to that." One of her English teachers, Lauren said, puts strong and weak paragraphs from students' papers on an overhead, showing them, at the sentence level, what was strong and how to fix what was weak. Similarly, in an NCC class where projects were done in groups, Lindsay described a professor using an overhead projector to comment on work from each of the groups, "either naming the groups or not, and saying what's working and what's not. That way the class as a whole gets an understanding of how their group is doing and how their work compares to the work of other groups." Another NCC professor passed around sample portfolios that demonstrated excellent work.

While students who receive prior information about expectations and grading standards find it useful, they, along with nearly all our focus group informants, said they feel at least some degree of anxiety when they write the first paper for a new professor. "In all my courses," Grace said, "each teacher prefers a certain tone and style and that's what you learn after you turn in the first paper. The first paper they grade, you know what they want, and that's why it's so important." Even in relatively compact disciplines like psychology, as Robyn noted, teachers' expectations can vary from course to course. In more diffuse disciplines, differing approaches to the same material mean that even the most confident writers, like Courtney, a government major, need to know teacher expectations: "I'm taking political analysis and research and this kind of writing is very different from what I've been trained in so far; it's much more technical and it involves data and statistics, which I haven't been trained in using. So I'd say that I have some anxiety about writing for this class even though my writing has been reinforced well so far." What we can see in these comments is that in order to develop a sense of themselves as writers in a discipline, students need feedback that pertains not only to the assignment but also to the larger concerns of the discipline or subdiscipline.

The Cumulative Effect of Feedback

Even the most minimal feedback, we found, can help students intuit some of these concerns. This is understandable since students' sense of how to write in their discipline is cumulative, as we've already discussed, with proficiency and confidence gained through multiple and varied opportunities for writing and reflecting on their writing. "I was just thinking that in a lot of upper-level communication classes I've taken," Laura said, "teachers always make notes like 'try to simplify,' and if I try to write clearly and concisely they always say 'good, simple, good job!' And I think that's mainly how I've learned those characteristics of good writing." Similarly, students found that "cross outs" and comments like "'Expand on this'" helped them understand what was missing or where they were "going off on the wrong angle." Once they have even these sparse comments on the first paper, many said, they could use the comments as "a model for the rest of the work in that course, because you do get a sense of what's expected of you," as Shabnam, an engineering major, noted.

Many students stressed the importance of having a teacher point out their strengths as writers, as well as what needed to be improved. "When you turn in a 20-page paper you've been working on all semester and sweat is pouring off your face, you need someone to say 'good job,'" Jess explained. Yet that kind of generalized praise isn't necessarily enough, she added. "If a professor just writes 'Excellent job' and gives you back your paper and you notice that there are a thousand mistakes that she didn't say anything about, it makes you feel a little bit less. I think that if the professor marks up your paper and gives it back to you and points out your weaknesses and your strengths at the same time, it gives you a lot more confidence." Similarly, Shabnam said, "It's not just a good grade; you can get the highest grade, but for me what matters is if a professor mentions my strengths and then says what I should work on. Then the next time I write a paper I have a sense of my strengths and know that he's going to be noticing the strengths, too, and that increases my confidence."

When only one paper was assigned in a class, the students especially appreciated having opportunities for revision with feedback. Some mentioned the value of peer writing groups, though they tended to see peer review as a way "to gauge what others say and bounce that off what the teacher says." One informant explained that the most effective feedback she'd received in her health and fitness classes came from a teacher who broke the paper into sections, each of which was commented on and graded. This process, Danielle said, "makes you think about what you wanted to revise in the first part while you're writing the second part, so the teacher is always challenging you to create new ideas. It's stressful but it's apparent that she cares about what we're writing." Almost to a student, our psychology majors explained that they gained confidence with the APA "template" of the experimental report by writing individual sections and revising with feedback. "The TA was really good about saying that there are all these rules that we had to follow and making it clear that it's a pretty prescribed method of writing. So we actually practiced how to write in that style and submitted sections for review," Huan said. While he received helpful comments about where tables should go and how results should be discussed, he noted that "in terms of the writing, I think I was a little too verbose, so I got comments on that. The major thing I remember learning is to use 'whereas' instead of 'while.'" Though Huan didn't say that he found the "whereas" advice particularly arbitrary, he, like Robyn, realized that even within a prescribed template teachers will vary in their stylistic preferences.

Who Pays Attention to Style and Mechanics

That teachers will vary widely in their attention to a student writer's style and mechanics was, we discovered, an opinion held by many of our informants. In response to a survey question on whether they find teachers' expectations to be generally similar, the majority of students replied "yes"; however, those who said 'no' listed attention to grammar and mechanics as the most frequent instance of difference. When we probed this response further in our focus groups, we found that the student writers seemed to pay close attention to feedback on style and mechanics, regarding it as an important indicator of a teacher's preferences and also a key explanation of the grades they'd received. "Some econ professors are like 'I just want your ideas; you could scribble them out on a cocktail napkin, I don't care,'" Eric observed, while "others want to see that you've put a lot of time into how you're presenting the material and that everything is punctuated and spelled right. So you have to go by their comments." In psychology, Robyn said, "It raised my anxiety when one teacher just graded on content but for another one you knew it was going to be critical if your punctuation wasn't correct."

A number of students noted that English teachers—rightly so, they believed—had "more explicit" and "higher standards" for the quality of the writing. Laura, a double major in English and history, said her English teachers' attention to her sentences and word choices helped her become more stylistically "sophisticated," which she'd not found a priority in her history classes. In her proficiency exam essay, Laura wrote at length about how one English teacher helped her develop as a writer. Not only did this teacher attend carefully to his students' prose, he also showed them how to read literature from a "macro to micro" level. "First," she explained, "you read for the story. Then, at the micro level, for the details, like the names of characters, towns, the spaces (inside/outside, kitchens, trains, bridges, south/north), the time, colors, verbs, repetition of words, images, spelling, the ways words are physically printed on the page." When she learned to read this way, she said, she understood that you can "choose effective words at every step to create effective sentences."

The Role of Reading in a Writer's Development

In addition to teacher feedback on their writing, reading was frequently noted by students as an important factor in their development as writers in a discipline. Reading widely and deeply, many students said, helped them understand not only the subject matter of the discipline but also the ways in which it can be/should be presented. We've already mentioned the value of students being given explicit models for their writing, whether these be experimental lab reports in psychology, sample papers written by teachers or peers, or literary prose. But we also found that students can infer style from reading professional writing. Amanda and John, both in technical majors, said that they look to see whether the authors "drag things out or get to the point," "what you can get from skimming the first and last paragraphs," as well as "what extra information they give and what they assume the reader knows." Kristen said she has learned the necessity of "careful, deep reading" in philosophy and, because of that training, "I take a lot of time on revision, which is where my papers come together. I push myself to say, 'This is what the philosophers are doing, so shouldn't I be pushing myself to do the same?'" For Kristen, as with many of the highly proficient writers we've cited earlier, it is very important to find a topic that "gives me pleasure" in order to be motivated to spend time on otherwise "tedious" reading. John, who reads widely in history, said he looks to see "how the author has reached me, even though he may not necessarily reach other people, and how that style works."

Reading outside of their disciplines has also helped many of the students, particularly those we would call third-stage writers, appreciate the rhetorical differences that distinguish one discipline from another as well as the comfort level they've achieved as readers and writers in their chosen field. Courtney, for example, told us that she realized how comfortable she'd become with even the most difficult discourses of government when she compared her ease of reading in her field with the trouble she was having with the "jargon" in her film studies course, which "is like Greek to me." With that realization of difference, as we've noted in earlier sections, also comes a much clearer understanding of the styles and strategies that are appropriate to one's own discipline. Sara, for example, said that her experience with the "high threshold of evidence" required in a physiology course made her appreciate the "out of the box" analysis that's encouraged in her government major. Some students said that they applied a particular way of thinking and/or researching that they had learned in one discipline to another. Both Sayeda, an English major, and Richard, a sociology major, said they have found the ethnographic methodology they learned in courses outside their major to be a useful tool for thinking, researching, and writing in their majors.

When we asked our focus group informants the advice they would give to new students in the major, they responded: "Read a lot." "Ask questions." "Take good notes." "Give yourself time to write." "Don't be afraid to ask teachers about how to improve your writing." While these responses are not so different from the generic advice they've no doubt been given by most of their teachers, they reveal, we think, that these more experienced writers understand that knowing a discipline occurs gradually and involves much more than imitation of forms, templates, and styles. We can't expect that students will develop from first- to second- to third-stage writers unless teachers give them the instruction and support they need to construct for themselves a nuanced, coherent sense of the discipline. It is not accurate for teachers to say that their expectations for good writing are the same as everyone else's nor, conversely, that their preferences in student writing are merely personal ("other teachers may not care, but for me, don't do ___"). Whatever we teachers convey to students about our expectations for their writing is grounded in our sense of what is appropriate to or allowed by our disciplines, so our instruction and feedback to student writers should help them understand this larger context.

How Student Perceptions Relate to the "Taxonomy of Alternatives"

In the previous sections, we discussed what students say they have learned about writing and themselves as writers in their majors. We've also been interested in their perceptions of teachers' practices in assigning and responding to writing. As we probed those perceptions, on the survey and in our focus groups, we noted whether the students expressed feelings of being inhibited by an assignment or a teacher's response to their writing, or if they felt surprised by an assignments falling outside their conception of the discipline. In this section, we relate their responses to the taxonomy of alternatives we've discussed in preceding chapters.

- *Alternative formats*

Our questions in the survey, the focus groups, and the proficiency essays did not pursue explicitly this aspect of alternativeness, except in regard to "autobiographical detail," about which focus group students had a good bit to say, as we report in detail in "Passion and the Discipline." Our concrete data about format experimentation and variety are therefore scant. We focused on student perceptions; we did not view student written products as part of the research, except for the proficiency essays—which in every case stick religiously to the prompt, which asks implicitly for a first-person descriptive analysis. But the lack of explicit questions about audience on either this prompt or on the survey had not stopped the students from spontaneously discussing the nuances of adapting their writing to diverse readers. Therefore, the lack of clear evidence of formal experimentation, combined with our survey respondents' consensus view that they had not been "discouraged" from writing alternatively by their teachers, indicates that our upper-division writers have by and large been satisfied to write according to their instructors' guidelines; most seem not to have experimented outside these guidelines because they have not felt the need for such experiments.

But the reader should keep in mind the variety of formats that our faculty informants (see Chapter Three) had noted in describing their assignments. To the extent that our informants are representative of faculty, "instructor guidelines" may mean a more significant variety of formal structures than the student data easily reveal. Thus, even if most of our student informants did not define themselves as stylistic risk-takers, they may have had to be inventive in meeting the varied formal demands of assignments in regard to audience and purpose. To cite one prominent example of stylistic difference, remember that 11 percent of our survey respondents had noted "journal or reflection" as their most common assignment. On the other hand, when our proficiency essayists describe the assignments that have had the most profound impact on their learning to write in their disciplines, their lengthy summaries of analyses and researched arguments rarely imply stylistic risk-taking—even as the writers express the freedom they have felt to think originally.

Thus, we need to remember the distinction between the use of unconventional formats in order to meet an audience's needs, including the criteria for a professor's assignment, and the student's desire to be "alternative"—a distinction we first posited in Chapter One. That our student informants by and large did not feel the need to resist the formal demands imposed by faculty does not mean that they did not invent or vary forms in meeting assignments—indeed, the spontaneous attentiveness to audience variation by our focus group and proficiency writers suggests otherwise.

- *Alternative ways of conceptualizing and arranging academic arguments*

Although our student data don't really speak to the question of format alternativeness, they do give us insight into students' ways of conceptualizing and arranging arguments—particularly as they attempt to reach diverse audiences. Again, the motive for experimenting may come more from the teacher than the student, but de facto our informants are having to think about what to present and how to present it, in order to convince a range of teachers and, in many cases, a range of nonacademic readers. Our proficiency essayists had the chance to expound on this struggle, and the many examples we excerpt throughout the chapter show them doing so inventively. Indeed, as third-stage writers, they see the writing of their fields as always involved in this effort to find the appropriate evidence, method of inquiry, arrangement, and voice to meet the needs of the particular reader. We find them transferring the writing styles and approaches they've learned in one course and/or through their reading to other contexts; they modify arrangements, language, and approaches; they develop the professional's sense of the alternative ways of conceptualizing and arranging that exist within the discipline—and that shape it for the future.

- *Alternative syntaxes (language and dialect differences)*, which we have characterized as varying in their acceptance by academic readers

The survey asked students to identify themselves as native or nonnative speakers of English. A follow-up question asked whether a teacher had ever criticized a piece of writing for something other than grammar; organization, for example. As expected, about 25 percent of the respondents identified as nonnative speakers, but less than 10 percent of the respondents answered "yes" to the follow-up question—and those who did noted grammar and mechanics, no other factors, as the key factors in teacher critique. That teachers expect conformity to standard edited syntax came through in survey respondents' answers to the earlier question on the survey in regard to differences in teacher expectations in their majors: as we mentioned earlier in the chapter, teachers' attentiveness to "grammar" was, they noted, the primary element that distinguished one teacher's expectations from those of another. When we asked focus group students to give writing advice to hypothetical students just entering their majors, "use correct grammar" was a frequent rec-ommendation. Not unexpectedly, the proficiency essay writers by and large ignored "correct grammar" as a characteristic of writing in the major, pre-sumably because they did not see it as discipline-specific and perhaps because their own sense of control of syntax made it a non-issue for them.

There was no sense from the data that students regard nonstandard syn-tax as a "choice" in academic writing. Faculty are more or less stringent in marking it, but there was no evidence that students feel restricted or discour-aged by this stringency. As we noted in Chapter Three, all our faculty inform-ants valued grammatical correctness, with four of them emphatic about its importance. This same expectation shows up in all the departmental assess-ment rubrics. Whether influenced by teacher attitudes or not, our student informants gave no evidence of resisting this expectation. That said, we must remember that all our informants are upper-division students; our sample thus does not include writers whose deficiencies in the standard dialect, or attitudes toward it, had either kept them out of the university or kept them from passing lower-level courses.

- *Alternative methodologies,* which entail experimenting with methods and ways of thinking outside one's disciplinary tradition

With few exceptions, student attitudes toward methodology and ways of thinking corroborated their attitudes toward format and arrangement. The proficiency writers, by and large our most mature group of informants, revealed in their essays knowledge of the range of methods and modes of thought characteristic of their fields, as well as a pragmatic ability to tailor modes of inquiry and search strategies to differing topics and rhetorical situ-ations. While some of our focus group informants expressed the wish to be more creative and less conventional in their approaches to writing, the con-sensus was that they were given sufficient opportunities to be original. The survey respondents by a large majority expressed satisfaction with the free-dom their teachers gave them to choose topics; an even higher percentage (over 80 percent) said they had never been discouraged by a teacher from "using a style that . . . would be a more original and/or individual way" of writing to an assignment in the major.

Just as our faculty informants (in Chapter Two) spoke of their disci-plines as dynamic in accommodating a range of alternative methods and styles, so our proficiency essayists were frequently eloquent and enthusiastic in describing the different approaches they used to different problems and issues, often with the encouragement and guidance of their teachers. Although we would not expect even our most mature undergraduate writers to have as clear a sense as faculty do of the range of alternative styles and methods "allowed" in the discipline, we saw in these essays a similar excitement about possibilities, as well as a similar blending of perceived convention and individual passions to know and express.

- *Alternative media* (email, hypertext, digitized text and images, video)

As we noted in the previous chapter, we did not set out in this research to study technologies. So, just as our faculty data contain relatively few explicit references to digital media—except in the remarks and materials of media specialist Lesley Smith—our student data are relatively silent on the role digital technologies played in teaching disciplinary writing conventions. Even the students in the focus group representing New Century College, the media-intense unit where Lesley Smith teaches, did not attribute their attitudes to digital technologies, though we know that course syllabi and other materials emphasize web design and electronic collaborative tools. Certainly we can posit that the NCC students' obvious sophistication, self-awareness, and confidence as communicators derive in part from the rhetorical challenges posed in courses such as Information in the Digital Age; but our data do not suggest that the technological possibilities themselves are sufficient to explain this growth. As we suggest above, the commitment by NCC faculty to develop rhetorically versatile, culturally aware students better explains the students' sophistication.

All three of our data sources emphasize academic/disciplinary characteristics and personal agendas that are as likely to be expressed on paper as on screen. Conventions of linear written discourse predominate; the importance of correct grammar, for example, is the primary way that survey respondents differentiate the expectations of their major teachers. "Paper" is the common term students use for their assignments. The comments on "clarity," "use of sources," and "analysis" that are repeated from essay to survey to focus group imply the academic conventions of the formal essay. No student on the surveys mentions, for example, integration of sound and/or visuals with text as a major expectation. As might be expected, some students, such as computer scientists and majors in Art and Visual Technology, state that they write using digital tools; however, assignments involving Web design or other multimedia approaches remain uncommon across the curriculum. A program such as New Century College is still an exception.

Nevertheless, as with our faculty informants, student reliance on many aspects of digital technology has become so commonplace that students find it unworthy of mention. The "research" of which the students in all our data sources speak no longer occurs without email, word processing, file transfer, Web browsing, and electronic database searching—the basic IT skills that all GMU students learn in required courses. If at one time such skills constituted an "alternative discourse," they have long since been assimilated into the reigning concept of academic discourse at a school such as ours.

Conclusion

The students on whose words, spoken and written, we have relied for our data in this chapter have enabled us to achieve insights into the attitudes and development of writers across many disciplines. We have focused on four areas of inquiry:

- Expectations for writing in students' disciplines
- How students gain confidence to write with passion and voice
- How they learn to write in disciplinary ways
- How our findings relate to the taxonomy of alternatives we've previously generated

In regard to the first, we've noted ten generalizations about writing in disciplines based on our data. In addition, we are positing three "stages" in the development of undergraduate disciplinary writers—a progression dependent on the frequency and variety of writing experiences, as well as on writers' reflectiveness about both the field and their growth into it.

As for our second inquiry, we have seen that for "third-stage" writers there is a merging of the writer's personal goals and preferred styles with the discipline's expectations, as the writer understands them. Similar to our faculty informants, students with the most experience writing in their majors understand how the discipline, in its dynamic variety of voices and exigencies, can accommodate original ideas and new perspectives. These students see their most influential teachers inspiring and encouraging their own passions, and they are confident that they will have a role in shaping the discipline.

That teachers play an essential role in this process of growth is one of our most emphatic findings. While the teacher as lecturer and as published writer is credited by our student informants as sparking understanding, it is the teacher as guide, interested reader, and commentator on student writing that is most often mentioned. Third-stage writers also credit the broad and varied reading they do for their courses as helping them understand how to write in their fields, but time and again students note the teacher's guidance in the process of revision as most vital to their development.

Few of our informants saw either the teacher or the discipline as inhibiting their writerly choices, so the idea of "alternative discourse" as resistance to either a "generic academic" discourse or a disciplinary discourse was not played out in our data. The student data, corroborating the faculty data from earlier chapters, revealed a range of options for student writers, options that seemed to accommodate both their personal and academic goals. Also, as with our faculty, nonstandard usage and/or grammar were not considered legitimate "alternatives" by our student informants, even though students distinguished between faculty who were more "picky" and those who overlooked errors. Finally, while some electronic compositions, such as hypertext documents and Web pages, are still "alternative" in that they are not mentioned by most students as part of their discipline's expectations for writers, other aspects of electronic media have now been assumed into the generic construct of academic writing.

In our final chapter, we discuss the implications of these student findings, as well as the implications of our research with faculty. We offer recommendations for writers, for teachers, and for program leaders across the disciplines.

Chapter Five

Implications for Teaching and Program Building

In this final chapter, we summarize several conclusions we have drawn from our research, particularly those that we feel make a contribution to theory on the growth of writers in and through the academy. Then we describe practices that apply to these conclusions both to the classroom and in faculty development programs.

> It's clear when you're writing something you really care about. You're impassioned, but you're also logical and you're making your point and you underscore it. When people can't find the part of their work that they care about, they just pile words and sentences together.
>
> —*Roger Lancaster, Anthropology*

The Discipline and Passion

We begin with Lancaster's observation because he speaks to one of the most important insights we've gained from our research with faculty and students: good writing, whether it adheres to established conventions or takes risks with form and structure, grows out of a writer's sense that the work he or she is doing matters, both professionally and personally. All the faculty we interviewed are deeply engaged in their scholarship, though their motives for writing, the audiences they envision, and the shapes their writing takes in response to motive and audience may vary enormously. Similarly, in teaching with writing, these faculty devise assignments that reflect not only their sense of the kinds of writing undergraduates should be doing, but also their sense of topics and materials that will engage the students. For some of our faculty informants, what they ask students to do, as we have discussed, mirrors their own interests and passions, and they want students to be inspired as well. So important is this connection between "good writing" and individual vision that the rubrics our departments have designed to measure student writing usually include "original thinking" as a key component.

Alternative Discourses

The idea of the "alternative" in academic discourse is closely related to this idea of individual passion and intention, either the student's or the teacher's. We began this research imagining that we might identify clear "alternatives" to a recognizable academic discourse. But as the study went on, we saw more and more that the versions of the alternative we delineated in the taxonomy in Chapter One could better be understood as *variations within* academic expectations. What might be regarded as an "exception" in one teacher's view of the rhetoric of the discipline might be essential in the view of another practitioner in the same field. Further, the dynamism of disciplines that our faculty informants revealed works toward the acceptance of new methods and concepts, as well as a blurring of disciplinary borders. Hence, whatever might appear out of bounds to some members of the academy will likely show up in course syllabi and in articles in some journals, so a teacher preparing students for academic writing would be hard pressed to label any discursive practice always unacceptable. Certainly yes, both student and faculty informants cited thesis-driven essays supported by evidence as the most popular academic form, but other forms are also common; moreover, the range of purposes, audiences, contexts, and formats for these "research-based" assignments is great, and will vary significantly depending on course level and the subject of the course.

This great diversity notwithstanding, we hold to the three principles of academic writing that we described in Chapter One:

- Clear evidence in writing that the writer(s) have been persistent, open-minded, and disciplined in study
- The dominance of reason over emotion or sensual perception
- An imagined reader who is coolly rational, reading for information, and intending to formulate a reasoned response

But these broad principles, while they can help teachers explain the most common rhetorical attitudes of academics, won't relieve teachers or students of the responsibility to observe the myriad ways in which disciplines, specialties, and individuals embody these principles in language and media.

Five Contexts for Writing Assignments

Our research with faculty and students has also given us insight, we think, into the reasons for misunderstanding and miscommunication about expectations for writing. We observed over and over almost all our informants—teachers and students—using the same short list of terms to describe good writing, but meaning, as we came to learn, very different things by them. Some insight into this phenomenon is offered by activity theory, which describes the ecology of the classroom as often, perhaps inevitably, revealing conflict between teachers and students in terms of their motives and objectives. Students don't give teachers what they want in writing because they perceive the tasks and goals differently. Likewise, genre theory tells us that, as writers' motives or "exigencies" differ, all aspects of the writing may differ. Further, by their very social nature, genres may differ even within communities bound by similar interests and goals (see Devitt, for example).

As we have listened to faculty and students talk about their writing and learning, we have come to a better articulated understanding of this conflict of motives—one that we hope can help teachers craft clearer assignments through their own clearer awareness of their motives and expectations. We see up to five contexts at work in a teacher's design of any assignment, and these same contexts influence how the teacher will respond to and evaluate the student's work. These contexts are

- The academic (pertaining to the broad principles described in Chapter One)
- The disciplinary (pertaining to the methods and conventions of the teacher's broad "field")
- The subdisciplinary (pertaining to the teacher's area of interest, with its own methods and conventions, within the broader discipline)
- The local or institutional (pertaining to the policies and practices of the local school or department)
- The idiosyncratic or personal (pertaining to the teacher's unique vision and combination of interests)

We have found that when teachers talk about their expectations for student writers, they will invoke one or more, usually several, of these contexts.

As we talked at length with teachers, all the contexts emerged in their reasoning. However, written assignments almost never explicitly reveal how these contexts have been blended in tasks and criteria; we suspect that few teachers, ourselves included, have been aware of the interplay of these multiple influences on their thinking. How can we teachers expect students to share our complicated sense of expectations for writing, when we have not articulated them ourselves? Later in this chapter, we describe a teaching practice that applies the "five contexts" to revision of an assignment.

Stages of Writing Development "into" a Discipline

In the previous chapter, we described "three stages" of students' development as they learned to write within a disciplinary framework. In the first stage, the student uses very limited experience in academic writing, one or two courses perhaps, to build a general picture of "what all teachers expect." If, for example, a composition teacher or textbook imposes a list of "dos and don'ts in college papers," such lessons are apt to stick, especially in the absence of contrary experiences in the first year.

In the second stage, more advanced students, such as some of those third- and fourth-year students we interviewed in our focus groups, move to a radically relativistic view ("they all want different things") after they have encountered teachers' differing methods, interests, and emphases. Students in this stage see teachers as idiosyncratic, not as conforming to disciplinary standards, and they are likely to feel confused and misled as teachers use the same terms to mean different things. Using the "five contexts" as a frame, we see such students being overwhelmed by the idiosyncratic dimension of a teacher's thinking, and so ignoring the disciplinary and even generic academic consistencies of teachers' expectations.

In the third stage, which not all students reach in their undergraduate years, the student uses the variety of courses in a major: varying methods, materials, approaches, interests, vocabularies, etc., toward building a complex, but organic sense of the structure of the discipline. Some of our focus group informants and virtually all the proficiency essay writers demonstrated this sense of coherence-within-diversity, understanding expectations as a rich mix of many ingredients, as they wrote or spoke about how individual teachers' assignments and responses had led them to this nuanced construct of the discipline.

A crucial element of this third-stage vision is the student's sense of his or her place within the disciplinary enterprise. As noted first in this chapter, the writer's passion for the subject is essential for good academic writing. All the proficiency essay writers we studied wrote with passion about specific courses and projects. We might express the connection this way: once a student learns that the flexible principles of the discipline offer room for his or her desires, then the student can appreciate how the passions of other scholars, perhaps organized into subdisciplines, contribute to and continually shape the larger discipline. We saw this process enacted in the careers of our faculty informants, just as we saw its early flowering in the essays of the proficiency writers.

We might indeed envision fourth or higher stages in this development; for example, our faculty informants' appreciation of the influences of other disciplines, new technologies, etc., on any field, and how the individual scholar/writer can negotiate among disciplines to forge new directions—not only for him- or herself but for others and even for the field at large. Certainly we saw this cross- and interdisciplinary movement in the work of Jeanne Sorrell, Chris Jones, or Lesley Smith. We see the beginnings of this development in those of our students who had chosen double majors or who had crafted interdisciplinary majors. Indeed, we see in these students often a quicker grasp of the flexible dimensions of any field, as if by ongoing and focused comparison of fields they come to understand both a field's central principles and where it is open to alliances and mutual influence. Bright examples include our informants from New Century College and individualized studies major Melanie; their self-possession is shown in an appreciation of how each course and discipline can contribute to their goals, but whose careful comparison of fields has shown them how they must limit the influence of any one disciplinary tradition.

While passion for inquiry into a subject is one crucial virtue of the third-stage writer, the ability to analyze the goals, methods, and genres of the discipline is another. The maturing academic writer achieves that awareness of coherence-within-diversity by *writing to a variety of assignments under the guidance of a range of committed teachers*. The practices that follow demonstrate that principle. But perhaps just as important is the regular opportunity and encouragement to reflect in writing on the connections and distinctions among those many experiences. For instance, what do these assignments in major courses have in common? What principles lie at the heart of my major? How can I find a place for my goals in that structure? What other modes of inquiry attract me, and can I borrow from different fields to achieve my goals? We have seen in the New Century students and in the proficiency essay writers the results of this written reflection. It is not uncommon for these essayists to comment on the value of the written reflection toward their understanding of the writing they have already done. The NCC students in particular spontaneously credit regular critical reflection as a key to their maturity. The practices that follow demonstrate the importance of students developing an awareness of genre as motivated, social, and situational and of themselves as active participants in shaping the genres they encounter.

Tension Between Individual Desire and Academic Convention

The practices we will suggest imply what we consider a productive tension between the student—a passionate individual with interests to cultivate and express—and an academy that imposes expectations on individuals, even though that academy is made up of dynamic and diverse disciplines and areas of interest. To illustrate, the departmental rubrics in Chapter Three emphasize both "original thinking" and conventions of form and method. This tension means that the teacher needs always to guide students with respect for both exigencies: thus, the teacher helps students to identify and express their passions for learning and teaches conventions of the academy.

Inevitably, however, if teachers enact the former successfully, students will sometimes write in ways that run counter to academic convention. For example, our second principle of academic writing is that reason controls both emotion and sensation; but a student writing enthusiastically about a favorite subject—as teachers often want students to write—will come across as more passionate than analytic. The writer will also likely ignore Principle 3—to address a reader who is by training skeptical—and so never think of objections such a reader might raise. How can the teacher help guide this student?

As our recommended practices will show, we prefer that teachers respect and encourage both passion and discipline. To apply what we see as this balanced perspective, we suggest that our taxonomy of alternatives (see Chapter One) and writers' motives in using them can help teachers productively respond to student writing. For example, the student in the first-year course who writes passionately but not analytically may, as the taxonomy of alternatives suggests, be ignorant of academic convention—but should teachers presume such ignorance? We encountered students in all three research samples (survey, focus groups, proficiency essays), albeit not many, who claimed a high level of self-possession even as they entered college, whose writing choices were informed and deliberate, and who complained about teachers' failure to imagine that the students knew teacher objectives and had carefully thought about what they were doing. A premise of this chapter is that students learn about expectations and options in the "five contexts" ethnographically, not by rote, and that individual variations are an indispensable component of the progress of disciplines. We feel that teachers can adapt this ethnographic perspective to their reading of student prose. Rather than the teacher's assuming that an alternative format, arrangement, voice, etc., represents either ignorance or merely a failed effort, we'd recommend a more flexible, investigative attitude.

Practices for Teachers

In this section, we describe 12 practices that apply the conclusions described above and other findings from the research. The first seven of these are intended for college teachers of courses across disciplines. Although all seven can be adapted to a range of disciplinary environments, the latter three may be more applicable to the composition classroom, where the teacher's primary focus is the students' writing. The final five practices are intended for faculty development workshops and seminars, either in the cross-disciplinary environment of the most common WAC/WID workshop or in discipline-specific workshops. These practices are intended to add to the already considerable literature of exemplary practice contained in WAC/WID pedagogy texts[1] and online at the WAC Clearinghouse (wac.colostate.edu).

Practice 1: Define expectations clearly and place them in the context of the discipline or in other contexts meaningful to you.

Our study of both faculty and student behavior has revealed to us the difficulty that almost all faculty, including composition faculty, have in articulating more than the "generic academic" expectations for student writing. The rubrics that our departments at Mason have created as part of our state-mandated writing assessment, described in Chapter Three, characteristically reiterate, with varying emphasis, the same twenty or so terms. The departmental faculty committees making these judgments understand the discipline-specific connotations and exigencies of a term such as "research" because they are insiders to these connotations; but students—largely through painful trial and error, usually manifested in low grades—come to see that "research" in one context can be very different from "research" in another. These findings have been replicated in other workshop settings with faculty, when we have asked faculty to articulate their expectations.

Conversely, when teachers do articulate more precise criteria and procedures in their assignments, or in their responses to student papers, students

[1]For a good explanation of a variety of WAC "how-to's," see John Bean's *Engaging Writers: The Professor's Guide to Integrating Writing, Critical Thinking, and Active Learning in the Classroom;* Barbara Walvoord and Virginia Anderson's *Effective Grading;* and Christopher Thaiss's and Art Young's guides to teaching and writing across the curriculum.

often do not see the criteria as inspired by the discipline or by a subdiscipline within the larger concept; rather, they see these specific criteria as merely idiosyncratic. A significant minority of our survey respondents and focus group members expressed this interpretation of differences among faculty. The first-stage writers—the least experienced among the informants— expected all teachers in the discipline to operate by the same standards and saw differences as mere aberrations; second-stage writers had enough experience of difference to see idiosyncracy—"they're all different"—as the explanation for a mainly unpredictable experience. Our histories in faculty development give us many examples of faculty who contribute to this confusion by explaining their expectations in purely personal terms: "This is what I want" or even "I don't care what you did in your other classes—this is what you do in mine."

We don't wish to imply that students can't succeed as writers in fields without a better-contextualized explanation by all faculty. Nevertheless, we do have the impressive evidence of our proficiency essayists, who have learned a nuanced, inclusive understanding of the discipline—and who credit the care by some of their teachers to explain their expectations in terms of the particular mode of thought that identifies the field.

Given the difficulty faculty have in articulating criteria, our merely saying "define expectations clearly and place them in the disciplinary context" may not help. Then again, the mere challenge of explaining *why* you are requiring "research" to consist of certain operations and certain types of data will surely help students understand both what to do and how your expectations relate to those of other teachers. We found in our interviews with faculty that the more we asked about their careers as writers and teachers—what they did and why—the richer and better articulated their portraits of their disciplines became.

To go beyond the mere imperative to be *clear* and *contextual,* we suggest the usefulness of the framework of contexts we introduced early in Chapter Three:

- Generic academic
- Disciplinary
- Subdisciplinary (area of interest)
- Local or institutional
- Idiosyncratic

We suggest that, in designing assignments, teachers can clarify expectations for themselves and students by analyzing how their procedures and criteria draw from each of these contexts. Whether or not this thinking ever makes its way into an assignment description, the exercise can help teachers in the design process and in explaining criteria to students. This analysis can be done as quickly or as thoroughly as one wishes. In the following example, Chris considers one of his own assignments for an advanced composition course in business writing.

Sample Assignment: "White Paper" Based on Team Field Research

In the course of your team field research on the writing culture of a business organization, each team member will identify a communication issue or problem at the company/agency/business that will form the basis of a "white paper" (i.e., a position statement or formal recommendation). The white paper is an important form of business report that is used in both university courses and the workplace.

Each member of the team will write a separate white paper on a separate issue. I must approve topics. Your white paper should be addressed to a relevant manager with the firm (though whether you indeed deliver the white paper is up to you!), rather than to me as an interested outsider. Your white paper will need to

1. Succinctly describe the issue or problem, including any relevant background the reader needs;
2. State your position on the issue and/or make recommendations toward solving the problem;
3. Support your position and/or recommendations with all relevant data and sources;
4. Cite sources using APA style.

Source material may include your own relevant experience and observation and that of others whom you can accurately and specifically cite; sources may also include print or online articles or product specifications that you must accurately cite and document. Databases may come in handy in this project. A table (e.g., of data, options, or pros and cons) must be included somewhere in the document, as appropriate to your subject.

As customary in this course, use standard memo format for the heading. Your final draft should be between 1200 and 1500 words. Include your first draft, critique sheets, and a change memo in the final packet.

Chris's thinking-out-loud analysis of the assignment using the contexts listed above:

Generic academic: "Even if students haven't had other business courses (most of them take this course as rising juniors), they should have written papers that required them to support a position with evidence. They'll have done so earlier in this course. But they may have trouble knowing what

(continues)

---

constitutes evidence in a business environment. They should also know that teachers require correct use of standard edited American English—do I need to include this in criteria? I'll include it on the critique sheet that the groups use, but I wonder if I can assume that they know the requirement is an academic standard, not just the preoccupation of an English teacher."

Disciplinary: "I need to be clear that the primary context here is not an academic business environment but the workplace itself. Memo formatting is one aspect of that. Sure, the actual audience of the writing will be me, an academic, but I really intend this assignment to test their close observation of the research site and their sense of the manager they'll be addressing. Students have used this assignment in the past to propose actual changes in their workplaces, and I want them to entertain that as a serious possibility. I'll also make it clear that the APA documentation is a nod to business school practice, not to workplace practice. And my requirement of a table is just to give them practice in presenting data that way, because the business discipline expects it."

Subdisciplinary: "Business writing classes straddle the shifting line between academic management study, which is a social science field, and workplace practice. I know I don't address this specifically enough with my classes. Some of my assignments, methods, and criteria are fully academic in nature—e.g., the news analysis and the entire research project—while the formal memo writing and the online short reports and approvals characterize 'our' workplace. The 'subdiscipline' of business communication seems to be a strange amalgam of academic analysis and pragmatic business practice. One thing I like about the 'white paper' assignment, as I've constructed it, is that it gives students practice in a flexible form that straddles that same border."

Local or institutional: "I realize that my syllabus could be much clearer about the connections between my sections and the objectives of the advanced comp program at Mason. I include a link on my syllabus to the program's description of the course, but I should include the objectives in my course description itself. In addition, my expectations are local—appropriate for this community—because almost all the students have jobs and commute to school; therefore, it's relatively easy for me to set up a business-writing course that takes advantage of their familiarity with workplaces and their mobility to perform on-site research. That this type of requirement is part of a number of sections is something they should also know—just as they should also know that case studies and ethnography are part of social science practice. They also need to know that my requirement of APA style is part of social science practice, not a requirement of our business school. Indeed, our business faculty have no policy on documentation in student writing, and the required course that follows this one uses MLA—only because most of the students have had it in some English classes."

(continues)

Idiosyncratic: "Students get lots of reinforcement of the individuality of their teachers in their interactions with them, and a lot of what students perceive as idiosyncrasy the teacher is probably not aware of—body language, conversational turns, and the like. Am I naive to think that my assignments and criteria derive wholly from the contexts I've described above and not from just me? Of course, I put those various influences together in a way that's somewhat different from other teachers, so that's the idiosyncrasy. But it's important for students to know that I just didn't 'make them up.' I can surely do a better job of communicating that interplay of contexts clearly."

We have already defined the growth from the second to the third stage by students as a shift from their dominant expectation of the idiosyncratic to their understanding of the disciplinary contexts in which individual classes and assignments occur. Surely, teachers in any discipline can aid this process of growth by showing students that what appears to be uniqueness, even caprice, by teachers is largely a deliberate blending of influences and demands from the academy, the discipline, the area of interest, and the local/ institutional communities.

This articulation of contexts can occur anywhere in a course, not just in the syllabus or in the assignment description. For example, we suggest that teachers make the methods and discourses visible in the readings they assign, as, for example, environmental scientist Chris Jones does in his comparisons of "newspaper science" and the explanations in the textbook. When exigencies are truly personal or when an assignment privileges one vision of the discipline over another, as in Sorrell's paradigm cases for her writing-intensive course, teachers should let the students know.

Practice 2: Reflect on your own developing career as a scholar/writer and as a teacher.

Chris's exploration of the "five contexts" in relation to his business writing assignment, in the preceding box, illustrates one kind of reflective teaching. But what we are suggesting here is a broader, less specific consideration modeled on the core questions we asked our faculty informants (see chapters Two and Three). This model relies on the experiential link between one's growth and practice as a scholar/writer and the values and expectations one communicates to students. Our interviews with faculty and the teaching materials we reviewed showed us clear connections between a faculty member's priorities in scholarship and priorities in teaching—even though some of our informants seemed not to be aware of this parallel. For example, as we describe in Chapter Three, several claimed that their goal in undergraduate teaching was not to inculcate the specific values of their disciplines, but to teach a broader "good" thinking or writing. But as they talked, particularly about assignments, we could see that their descriptions of objectives matched those of their fields and interest areas, not of the generic academy.

While one goal of this broader, blended reflection would be general self-awareness, our specific goal for the teacher would be to clarify and articulate expectations for students. A possible rubric for this reflection might include:

- How would you describe the expectations for good writing in your discipline? How do these compare with the expectations for good writing in your area(s) of interest in this field? How did you learn them? Who and what have been the most important influences on your learning of these expectations?

- Looking at your career as a scholar and writer, how have your own values and preferences as a scholar and writer compared with the expectations you described above? Have you ever done work you'd consider "alternative" to the mainstream? Why or why not? What risks has this "alternative work" entailed for you? How do you see your field changing over the years to accommodate or exclude different ways of thinking and writing?

- What are your expectations for students as scholars and writers? How do these vary from course to course, level to level? What links or divergences do you see between your values and preferences in your own scholarly writing and those you have for students? How do you describe your expectations to students, or carry out a process in your teaching, so that students can understand and meet these expectations?

Not only will this kind of reflection on writing and teaching-with-writing practices help the teacher achieve greater clarity in what students are told up front—in the syllabus, in assignment directions and accompanying evaluation rubrics, and in class discussions—it will also save time when responding to student papers. Perhaps more importantly, students will have a context for interpreting the feedback the teacher gives on their papers.

Practice 3: Provide students with contextualized feedback on their writing, especially early in a course.

That students rely heavily on teacher feedback, particularly on their first paper in the course, was one of the more dramatic findings from our focus groups. As WAC program leaders, we were gratified to learn that students had come, by experience, to expect their teachers in disciplinary courses to give them an articulated response even though they also expected that the feedback they received would be different from that given by a composition teacher.[2] While, as we describe in the previous chapter, students are adept at picking up clues about teacher expectations even from minimal feedback— e.g., a crossed-out word, a brief note of approval in the margin of a draft— they especially appreciate those teachers who give them detailed feedback. Student after student in the proficiency exam essays, for example, readily credited their understanding of the rhetorics of their fields to teachers who took the time to respond in detail to their writing.

At the same time that we are pointing out the importance of detailed, nuanced feedback, we also realize the time commitment that this kind of feedback requires, particularly for those teachers who give writing assignments in all their courses and/or who teach large numbers of students. As we've noted, the WAC literature is filled with advice on how teachers can give effective feedback while managing their paper load, among other useful practices, so we want to focus here on the benefits that accrue to students when teachers talk with one another about their expectations for student writers. Teachers who understand where their feedback practices are situated—in the discipline or subdiscipline, in the seemingly generic academic, in personal preferences, or in some combination of all of these—are better able, we think, to give effective advice to students, both prior to the assignment and in their evaluative commentary. In turn, students will gain a clearer understanding of why and how their teachers' expectations may differ, as well as a greater appreciation for the central role of the reader in the construction of a piece of writing. As we explain in the latter half of this chapter on practices for program development, WAC workshops (e.g., the assessment workshops described in Chapter Three) offer one of the best venues for faculty to talk with groups of colleagues about how they use and evaluate writing in their courses, an experience they generally find, often to their surprise, both enlightening and enjoyable.

Based on what we hear from faculty across the campus, we think it's safe to say that faculty generally do not talk about their expectations for student writing, other than to note how poorly students are writing or, conversely, to praise an exceptional writer. Faculty often come to us, in fact, with questions about what their colleagues or those in the field might expect when it comes to, say, the use of first person or a preferred documentation style. A teacher in

---

[2] They expected composition teachers to be more attuned to syntax and mechanics (yes, they do expect this from English teachers), and also more conscious of the student as a "writer" (as in "wordsmith") than as a student of the discipline. This is not to say that some of our faculty informants from different fields are not as conscious of student creativity and rhetorical/stylistic choice as this stereotypical English teacher, not to mention as "picky" about grammar and commas, but students expect these types of feedback from the composition teacher. They expect the feedback from their disciplinary teachers to concern types of evidence, methods of argument, and appropriate terms.

biology, for example, asked Terry whether she thought it was okay to tell students that they could use "I" in their experimental reports. Would he be misguiding students, the teacher wondered, if he allowed "I" and his colleagues did not, even though there is clearly a move in the professional literature to the use of first person? In response, Terry asked whether he explained to students the way first person is functioning in the literature and how they should similarly position the "I" in their writing; she suggested that he might share with them reservations about how his colleagues might react when they see students writing in first person. She also recommended that he talk with his colleagues about their preferences.

In another instance, an undergraduate associate dean inquired of both of us what documentation style is preferred in business schools, since faculty differed in the styles they were assigning and students were often confused. In this case, too, we suggested that the best way to determine a preferred style is to have faculty talk together about the styles they recommend to students, why they preferred one style over another, and the epistemological differences the preferred styles might represent.

Bringing faculty together for these kinds of conversations can be difficult, we realize, so it's useful to think about alternatives to face-to-face encounters. Some of these might be, for example:

- Brief queries on departmental listservs asking faculty to respond to questions like "What documentation style do you require your students to use? Why?" Or "Do you allow students to use first person? What directions do you give them for using 'I'?" Faculty can also be invited to paste in syllabi or assignment instructions related to the queries.

- Online writing guides for students, such as those we feature on the George Mason WAC website (http://wac.gmu.edu), which include interviews with faculty about their preferences, pet peeves, and "do and don't" writing tips. The writing guides may also include a sample paper with several teachers' commentaries on what the student has done well in terms of the assignment and the discipline.

- Lists of writing guides that individual faculty have created. Many of our faculty, we've discovered, have created their own writing guides for students. A number of them have also posted their guides on their websites. Yet, as we've also found, they typically have not shared their writing advice with others on the faculty, whether out of a sense that others will think they're being immodest or will be critical of the advice. We tend to find out about the work they've done in offhand conversations during WAC workshops, for example, which they see as sanctioned places for exchanging teaching advice.

However the sharing among colleagues occurs, it needs to be translated by the teacher into feedback for students that gives them a clearer sense of the discipline, of the area of interest represented by the course, of institutional requirements, and of the teacher's individual goals.

In the three practices described thus far, we focused on how teachers can better understand and articulate for students the contexts that influence their teaching-with-writing practices through reflecting on their assignments and expectations and talking about these with their colleagues, both informally and in more structured settings. Now we turn to another kind of reflective practice, which, based on our research findings, we think will help teachers in guiding students to become third-stage writers.

Practice 4: Help students find their own "passions" in learning and to realize their passions in your discipline. Seek ways to validate the student as "expert"— as potential contributor to the field.

One of the things that impressed us the most about the students we're calling third-stage writers was their sense of passion for the material they were studying and the confidence with which they spoke about themselves as writers, even as they also sometimes described the difficult learning process they went through to gain that confidence. In focus groups and proficiency exam essays, these students frequently credited teachers for helping them understand what it means to be original and how to make rhetorical choices that reflect their own interests and ideas and not simply what they think the teacher wants. As we explained in the previous chapter, when teachers trusted them to express interesting ideas and/or made them feel that they had some expertise to share, the student writers learned to trust themselves as well, even to break the rules if their writing goals seemed to demand alternative expressions. When they glimpsed a teacher's passion behind the scholarly prose—by reading a teacher's writing, through commentary on their texts, in conversation—they understood that academic writing doesn't rule out passion, but rather gives it a disciplined voice.

Based on these findings, we recommend that faculty consider ways that their teaching will help students to see the discipline not only as a system of terms, texts, expectations, and procedures, but also as a dynamic realm that can accommodate and nurture different personalities, passions, and visions. In practices 1 and 2 above, we've given systematic sets of questions that teachers can use to examine and reflect on their work with student writers. Now we turn to questions that might help teachers think about how their teaching-with-writing practices facilitate such growth and investment for students. We also recommend some methods teachers might use to help students articulate and reflect on their investment in the course and the field.

When students in the focus groups and in their proficiency essays mentioned teachers who helped them understand how to be passionately engaged and, at the same time, controlled writers, they usually gave the names of one or two teachers; never did they indicate that their teachers routinely made their scholarly passions explicit to students. We think it might be useful, then, for teachers to ask themselves the following questions as a sort of self-check on their practice and also a reminder of the importance of the practices we detail in the questions:

- Do you talk in classes about your own decisions to concentrate in your field—your earlier interests, the influences of teachers, turning points, etc.?

- Do you share examples of your writing with students and have them ask questions about your research?

- If one of the goals of your teaching is to inspire students to become majors in your field, how do you try to achieve that goal? How do you balance in your teaching the need to teach conformity to method and to standards of precision with appreciation/cultivation of your students' interests and professional desires—even if those seem at odds with the standards?

- How do you tend to talk about your field—more as a system of rules and accepted practices or more as a community of passionate scholars who are attempting to shape the future? How do you think your students see you? How do you want them to see you?

- How do your answers to these questions translate into your uses of writing in your teaching—to the assignments you write and your objectives for those assignments, to the instructions you give, to your grading criteria, to the feedback you give writers?

Like teachers, students bring to the course their own goals, objectives, and prior learning experiences. We think it is important, then, for teachers to give them a similar opportunity to reflect on how the course fits with their goals. In the first week of the semester, teachers might invite students to write about the course objectives, the knowledges they already have related to these objectives, and, perhaps most importantly, what their own goals are for learning and writing about the course material, which may well extend outside of the academy and even the workplace. We showed, for example, in Chapter Two on faculty as writers and in Chapter Four on students as writers, that many of our informants have writing goals related to self-discovery and to the relationship of the self and/or the discipline to larger social issues.

Further, we think there is great value in giving students the opportunity at one or more points in their college experience to reflect on their writing during a course, an entire major, and their college careers. We saw this point borne out, to give one example, in the essays students wrote to accompany the portfolios they submitted for proficiency credit in advanced composition. Many noted that they had never been asked to write about themselves as writers in their field(s) and, at first, felt intimidated by the prospect. As they wrote the essay, however, they discovered, to their surprise, the ways they had successfully assimilated and applied to their writing the implicit lessons learned from teachers' lectures, assigned reading and writing, and responses to papers. To give another example, the focus group informants from New Century College, as reported in Chapter Four, impressed us with their insights on the importance of the reflective writing they do at the end of each year, which culminates in a reflective capstone portfolio. Before we leave the topic of portfolio reflection, we want to mention the potential of electronic eportfolios, which allow students to create a dynamic portrait of themselves as writers in college and to reflect not only on the writing they have included but also on the format itself as a vehicle for conveying their hypertextual identity.

Each of the preceding practices above focuses on ways teachers can examine and reflect on their own teaching-with-writing practices and motivate students to similarly question and reflect. Now we turn to a set of practices to help students better understand writing and themselves as writers, in disciplines, in the workplaces they want to enter, and in other, more personal, venues. Because each of these practices requires more time and attention than might be available in courses outside of English composition, we see practices 5, 6, and 7 as working best in composition courses where adequate time can be given for students to reflect on themselves as writers, to investigate the expectations of teachers in courses inside and outside of their major, and to report on the results. Teachers in any course, however, may find that they can incorporate aspects of these inquiries to the degree that time allows.

Practice 5: Give students opportunities for reflecting on their own growth as writers and rhetors, in the academy and as related to the workplaces they will enter.

Far from presuming the student a tabula rasa in knowledge of written rhetoric, asking students to think systematically about how they have changed and matured as writers respects their experience not only in prior schooling but also in any other context—family, workplace, community—in which they may have not only written but also been affected by the written rhetoric of others. It presumes that they have a history as writers: that they've developed assumptions about tasks, readers, and processes that can either help them in future situations or limit their understanding and performance. The assignment itself can be expressed several ways, among others:

- It may be constructed as a form of "literacy narrative," a single assignment early in the semester that asks students to respond in an autobiographical essay to a range of questions about their past (or past, present, and future) as writers, such as the kinds of writing that have come most easily; the turning points, major lessons, minor lessons, foolish misconceptions that have been outgrown; the advice these writers would give to others in their field; the challenges encountered in writing in new courses; the writing they imagine doing in five years. This kind of self-reflection might also be useful in preparing students for other courses. While writing about the self might be an "alternative" assignment in most disciplines, we saw among our 14 faculty informants five who consistently asked students to reflect on their learning and their relationship to the field—Lancaster in anthropology, Bergoffen in philosophy, Rader in sociology, Sorrell in nursing, and Lesley Smith in new technologies;

- It may be an ongoing log or journal that, perhaps, asks the writer to analyze current rhetorical tasks in the context of relevant challenges of the writer's past. Melanie, the individualized studies major described in Chapter Four, for example, already had a great deal of experience writing motivational texts for her female clients. She often resisted writing assignments if she was unable to see the relevance of the assignment in helping her fulfill the rhetorical demands of her work space.

- It may be part of an electronic forum in which the class responds to a series of prompts about rhetorical issues by writing about relevant current and past experience.

- It may be a blog, a website, or an eportfolio in which writers not only post their writing but add links, attachments, or images, and reflect on all these elements to create a fuller, more dynamic picture of the writer.

- It may ask writers to reflect on the ways in which typical rhetorical tasks of the discipline are manifested in the workplaces and social spaces they may enter. The NCC students, for example, frequently mentioned the value of their reflective writing for helping them connect their academic work with their career goals and sense of the field they wanted to enter. As noted in Chapter Four, these students were deeply invested in their projects and saw them not as academic exercises but as opportunities to prepare for the workplace.

Practice 6: Give students opportunities for exploring and understanding the variety of rhetorical environments they'll encounter in college and the workplace.

Many of the responses to our survey and some in the focus groups showed inexperienced writers putting together surmises about writing in the major from skimpy evidence: one or two courses, minimal feedback from a few teachers, hearsay, the style of a textbook. Even the more advanced students in the focus groups often revealed a cumulative sense of the field that, while slightly more sophisticated, was still based on accretion of partial and unreliable evidence. To help students acquire a better and more reliable sense of disciplinary conventions and teacher preferences, we suggest they investigate the field by questioning the "experts"—faculty, advanced students, and workplace professionals—and analyzing the documents that articulate the field to others—textbooks, journal articles, and course materials. Such a study is meant to take the student beyond the first stage we described in the previous chapter, wherein writers identify the disciplines with a few vague generalizations they assume will apply to all courses. "You can't use 'I' in science" is one example; "only English teachers care about good grammar" is another. The inquiry should actually begin to move the student to the third stage, wherein the writer sees the discipline as maintaining some consistent principles of method and rhetoric—but also accommodating a range of subdisciplines and areas of interest, local and institutional variations, and preferences particular to the given teacher/scholar. The boxed questions suggest some areas that the inquiry might explore.

A. Questions students can ask professors

- What is your discipline and how would you describe it?
- What is your subdiscipline or areas of interest in your field and how would you describe them?
- What kinds of writing do you do in your work in this discipline?
- What would you say are the characteristics of good writing in your discipline? What do editors of journals expect?
- How is the writing you do in your area of interest different from the writing that others do in your discipline?
- Is there any other kind of writing that you do? Does it relate to the writing you do in your field or is it different?
- Have you ever done writing in your area of interest that you thought took a risk? Was it in a way that you thought was alternative to what editors usually expect?
- How do you think your discipline is changing in terms of how people are writing within it?

(continues)

- What is the most exciting thing for you about working in your discipline?
- How do you express this excitement in your writing?
- May I see examples of your writing in your field? May I see examples of writing by others that you think is typical of your field?

B. Text Analysis Questions

- *Journal article:* Who are the readers of this journal? To understand and use this article, what would the reader already have to know? (For example, look for key terms the reader would have to understand.) How is the article organized? If you look at more than one article, do you see characteristics of organization that are standard? How does the article reflect what the professor told you about the discipline and its expectations? Differ from what he or she said? Can you tell why readers of this article might find it important?

- *Course syllabus:* What does the syllabus tell you about the goals of the course? The most important methods you'll learn? How do these relate to what the professor told you about the discipline? About his or her area of interest? How does the teacher convey a sense of what he or she finds important and exciting about this subject? How does the syllabus help you understand the expectations for writing that (1) your professor has, and (2) that the discipline has?

- *Written assignment:* What does the assignment convey to you about the professor's expectations for research, thinking, and writing? How do these expectations reflect or relate to (1) what the professor said about the discipline or area of interest, (2) the goals and methods described in the syllabus, (3) the characteristics of the journal article?

- *Workplace documents:* What do sample documents from workplaces you already inhabit or hope to enter tell you about the culture of writing in that space? (See Chris's sample assignment earlier in this chapter.)

Practice 7: Teach students, through guided practice, the "generic academic" principles that all majors share and how to distinguish between these principles and the variations that derive from the five rhetorical contexts we also described: generic academic, disciplines, subdisciplines, local institutions, and individual teachers and courses.

If you have students conduct systematic inquiries such as the ones recommended in the box, they will enact the "disciplined study" identified as the first principle of academic writing in Chapter One. They will also move toward understanding the expectations of their majors. We also recommend that students be explicitly presented the five contexts as a framework for interpreting the assignments and teaching methods they encounter in different classes—including yours. For example, knowing that they can count on their teachers, regardless of the course, to appreciate the three broad principles of academic writing described in Chapter One can help them see the kernel of consistency in academic work amid the variety of exigencies, formats, and methods they will encounter.

Similarly, students can more readily understand the "generic academic" if the teacher presents the list of common terms gleaned from the departmental assessment rubrics summarized in Chapter Three. These 20-plus common terms not only show the values consistent across the academy but will also alert students to probe for the variations that are in play in a specific class. What, for example, does "research" mean in an introductory psychology course? In an introductory literature course? What does "original thinking" mean in those two courses?

Unlike Practice 6, which probes detailed features of specific teachers' attitudes and practices, this inquiry asks students to look for similarities across courses and teachers. Students might be asked to collect the assignments for research and/or writing in all the courses they are taking (including those in your course) and look for the following:

- Certainly there are many differences among these assignments, but in what ways are they similar? For example, in the kinds of things students are asked to study closely? In the attitude they are supposed to take toward the material? In how the paper will be graded?

- What terms do the assignments have in common or that seem to be closely related? In what way do these terms seem to be used in the same way across courses?

- Based on the similarities you've detected, how would you define "writing in college"?

Practices for Faculty and Program Development

All the practices described above should be and can be developed and adapted in a cooperative faculty environment. There are a plethora of materials available for starting or enhancing faculty development according to WAC and WID principles (see, for example, McLeod and Soven; McLeod, Miraglia,

Soven, and Thaiss; and Yancey and Huot). In addition to the thoughtful advice in these many sources, we have used our methods and findings to suggest the following models and practices.

Practice 8: Workshops for teachers should ask them to talk/write about their values/growth/passion as writers as well as their values/growth/passion as teachers.

We describe this method in detail as an individual exercise for teachers in Practice 3. In a workshop setting, an opportunity for teachers to hear one another's stories and reflections can be mutually exhilarating and enlightening, as the writing and reading open up the academy's richness as a community of dedicated, imaginative scholars/writers/teachers.

Valuing workshop participants as writers and scholars, as well as teachers, can be extended by workshop organizers through such activities as planned time for participants to write about their current scholarly or creative projects. These writings can then be shared in small groups or summarized by each writer for the entire group. Alternatively, workshop participants might be asked to bring with them a piece of work-in-progress to read to the cross-disciplinary workshop group. Such workshop activities can be structured to emulate the peer response groups that are a staple of process-based composition classes. This mingling of attention to faculty writing and attention to student writing harks back to many of the first programs in WAC faculty development, influenced as many of them were by the principles of the National Writing Project, as Chris has written about elsewhere (Thaiss, 2006).

Indeed, when cross-curricular faculty development in writing began at Mason in 1978, the first program was named the Faculty Writing Program, to recognize the relationship between faculty as writers and as guides for their students in learning the discourses of their disciplines. Faculty from diverse fields would bring to workshops pieces of work in progress that they would read to other participants in small groups. In addition to giving each scholar/writer a new and different audience for their writing, these group sessions had the further effect of requiring writer/teachers to explain to colleagues from other fields enough background of research, methods, and terms to enable these audiences to understand their work. In other words, the sessions became another teaching context that depended on each professional's ability to articulate features of their disciplines that they did not need to articulate when writing or speaking to colleagues in their research areas. So the writing groups reinforced the goal of the teaching workshop to make faculty better able to articulate expectations to an unfamiliar audience, whether student or fellow scholar.

Practice 9: Teachers should regularly engage in group assessment of sample papers as a faculty development technique.

A typical feature of WAC workshops is the group-grading exercise, in which one or more sample student essays are evaluated and teachers' criteria discussed. Usually the main purpose is to help teachers discover useful practices for themselves in assessing student writing, as the teachers discuss options with peers and hear advice from the workshop leader. A significant by-product of the interaction is that academics come to see that they do not all share the same standards and expectations—that disciplines and individuals differ in their definitions of "good" writing.

We see other purposes for the exercise as well. In the creation of department-based rubrics that facilitate formal assessment of student writing in the major, such group evaluation of sample student work can efficiently help faculty identify points of consensus and points of difference. The differences lead to fruitful discussions of options within a major, and they often help faculties articulate expectations for students, as we've already explained in the section on classroom practices. We have conducted such "consensus-building" workshops for many years with our English Department writing faculty, but when we adapted the model to departments across the university several years ago, we saw that the give-and-take served not only the immediate practical purposes but also (1) led teachers to learn about and appreciate one another's commitment to student learning, and (2) led faculty to consider department-wide changes in policy, requirements, and services. In other words, the exercise served both basic and advanced purposes of faculty development.

We have used assessment of sample papers with cross-disciplinary groups of faculty and with members of the same department. The cross-disciplinary assessment workshops have occurred both at George Mason and at other colleges where we have consulted. At Mason, one forum for these assessment procedures has been what we call the "training of trainers" workshop, because we expect those who participate to return to their departments to teach this assessment method, or a modified version, to colleagues.

For the exercise, we use a set of four sample essays written to the same assignment in an advanced composition course. We preselect the sample papers to represent what we judge to be a range of proficiency and approaches; but we want the samples to be close enough in quality to test the ability of the participants to articulate their priorities and criteria in evaluation. Then we ask the group to read two of the four and judge which is the "better" of the two; we give participants the chance for an extended discussion of their reasons for preferring one to another. As the discussion proceeds, the workshop leader records (on board or overhead) every criterion that is named.

Once this part of the exercise is completed, we repeat the process with the other two essays, and ask the participants to add to the list of criteria already recorded. Then we ask them to rate all four against one another and to elucidate any criteria not previously mentioned.

As a final act, we have the group review all criteria that have been named and to vote, by show of hands, for the criteria that they regard as "important." In this part of the exercise, some criteria that had been named in the discussion fall out for lack of group support.

Always, the exercise produces a long and relatively nuanced list of criteria. Since the group is cross-disciplinary, the consensus reached represents what we termed in Chapter Three the "generic academic" expectations for student writing. However, by taking part in the discussion, each faculty member can see where and how the predilections of the specific disciplines vary from one another and from the generic.

As we described earlier in this chapter, when we conducted the same process in individual departments, it has produced both a disciplinary consensus and an articulation of differences that play out across disciplinary subspecialties.

Indeed, the benefits of this exercise for faculty development can be so great that program builders might think of it as one starting point—an initial draw—for WAC/WID workshops. Faculty who might be resistant to or skeptical of workshops based on less formal "writing to learn" techniques are often drawn to workshops that promise immediate aid in evaluating student work and in affirming formal standards. Addressing these faculty's concerns, as this workshop structure does, may encourage future participation in workshops on other uses of writing in teaching. Even if it does not lead to further participation by some, the rubric-building exercise will still have the effects noted above. Detailed information on the assessment process can be found at: http://wac.gmu.edu/program/assessing/phase4.html.

Practice 10: Enhance the effects of Practice 9 by considering the "five contexts."

If the collaborative rubric-building workshop can help teachers become more articulate in explaining expectations to students, an exercise that applies the "five contexts" (academic, disciplinary, subdisciplinary, local, and idiosyncratic) can enhance this articulation. The exercise can be conducted individually, with each teacher practicing on a favorite assignment, as illustrated in Practice 1. The results can be discussed in small or large groups.

But the exercise can also be structured collaboratively, with, for example, a sample assignment (hypothetical or real) as the material for the entire group to discuss. As a further option, the five contexts can be used by small groups as a matrix for design of a new assignment. (See Figure 5–1.) In such

Generic academic	For instance, thesis supported by evidence, original thinking, correct use of English grammar
Disciplinary	
Subdisciplinary	
Local/institutional	
My preferences	

Figure 5–1. *Grid of criteria representing the "five contexts" for an assignment*

an exercise, group members would describe expectations for students that fell into each of the five categories.

Practice 11: Consider how to spark and nurture students' desires/passions in their disciplines—helping students achieve the third stage.

Based on our research, we advocate a faculty development structure that keeps in participants' minds the individual student's goals and intellectual passions, even as faculty also tackle the clearer articulation of their expectations for students. A workshop that uses versions of both Practices 1 and 2 (or 1, 2, and 3) can begin to achieve this balanced emphasis on the individual and the discipline. But we also recommend that Practice 4 be adapted to the group setting. Faculty can benefit from explicit discussion of the role of passion in learning, and ponder ways that their teaching does or could help students to see the discipline not only as a system of terms, texts, expectations, and procedures, but also as a dynamic realm that can accommodate and nurture different personalities and visions. We are beginning to share with colleagues in workshop settings the idea of the third stage of student growth through writing in disciplines, and we are finding it a powerful image of the productive coming together of individual passion and disciplinary standards.

Practice 12: Create unified program development in writing that coordinates goals of the composition course(s) with those of courses in majors.

The first section of this chapter describes practices for teachers without regard to the specific discipline and without distinction between courses that focus primarily on the craft of writing (e.g., English composition) and those that ask students to write as part of their learning the methods and materials of fields. In fact, an early draft of this chapter separated practices for English composition courses from practices for all other undergraduate courses, but so much of what applied to one context applied to the other that we melded the two sections. Nevertheless, here we want to revisit the distinction, because for most of us, at least in the United States, who are charged with building college and university writing programs, the distinction is a fact of life administratively and in terms of faculty assumptions about curriculum.

Too little has indeed been written about the active relationship of the English composition course(s) and the teaching of writing that occurs explicitly and implicitly in courses across the curriculum. Administration of the composition courses is usually, though not always, separate from that of WAC and WID programs—even if the administrators both come from the English department, as is often the case—and while the composition administrator most often reports to the English chair, the WAC/WID coordinator usually reports to a dean or a provost/vice president. If there is a concerted effort at a school to create a unified vision for both programs, it happens because of the mutual good will of the directors, via a committee structure that enables such collaboration (as we have at George Mason).

In this chapter we are not concerned with the mechanics of the administrative relationship. Rather, we want to focus on the relevance of our research to the de facto relationship between composition and all other courses that exists for every student who moves through the curriculum. We repeatedly saw in the survey responses, the focus groups, and (to a limited extent) the proficiency essays that students build their visions of writing in the academy from all their course experiences. Unaware of and not concerned with the administrative separation of composition from courses in the major, they tend to see, depending on their experience, either (1) a complementarity between required writing courses and writing in their majors or (2) a disjunction, which they attribute to the differences between "English" as a field and their major discipline. Some of our respondents are mystified by the disjunction and complain, while some relish the opportunity to do something different in "English" from what they do in usually more advanced courses in the major discipline. But there is no doubt that students juxtapose the experiences and see them all as influential. Thus, there is reason for program leaders—as well as individual teachers—to consider the de facto link a reason to plan collaboratively and toward a unified vision of writing in the institution. We'll briefly project three models of what that relationship might be.[3]

Model 1: Composition as "Generic Academic"

This most common model of the composition course, reified in most composition texts, has as its mission the preparation of students for the tasks of

[3] For a good overview of major composition pedagogies, see Tate, Rupiper, and Schick's *A Guide to Composition Pedagogies*.

academic writing they will face in later coursework. Its objectives are captured in the list of common terms that we gleaned in Chapter Three from the departmental assessment rubrics and that were matched by the consensus criteria from the student survey (Chapter Four). Most basically according to this model, student prose should observe the principles of academic writing we presented in Chapter One:

- Demonstrating disciplined study
- Privileging reason over emotion and sensation
- Projecting an informed reader who will make an analytical response

The dedicated composition course has a great opportunity to affect expertise in development of these generic academic writing characteristics because written rhetoric is the focus of the course. Recall, from the previous chapter, the students in focus groups who credited this rhetorical centeredness of the advanced composition course for a significant part of their understanding of writing expectations in the major.

Our study supports a definite role for the stand-alone composition course, whether first-year or advanced. The findings suggest that the writing course can be important in the student's development in the academy if it attends to some specific practices, including:

- Providing opportunities for students to observe their own writing/ rhetorical development, to write reflectively about the different rhetorical situations they face and how they have changed as writers
- Giving them tools for exploring and understanding new rhetorical environments, especially the different genres they'll encounter in their studies
- Helping them to understand, through guided practice, the "generic academic" principles that all majors share, and to distinguish between the common principles of academic writing and the local variations, emphases, and adaptations that define the rhetorics of disciplines, sub-disciplines, and individual teachers and courses
- Encouraging them to identify their "passions" for learning and how those might be nourished and refined in academic study
- Guiding and evaluating them based on an understanding of the varieties of the "alternative."
- Educating them to the variety of evaluative criteria that apply to academic writing

Each time a student enrolls in a dedicated academic writing course, from the "developmental" (pre-101) to the upper-division, these principles should apply. When they do, students will learn over time, through a complementary structure of courses, the discursive rhetoric of the academy and the fields within it.

The students in our focus groups most frequently portrayed the English composition course as serving this complementary function in relation to their courses in the major, especially in their expectations for teacher feedback. The composition professor attends to particular features of academic prose: syntax and mechanics, thesis and support, search tools and documentation, etc., some knowledge of which all disciplines expect students to bring with them into more advanced courses. Graphically represented, the basic relationship might look something like this:

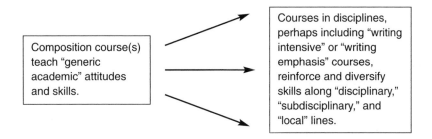

Of course, WAC theory assumes that this model of the composition course only succeeds within a framework that acknowledges the limitations of the composition course. A unified vision of writing in college, one implicitly corroborated by our proficiency essayists, includes the practices in the first section of this chapter, as enacted by teachers in all fields at all levels; these courses build on the emphases of the composition course. The comp course teaches the "generic academic" attitudes and skills; courses across disciplines modify, refine, and interpret the "generic academic" in a multitude of ways that enable the student to achieve versatility and a complex awareness of possibilities. At some schools, this role of writing in disciplines is embodied in designated "writing intensive" or "writing emphasis" courses in diverse fields (Townsend 2001); such courses ask teachers to go beyond the practices described in the first section of the chapter in order to pay increased attention to providing instruction in disciplinary writing, commenting in detail on student work, and promoting revision. These courses do not replace the composition course (as our students' comments illustrated), but they are meant to play a special role in the major.

Model 2: WID- or Interdisciplines-Focused Composition

A different vision of the college/university writing program stresses the discipline, broadly or narrowly conceived, as the locus of writing development. In this model, which has many variations, the English composition course, if it exists at all, becomes subdivided into "versions" (the term we use at Mason) or "tracks" that serve the expectations of areas (e.g., humanities), disciplines (e.g., history), or sub- or interdisciplines (e.g., Western civilization). For example, our advanced composition course, divided into sections for business, arts/humanities, social sciences, natural and physical sciences, and technology fields, illustrates division by area. Special sections of this course that we offer for history, music, nursing, and law enforcement majors illustrate division by discipline, and so on.

Some programs eliminate separate first-year composition and teach writing in "freshman seminars" housed in disciplines or gathered administratively into a disciplinarily diverse first-year writing program. The Cornell program is the best known of these; it features pedagogy courses for instructors similar to those for graduate teaching assistants in many composition programs (see Monroe, for example). A variation is what Chris has called the "pure WAC" model (Thaiss 1992), in which writing is taught to first-year students within interdisciplinary sets of courses, such as the "learning communities" that make up George Mason's New Century College, about which Terry has written (Zawacki and Williams 2001). Another variation, really a hybrid between the WID and generic models, links sections of first-year composition with introductory sections of courses in other fields (Zawacki and Williams 2001; Graham 1992). At Mason, our Mason Topics Program demonstrates this model for some first- and second-year students (mason-topics.gmu.edu).

Within the WID- or interdisciplines-focused model, a school's writing center often plays a pivotal role (Mullin). It provides individual tutoring for student writers; runs frequent, brief workshops on academic writing topics (e.g., editing, research paper design); it can also train undergraduate "peer tutors" or "writing fellows" to assist disciplinary faculty (Soven). By these functions, the writing center provides essential support for faculty across fields who cannot give the concentrated attention to student writing that the composition courses often provide. Certainly, even in a college/university curriculum that includes the comp courses, the writing center is important as support for all courses that ask students to write. (For additional information on the "writing fellows" variant, check the *WAC Clearinghouse* website, at wac.colostate.edu, under "Writing Fellows.")

The WID Focus and Its Variants

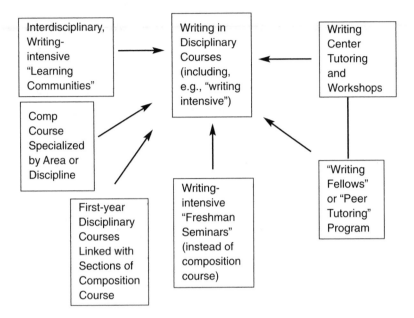

Model 3: Composition as Independent of WID

A school that places full responsibility for academic writing skills in disciplinary courses (Model 2) may choose not to eliminate the freestanding composition course, but to reconceive it to meet objectives not met elsewhere in the curriculum, and that all agree are important. These other forms of the course might include

- A required or elective first-year course that emphasizes student creativity with language: regular writing, much of it informal and experimental, and open-ended assignments that validate student life experience and opinion (See Elbow, for example.)

- A required or elective course that links the college with the larger community through service-learning projects or political-action projects, with some writing assignments (e.g., news articles, brochures) that serve the project and some that have students reflect on values, people, and issues (on service-learning, see Jolliffe 2001 and Adler-Kassner 1997, for example; on critical pedagogy, see the Hurlbert and Blitz collection and Bizzell and Herzberg).

- A required or elective course that uses writing primarily to improve students' critical/analytical reading ability (See Bartholomae and Petrosky).
- A required or elective course that uses writing primarily to improve and diversify students' abilities to use new technologies (for examples and applications, see the Wysocki et al. collection).
- Elective courses in technical writing, business writing, poetry/fiction/ memoir writing, etc., any one of which might fulfill a requirement

The list of possible emphases is limited only by the curriculum planners' sense of the students' needs. But the basic concept is this: if curriculum planners feel that writing in disciplines is sufficiently developed at a school so that disciplinary courses teach the *generic and more specific* academic writing skills and attitudes, then the composition course can be reconceived to meet other needs. Graphically, the relationship looks something like this:

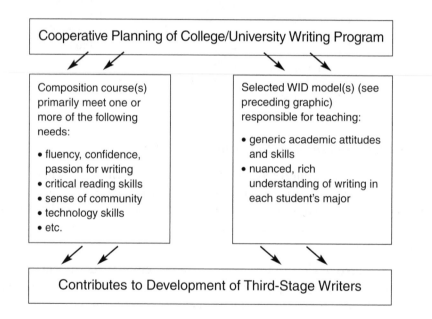

For example, those students in our focus groups who relished the opportunities in their English composition experiences to write more creatively and personally than in their major courses were expressing this sense of other needs that a required writing course might meet. Their vision of such a course parallels that of Peter Elbow in his well-known debate with David Bartholomae about the aims of composition in the college curriculum (1995). Bartholomae prioritizes teaching the attitudes and skills that we characterize as the generic academic; Elbow stresses student self-expression, the growth of fluency and confidence through regular writing that validates student experience outside the classroom. Both are worthy aims that can claim status as "basic" in the development of writers, as could others that we've listed above.

We want to emphasize that making such choices can most usefully occur when planners work cooperatively in awareness of the entire college curriculum. This position seems obvious, but our experience as consultants and readers shows that relatively few institutions enact it administratively, either through a centralized writing program administration or through an integrative committee structure. Conversely, the listservs regularly include cases of noncommunication between central administrations and composition programs and even between composition directors and WAC directors. A clash of teaching philosophies can certainly occur even in a cooperative environment, but all too often the composition program, whether or not it is part of an English department, enacts its own vision of student development while a WAC/WID committee enacts its vision. Only later, in an atmosphere of student or faculty complaint, does each painfully learn that their visions are incompatible, then blames the other for not having been consultative.

Again, we are not advocating one vision of the composition course above another; we are not, as our diverse options at George Mason illustrate, even advocating that the separate composition course exist at all. But we are firmly advocating that, based on our study findings from both faculty and student informants, all institutions need to ensure structures of faculty practice that will help students grow toward that third stage of writing development. We advocate integrative, mutually consultative planning of a college or university writing curriculum, with all stakeholders regularly involved, in an atmosphere informed by study and ongoing review.

Directions for Future Research

We conclude by offering suggestions for future research. Just as our study has profited from the work of countless others, many of whom we have cited, so we hope that others can use our methods and findings as springboards to their own research. The suggestions that follow include part of our own "wish list" for work that we and colleagues want to continue at George Mason, as schedules and funding allow.

Replication of Current Methods, with Additions to Data

We would like to see our methods used (modified as necessary) at other institutions, especially those with different demographics and missions. We devote parts of every chapter to descriptions of the methods we have used in the diverse facets of our research for this book, and elaboration is provided on the GMU WAC homepage (wac.gmu.edu, "Assessing WAC/WID"). Keep in mind that when we began our project in 2000, our intent was merely to interview faculty, and our first publication of the research (Thaiss and Zawacki 2002) came out of the first set of those interviews. The research model became more elaborate as time went on and other sources of data came available. We believe that the findings become richer and more meaningful as sources of data multiply, but certainly replication of any portion of our model can provide useful results. (For ongoing or recent studies using interviews and focus groups to explore students' acquisition of disciplinary discourses, see Sommers and Saltz, Herrington and Curtis; Hilgers, Hussey, and Stitt-Bergh.)

Effects of New Media on Learning to Write in Disciplines

One limitation of our research, acknowledged in several places in the book, is its lack of emphasis on technology. When our informants made reference to technologies, we noted them, and certainly our lengthy analysis of the work of new media specialist Lesley Smith centers the impacts of technologies on her research and teaching. But for most of our study, "writing," "teaching," and other key concepts are treated as technology independent. Indeed, it surprised us that neither student nor faculty informants made more explicit references to, say, electronic research tools, blogs, message boards, downloading, Web design, multimedia. Nevertheless, in our own teaching we've seen a profound impact on, for example, student writing fluency brought about by the ubiquity of email and our uses of electronic discussion forums; so to treat "learning to write in disciplines" as if the choice of technologies is incidental is to miss an opportunity, to say the least. (See, for example, Yancey on new writing technologies contributing to the creation of new genres and literacies; Selber on multiliteracies students need to possess in a digital age; and Miller and Shepherd on the rhetorical work that blogs perform.)

As our research continues, one direction surely will be to talk with faculty across fields about their adaptations of technology in research, writing, and teaching. We could ask them to describe and evaluate the influences of these choices according to the categories we explore in the book. A possible model we might follow is to reinterview our faculty informants, asking them to consider their earlier responses to our questions in terms of the technologies they have chosen and that are now available. Given that our WAC program in the past seven years has grown up in collaboration with our TAC (Technology Across the Curriculum) program, another model would select those on the technological front lines, like L. Smith, and use our question clusters (see Chapters One and Two) as the interview frame.

Genre Theory, Activity Theory, Complexity Theory: Frames for Further Analysis

As evident, we have been influenced in our design and analysis by discipline and genre theorists (e.g., Toulmin, Miller, Devitt) and activity theorists (e.g., Russell "Rethinking" and "Big Picture" and Bazerman and Russell *Writing Selves*, among others), as well as, of course, by numerous WAC/WID theorists and practitioners. We feel that we have only begun to think about not only the applications of these frames to our data and findings, but also the explicit use of these frames to focus research and teaching. We are particularly interested in questions Miller has raised about genre and activity systems, for example, can students acquire genre knowledge without participating in the larger activity system and, conversely, to what extent can we teach an activity system by teaching its genres, like the lab report in biology, for example? If genres are always part of larger systems and "genre ecologies," what problems are caused for teaching when workplace genres are embedded in academic disciplines (Miller, personal correspondence)?

We are also intrigued by the possibilities of "complexity theory," as it is being worked out by our colleague Byron Hawk, for thinking about the "tipping point" that third-stage writers reach, when they understand that there is a disciplinary coherence among even the most diverse practices. In Hawk's formulation, a tipping point occurs when the interactions among the individual parts of a complex adaptive system—such as rhetoric, text, audience—produce a "qualitative change at the level of the whole." Further, he notes, the more interaction there is among diverse components of a complex system, the more the system will move "from linearity and stability to recursiveness and complexity." We saw how this process had occurred for many of the students whose proficiency exams we read, particularly those with double majors, when they reflected on their maturation as writers who had successfully negotiated the expectations of a variety of teachers and courses. We can imagine further research with students—interviews, focus groups, reflective essays—that probes key tipping points in their development as writers in and across disciplines.

Learning to Write for Academia and for the Workplace

Though our study focused on learning to write in the academy and the disciplines that comprise it, writing for the workplace—as well as for other nonacademic venues—kept appearing in all sources of data. A surprising number of our faculty informants wrote or imagined writing for nonacademic readers (including Sorrell, Trefil, Rader, Williams, Jones, both Smiths); several focus-group students spoke in detail about conflicts or connections between writing in school and writing on the job; a few proficiency essayists, particularly those from political science, wrote about the priority in that field of learning to persuade political stakeholders. As Dias, Freedman, Medway, and Paré have pointed out, there are basic differences between writing on the job and writing for a teacher, and surely we should question any assumption that academic writing prepares a student to write in a nonacademic career. But our informants' considered remarks indicate that the relationship is not simple, that there may be a closer connection than some would wish to grant, and that writing for readers both inside and outside the academy can affect all that a writer does and thinks. Focusing research on the nexus among these tasks and readers is needed to illuminate what we can mean by "learning to write," on the roles of teachers, and on the shape of curricula. (For related research see Henry's *Writing Workplace Cultures* in which he analyzes students' investigations of writing and learning to write in a workplace along with their reflections on their ethnographic processes.) Moreover, focusing on this nexus between writing in schools and writing in the workplace is needed to shed light—not just generate heat—on the ever more contested issue of the roles that education plays in the community it purports to serve.

Similarly, more research is needed on the relationship, if any, that exists in regard to writing values and practices among the various schools that make up a "community." The university is not a closed ecology; neither is the community college nor the high school. To what extent, for example, might there be continuity between what a student learns about writing in history in high school and what that student will be asked to practice in an upper-level course in college? In our research, we've shown that disciplines are dynamic, responsive to the desires of engaged practitioners, who in turn convey their vision of the discipline and their goals for writers to the students they teach. To develop an even fuller picture of how students come into their disciplines, we need to look at the progression from school to school as well as what occurs within the university itself.

Works Cited

Adler-Kassner, Linda, Robert Crooks, and Ann Watters, eds. 1997. *Writing the Community: Concepts and Models for Service-Learning in Composition.* Washington, DC: American Association for Higher Education.

Adler-Kassner, Linda, and Susanmarie Harrington, eds. 2001. *Questioning Authority: Stories Told in School.* Ann Arbor: University of Michigan Press.

Anson, Chris M. 1988. "Toward a Multidimensional Model of Writing in the Academic Disciplines." In Jolliffe 1988, 1–33.

Anzaldua, Gloria. 1987. *Borderlands/La Frontera: The New Mestiza.* San Francisco: Aunt Lute Books.

Bartholomae, David. 1985. "Inventing the University." In *When a Writer Can't Write*, Mike Rose, ed. 134–65. New York: Guilford.

Bartholomae, David. 1995. "Writing with Teachers: A Conversation with Peter Elbow." *College Composition and Communication 46*: 62–71.

Bartholomae, David and Anthony Petrosky. 2004. *Ways of Reading: An Anthology for Writers.* Boston: Bedford/St. Martin's.

Bazerman, Charles. 1992. "From Cultural Criticism to Disciplinary Participation: Living with Powerful Words." In *Writing, Teaching, and Learning in the Disciplines,* Anne Herrington and Charles Moran, eds. 61–68. New York: MLA.

Bazerman, Charles. 1994. "What Written Knowledge Does: Three Examples of Academic Discourse." In Bazerman and Russell, 159–88.

Bazerman, Charles. 2000. *Shaping Written Knowledge: The Genre and Activity of the Experimental Article in Science.* Academic. Writing Landmark Publications in Writing Studies [online]. Available: http://aw.colostate.edu/books/bazerman_shaping/. Originally published in print: Madison: University of Wisconsin Press, 1988.

Bazerman, Charles, and James Paradis, eds. 1991. *Textual Dynamics of the Professions: Historical and Contemporary Studies of Writing in Professional Communities.* Madison: University of Wisconsin Press.

Bazerman, Charles, and David Russell, eds. 1994. *Landmark Essays on Writing Across the Curriculum.* Davis, CA: Hermagoras.

Bazerman, Charles, and David Russell. 2002. *Writing Selves/Writing Societies: Research from Activity Perspectives.* Perspectives on Writing. The WAC Clearinghouse and Mind, Culture, and Activity [online]. Available at http://wac.colostate.edu/books/selves_societies/. Publication date: February 1, 2003.

Bean, John C. 1996. *Engaging Ideas: The Professor's Guide to Integrating Writing, Critical Thinking, and Active Learning in the Classroom.* San Francisco: Jossey-Bass.

Bergoffen, Debra. February 2002. Interview by Terry Zawacki and Chris Thaiss. George Mason University, Fairfax, VA.

Bergoffen, Debra. 1997. *The Philosophy of Simone de Beauvoir: Gendered Phenomenologies, Erotic Generosities.* New York: State University of New York Press.

Bergoffen, Debra. 1999. "I Never Imagined Myself a Philosopher." In *Portraits of American Continental Philosophers,* James R. Watson, ed. 1–12. Bloomington: Indiana University Press.

Bizzell, Patricia. 1992. *Academic Discourse and Critical Consciousness.* Pittsburgh: University of Pittsburgh Press.

Bizzell, Patricia. 2002. "The Intellectual Work of 'Mixed' Forms of Academic Discourses." In Schroeder, Fox and Bizzell, 1–10.

Bizzell, Patricia. 2002. "Preface." In Schroeder, Fox and Bizzell, vii–x.

Bizzell, Patricia, and Bruce Herzberg. 1996. *Negotiating Difference: Cultural Case Studies for Composition.* Boston: Bedford Books.

Bridwell-Bowles, Lillian. 1992. "Discourse and Diversity: Experimental Writing within the Academy." *College Composition and Communication* 43: 349–68.

Brodkey, Linda. 1987. *Academic Writing as Social Practice.* Philadelphia: Temple University Press.

Brodkey, Linda. 1994. "Writing on the Bias." *College English* 56: 527–47.

Clark, Keith. February 2002. Interview by Chris Thaiss and Terry Zawacki. George Mason University, Fairfax, VA.

Clark, Keith. 2002. *Black Manhood in James Baldwin, Ernest J. Gaines, and August Wilson.* Urbana: University of Illinois Press.

Code, Lorraine. 1991. *What Can She Know? Feminist Theory and the Construction of Knowledge.* Ithaca, NY: Cornell University Press.

Copelman, Dina. February 2002. Interview by Terry Zawacki and Chris Thaiss, George Mason University, Fairfax, VA.

Delpit, Lisa. 1997. "The Silenced Dialogue: Power and Pedagogy in Educating Other People's Children." In Villanueva. 1997, 565–88.

Delpit, Lisa. 1998. "The Politics of Teaching Literate Discourse." In Zamel and Spack, 207–18.

Delpit, Lisa 1986. "Skills and Other Dilemmas of a Progressive Black Educator." *Harvard Educational Review* 56: 379–85.

Devitt, Amy J. 2004. *Writing Genres.* Carbondale, IL: Southern Illinois University Press.

Dias, Patrick, Aviva Freedman, Peter Medway, and Anthony Paré. 1999. *Worlds Apart: Acting and Writing in Academic and Workplace Contexts.* Mahwah, NJ: Erlbaum.

Elbow, Peter 1995. "Being a Writer vs. Being an Academic: A Conflict in Goals." *College Composition and Communication* 46: 72–83.

Elbow, Peter. 2002. "Vernacular Englishes in the Writing Classroom? Probing the Culture of Literacy." In Schroeder, Fox and Bizzell, 126–38.

Engestrom, Yrjo. 2001. "Expansive Learning at Work: Toward an Activity Theory Reconceptualization. *Journal of Education and Work.* 14(1): 133–36.

Fleckenstein, Kristie S. 1998. "Resistance, Women, and Dismissing the 'I.'" *Rhetoric Review* 17(1): 107–25.

Flynn, Elizabeth. 1988. "Composing as a Woman." *College Composition and Communication* 39: 423–35.

Fox, Helen. 1994. *Listening to the World: Cultural Issues in Academic Writing.* Urbana, IL: NCTE.

Fox, Helen. 2002. "Being an Ally." In Schroeder, Fox and Bizzell, 56–67.

Freedman, Aviva, and Peter Medway, eds. 1994. *Genre and the New Rhetoric.* Bristol, PA: Taylor & Francis.

Fulwiler, Toby, and Art Young, eds. 1982. *Language Connections: Writing Across the Curriculum.* Urbana, IL: NCTE.

Gebhardt, Richard. 1992. 'Editor's Column.' *College Composition and Communication* 43.

George Mason University WAC Assessment. http://cas.gmu.edu/wac/program/assessing/phase3.html.

George Mason University. Writing Across the Curriculum Program Website. http://wac.gmu.edu/program/assessing/phase4.html.

Gilyard, Keith. 1991. *Voices of the Self.* Detroit: Wayne State University Press.

Graham, Joan. 1992. "Writing Components, Writing Adjuncts, Writing Links." In McLeod and Soven, 110–33.

Grant-Davie, Keith. 1992. "Coding Data: Issues of Validity, Reliability, and Interpretation." In Kirsch and Sullivan, 270–86.

Gurak, Laura, Smiljana Antonijevic, Laurie Johnson, Clancy Ratliff, and Jessica Reyman. Eds. (2004). *Into the Blogosphere: Rhetoric, Community, and the Culture of Weblogs.* http://blog.lib.umn.edu/blogosphere/blogging_as_social_action.html

Harding, Sandra. 1987. *Feminism and Methodology.* Bloomington: Indiana University Press.

Hawk, Byron. 2004. "Toward a Rhetoric of Network (Media) Culture: Notes on Polarities and Potentiality. *JAC: Special Issue on Mark C. Taylor and Emerging Network Culture* 24.4: 831–50.

Heilker, Paul. 1996. *The Essay: Theory and Pedagogy for an Active Form.* Urbana, IL: NCTE.

Henry, James. 1994. "A Narratological Analysis of WAC Authorship." *College English* 56: 8–24.

Henry, James. 2000. *Writing Workplace Cultures: An Archaeology of Professional Writing.* Carbondale, IL: Southern Illinois University Press.

Herrington, Anne. 1988. "Teaching, Writing, and Learning: A Naturalistic Study of Writing in an Undergraduate Literature Course." In Jolliffe 1988, 133–66.

Herrington, Anne. 1994. "Writing in Academic Settings: A Study of the Contexts for Writing in Two College Chemical Engineering Courses." In Bazerman and Russell, 97–124.

Herrington, Anne, and Marcia Curtis. 2000. *Persons in Process: Four Stories of Writing and Personal Development in College.* Urbana, IL: NCTE.

Herrington, Anne, and Charles Moran. 1992. *Writing, Teaching, and Learning in the Disciplines.* New York: MLA.

Hilgers, Thomas, Edna Lardizabal Hussey, and Monica Stitt-Bergh. 1999. "'As You're Writing You Have These Epiphanies': What College Students Say about Writing and Learning in Their Majors." *Written Communication* 16.3: 317–39.

Hindman, Jane E. 2001. "Making Writing Matter: Using the 'Personal' to Recover(y) an Essential(ist) Tension in Academic Discourse." *College English* 64: 88–108.

Hinds, John. 1987. "Reader versus Writer Responsibility: A New Typology." *Writing Across Languages: Analysis of L2 Text,* Ulla Connor and Robert Kaplan, eds. 141–45. Reading, MA: Addison-Wesley.

Hocks, Mary E. 2003. "Understanding Visual Rhetoric in Digital Writing Environments." *College Composition and Communication* 54.4: 629–56.

Hope, R. N. 2003. *The Magic Stethoscope.* Jeanne Sorrell, ed. Fairfax, VA: College of Nursing and Health Sciences, George Mason University.

Horner, Bruce. 2001. "'Students' Right,' English Only, and Re-imagining the Politics of Language." *College English* 63: 741–58.

Hurlbert, Mark, and Michael Blitz, eds. 1991. *Composition and Resistance.* Portsmouth, NH: Boynton/Cook.

Jarratt, Susan C. 1991. "Feminism and Composition: The Case for Conflict." In *Contending with Words: Composition and Rhetoric in a Postmodern Age.* Patricia Harkin and John Schilb, eds. 105–23. New York: MLA.

Jarratt, Susan C., and Lynn Worsham, eds. 1998. *Feminism and Composition Studies: In Other Words.* New York: MLA.

Johns, Ann M. 2001. "ESL Students." In McLeod, Miraglia, Soven, and Thaiss, 141–64.

Johns, Ann M., ed. 2002. *Genre in the Classroom: Multiple Perspectives.* Mahwah, NJ: Erlbaum.

Johns, Ann M. 2002. "Destabilizing and Enriching Novice Students' Genre Theories." In Johns, *Genre in the Classroom* 237–48.

Jolliffe, David A., ed. 1988. *Writing in Academic Disciplines.* Norwood, NJ: ABLEX.

Jolliffe, David. 2001. "Writing Across the Curriculum and Service Learning: Kairos, Genre, and Collaboration." In McLeod, Miraglia, Soven, and Thaiss, 86–108.

Jones, R. Christian. February 2002. Interview by Terry Zawacki and Chris Thaiss, George Mason University, Fairfax, VA.

Kirsh, Gesa. 1993. *Women Writing the Academy: Audience, Authority, and Transformation.* Carbondale, IL: Southern Illinois University Press.

Kirsch, Gesa. 1999. *Ethical Dilemmas in Feminist Research: The Politics of Location.* Albany, NY: State University of New York Press.

Kirsch, Gesa, and Joy Ritchie. 1995. "Beyond the Personal: Theorizing a Politics of Location in Composition Research." *College Composition and Communication* 46: 369–80.

Kirsch, Gesa, and Patricia A. Sullivan, eds. 1992. *Methods and Methodology in Composition Research.* Carbondale, IL: Southern Illinois University Press.

Lamb, Catherine E. 1991. "Beyond Argument in Feminist Composition." *College Composition and Communication* 42: 11–24.

Lancaster, Roger. February 2001. Interview by Terry Zawacki and Chris Thaiss. George Mason University, Fairfax, VA.

Lancaster, Roger. 1992. *Life Is Hard: Machismo, Danger, and the Intimacy of Power in Nicaragua.* Berkeley: University of California Press.

LeCourt, Donna. 1996. "WAC as Critical Pedagogy: The Third Stage?" *Journal of Advanced Composition* 16: 389–405.

Lu, Min-zhan. 1987. "From Silence to Words: Writing as Struggle." *College English* 49: 437–48.

Lu, Min-zhan. 1998. "Reading and Writing Differences: The Problematic of Experience." In Jarratt and Worsham, 239–51.

Malinowitz, Harriet. 1998. "A Feminist Critique of Writing in the Disciplines." In Jarratt and Worsham, 291–312.

Matsuda, Paul Kei. 2002. "Alternative Discourses: A Synthesis." In Schroeder, Fox and Bizzell, 191–96.

McLeod, Susan H., Eric Miraglia, Margot Soven, and Christopher Thaiss, eds. 2001. *WAC for the New Millennium: Strategies for Continuing Writing-Across-the-Curriculum Programs.* Urbana, IL: NCTE.

McLeod, Susan, and Margot Soven, eds. 1992. *Writing Across the Curriculum: A Guide to Developing Programs.* Newbury Park, CA: Sage.

McLeod, Susan. 2001. "The Pedagogy of Writing across the Curriculum." In Tate et al, 149–64.

Mellix, Barbara. 1998. "From Outside, In." In Zamel and Spack, 61–70.

Miller, Carolyn R. 1984. "Genre as Social Action." *Quarterly Journal of Speech* 70: 151–67.

Miller, Carolyn R. 1994. "Rhetorical Community: The Cultural Basis of Genre." In Freedman and Medway, 67–78.

Miller, Carolyn R. April 12, 2004. Personal Correspondence.

Miller, Carolyn R., and Dawn Shepherd. 2004. "Blogging as Social Action: A Genre Analysis of the Weblog." In Gurak et al.

Miller, Linda. February 2002. Interview by Terry Zawacki and Chris Thaiss, George Mason University, Fairfax, VA.

Monroe, Jonathan, ed. 2002. *Writing and Revising the Disciplines.* Ithaca, NY: Cornell University Press.

Mortensen, Peter L. 1992. "Analyzing Talk about Writing." In Kirsch and Sullivan, 105–29.

Mullin, Joan. 2001. "Writing Centers and WAC." In McLeod, Miraglia, Soven, and Thaiss, 179–99.

Myers, Greg. 2002. "The Social Construction of Two Biologists' Proposals." In Bazerman and Russell, 189–210.

Newkirk, Thomas. 1989. *Critical Thinking and Writing: Reclaiming the Essay.* Urbana, IL: NCTE.

Odell, Lee, and Dixie Goswami, eds. 1985. *Writing in Nonacademic Settings.* New York: Guilford Press.

Pare, Anthony, and Graham Smart. 1994. "Observing Genres in Action: Towards a Research Methodology." In Freedman and Medway, 146–54.

Pennycook, Alastair. 1998. "Borrowing Others' Words: Text, Ownership, Memory, and Plagiarism." In Zamel and Spack, 265–92.

Perry, William G. 1999. *Forms of Ethical and Intellectual Development in the College Years: A Scheme.* San Francisco: Jossey Bass.

Powell, Malea. 2002. "Listening to Ghosts: An Alternative (Non)argument." In Schroeder, Fox and Bizzell, 11–22.

Rader, Victoria. February 2001. Interview by Terry Zawacki and Chris Thaiss. George Mason University, Fairfax, VA.

Rader, Victoria. 1986. *Signal Through the Flames: The Homeless Advocacy of Mitch Snyder.* New York: Sheed and Ward.

Regan, Priscilla. March 2001. Interview by Terry Zawacki and Chris Thaiss. George Mason University, Fairfax, VA.

Rose, Mike. 1989. *Lives on the Boundary.* New York: The Free Press.

Royster, Jacqueline Jones. 2002. "Academic Discourses or Small Boats on a Big Sea." In Schroeder, Fox and Bizzell, 23–30.

Royster, Jacqueline Jones. 2003. "A View from the Bridge: Afrafeminist Ideologies and Rhetorical Studies." Reprinted in *Feminism and Composition: A Critical Sourcebook*. Kirsch et al, eds. 206–33. New York: Bedford/St. Martin's.

Russell, David. 1997. "Rethinking Genre in School and Society: An Activity Theory Analysis." *Written Communication*. 14.4. Accessed online.

Russell, David. 2002. *Writing in the Academic Disciplines: A Curricular History, 2nd Ed.* Carbondale, IL: Southern Illinois University Press.

Russell, David. 2001. "Where Do the Naturalistic Studies of WAC/WID Point? A Research Review." In McLeod, Miraglia, Soven, and Thaiss, 259–98.

Russell, David, and Arturo Yanez. 2002. "'Big Picture People Rarely Become Historians': Genre Systems and the Contradictions of General Education." Bazerman and Russell. http://wac.colostate.edu/books/selves_societies.

Schroeder, Christopher, Fox, and Patricia Bizzell. 2002. *Alternative Discourses and the Academy*. Portsmouth, NH: Boynton/Cook.

Selber, Stuart A. 2004. *Multiliteracies for a Digital Age*. Carbondale, IL: Southern Illinois University Press.

Selber, Stuart A. 2004. "Reimagining the Functional Side of Computer Literacy." *College Composition and Communication* 55: 470–503.

Smith, Lesley. February 2002. Interview by Terry Zawacki and Chris Thaiss. George Mason University, Fairfax, VA.

Smith, Robert. February 2001. Interview by Terry Zawacki and Chris Thaiss. George Mason University, Fairfax, VA.

Sommers, Nancy, and Laura Saltz. 2004. "The Novice as Expert: Writing the Freshman Year." *College Composition and Communication* 56: 124–49.

Sorrell, Jeanne. February 2001. Interview by Terry Zawacki and Chris Thaiss. George Mason University, Fairfax, VA.

Soven, Margot. 2001. "Curriculum-based Peer Tutors and WAC." In McLeod, Miraglia, Soven, and Thaiss, 200–232.

Struppa, Daniele. March 2001. Interview by Terry Zawacki and Chris Thaiss. George Mason University, Fairfax, VA.

Students' Right to Their Own Language. 1974. Monograph. *College Composition and Communication Special Issue XXV*. Urbana, IL: NCTE.

Swales, John. 1990. *Genre Analysis: English in Academic and Research Settings*. Cambridge: Cambridge University Press.

Tate, Gary, Amy Rupiper, and Kurt Schick, eds. 2001. *A Guide to Composition Pedagogies*. New York: Oxford.

Thaiss, Christopher. 1992. "WAC and General Education Courses." In McLeod and Soven, 87–109.

Thaiss, Christopher. 1998. *The Harcourt Brace Guide to Writing across the Curriculum.* Fort Worth: Harcourt Brace.

Thaiss, Christopher. 2001. "Theory in WAC: Where Have We Been, Where Are We Going?" In McLeod, Miraglia, Soven, and Thaiss, 299–325.

Thaiss, Christopher. 2006. "The History of WAC and the Northern Virginia Writing Project at George Mason." In *Creating a Community: The Early History of the WAC Movement.* Susan McLeod and Margot Soven, eds. West Lafayette, IN: Parlor Press.

Thaiss, Christopher, and Rick Davis. 1999. *Writing About Theater.* Needham Heights, MA: Allyn and Bacon.

Thaiss, Christopher, and John Hess. 1999. *Writing for Law Enforcement.* Needham Heights, MA: Allyn and Bacon.

Thaiss, Christopher, and James Sanford. 2000. *Writing for Psychology.* Needham Heights, MA: Allyn and Bacon.

Thaiss, Christopher, and Terry Myers Zawacki. 1997. "How Portfolios for Proficiency Help Shape a WAC Program" In Yancey and Huot, 79–96.

Thaiss, Christopher, and Terry Myers Zawacki. March 2002. "Alternative to What? Questioning Assumptions of Disciplinary Conformity and the Necessity of Resistance." Presentation at Convention of the Conference on College Composition and Communication.

Thaiss, Christopher, and Terry Myers Zawacki. 2002. "Questioning Alternative Discourse: Reports from Across the Discipline." In Schroeder, Fox, and Bizzell, 80–96.

Tompkins, Jane. 1990. "Pedagogy of the Distressed." *College English 52*: 653–60.

Toulmin, Stephen. 1972. *Human Understanding.* Volume 1. Princeton: Princeton University Press.

Townsend, Martha. 2001. "Writing Intensive Courses and WAC." In McLeod, Miraglia, Soven, and Thaiss, 233–58.

Trefil, James. 2001. Interview by Terry Zawacki and Chris Thaiss. George Mason University, Fairfax, VA.

Trefil, James, and Robert M. Hazen. 1991. *Science Matters: Achieving Scientific Literacy.* New York: Doubleday.

Villanueva, Victor, Jr., ed. 1997. *Cross-Talk in Comp Theory: A Reader.* Urbana, IL: NCTE.

Villanueva, Victor, Jr. 2001. "The Politics of Literacy Across the Curriculum." In McLeod, Miraglia, Soven, and Thaiss, 165–78.

Walvoord, Barbara E., and Virginia Johnson Anderson. 1998. *Effective Grading: A Tool for Learning and Assessment.* San Francisco, CA: Jossey-Bass.

Walvoord, Barbara, and Lucille McCarthy. 1990. *Thinking and Writing in College: A Naturalistic Study of Students in Four Disciplines.* Urbana, IL: NCTE.

Williams, Patricia. 1991. *The Alchemy of Race and Rights.* Boston: Harvard University Press.

Williams, Walter. February 2002. Interview by Terry Zawacki and Chris Thaiss, George Mason University, Fairfax, VA.

Wysocki, Anne, Johndan Johnson-Eilola, Cynthia Selfe, and Geoffrey Sirc. 2004. *Writing New Media: Theory and Applications for Expanding the Teaching of Composition.* Logan, UT: Utah State University Press.

Yancey, Kathleen Blake. 2004. "Made Not Only in Words: Composition in a New Key." *College Composition and Communication* 56: 297–328.

Yancey, Kathleen Blake, and Brian Huot, eds. 1997. *Assessing Writing Across the Curriculum: Diverse Approaches and Practices.* Greenwich, CT: ABLEX.

Young, Art. 2002. *Teaching Writing Across the Curriculum, Third Edition.* WAC Clearinghouse Landmark Publications in Writing Studies [online]. Available at: http://wac.colostate.edu/aw/books/young_teaching/. Originally published in print. Upper Saddle River, NJ: Prentice Hall, 1999.

Zamel, Vivian, and Ruth Spack, eds. 1998. *Negotiating Academic Literacies: Teaching and Learning Across Languages and Cultures.* Mahwah, NJ: Erlbaum.

Zawacki, Terry Myers. 1992. "Recomposing as a Woman—An Essay in Different Voices." *College Composition and Communication* 43: 32–38.

Zawacki, Terry Myers. 2001. "Telling Stories: The Subject Is Never Just Me." In Adler-Kassner and Harrington, 34–52.

Zawacki, Terry Myers, and Ashley Taliaferro Williams. 2001. "Is It Still WAC? Writing within Interdisciplinary Learning Communities." In McLeod, Miraglia, Soven, and Thaiss, 109–40.

Index

A

Academic standards (*See* standards, academic)

Academic writing, 2–23, 53, 54
  characteristics or principles of, 4–8, 58–59, 86, 114, 141, 162
  expectations for, 60, 96, 149

Activity theory, 17, 60, 138, 169

Adler-Kassner, Linda, 165

African American discourse (*See* discourse, African-American)

African-American Studies, 34, 42, 66–67, 114

Alternative arrangements, 12, 44, 90–91, 131

Alternative assignments, 75–83, 89–94
  "action project" as, 76, 78
  children's books as, 76
  "paradigm cases" as, 76–78, 89–91
  websites as, 81–82

Alternative discourse, 2–24, 137
  as resistance to convention, 20–23, 134–135
  defined, 8–12, 18–24
  taxonomy of, 12, 61, 96, 129

Alternative formats, 12, 89–90, 130–131

Alternative media, 12, 93, 133–134

Alternative methodologies, 12, 91–92, 132–133

Alternative syntax, 12, 91, 131–132

Anderson, Virginia, 142

Anson, Chris, 15, 25

Anthropology, 8, 34, 37, 43, 68–72, 89–90, 105

Anzaldua, Gloria, 21

Art history (major), 109

Art studio (major), 109

Assessment
  departmental workshops for, 1, 25, 30–31, 83–85, 157–160
  description at George Mason University, 85–88, 158–159
  rubrics (*See* Evaluation, rubrics)

Assignments
  alternative (*See* Alternative assignments)
  collage, 74–75, 89
  compare-contrast, 68
  essays, 68
  journals (*See* Journals)
  lab reports (*See* Lab reports)
  literary analysis, 67
  opinion paper, 68
  personal writing, 74, 153
  posters, 63, 89
  reflection paper, 72, 105, 153
  researched writing, 104–105
  white papers, 144–146

Audience
  academic, 48–50, 54, 59, 71, 102, 110–112, 120
  non-academic or popular, 33, 47–50, 56, 64–66, 68–70, 71, 77, 102, 110–112, 115, 170

B

Bartholomae, David, 119, 166

Bazerman, Charles, 15, 16, 18, 169

Bean, John, 142

Benner, Patricia, 43

Bergoffen, Debra, 28, 34, 41–43, 58, 61, 72–74, 89, 92, 153

Biology (*See* Environmental science)

Bizzell, Patricia, 4, 7, 19, 24, 165

Blitz, Michael, 165

Blogs, 12, 153

Bridwell-Bowles, Lillian, 21
Brodkey, Linda, 21
Business administration, 87–88, 111, 145, 149

C

Clark, Keith, 28, 35, 37, 42, 66–67
Code, Lorraine, 21
Collaboration, 26, 105, 120
College Composition and Communication, 20
Communication (major), 116, 125
Complexity theory, 169
Composition, teaching of, programs, 161–167
Computers and Composition, 51
Computer science (major), 123
Conference on College Composition and Communication, 2
    guidelines for technology specialists, 56–57
Contexts for academic expectations, 60, 95, 117, 137–139, 141–146, 148, 154–156, 159–160, 166–167, 169
    disciplinary, 60, 95, 104, 145
    "generic academic," 60, 62, 95, 104, 109, 144–145, 161–164, 166–167
    idiosyncratic or personal, 60, 95, 108–109, 146
    local or institutional, 60, 95, 145
    subdisciplinary, 60, 95, 145
Contrastive rhetoric, 3, 10, 22, 113
Conventions, 7, 35–36, 45–57, 59
Copelman, Dina, 28, 34, 36, 37, 40, 42
Criminal justice (major), 111
Critical pedagogy, 3, 165
Cultural studies, 3, 42, 55
Curtis, Marcia, 168

D

Dance, 34, 36, 49–50, 52, 67, 85
Deconstruction, 42
Delpit, Lisa, 23
Derrida, Jacques, 43
Development of disciplinary writers, 109–110, 121, 123, 128–129, 134–135, 139–141, 154, 166

comparison of majors toward, 128–129
importance of teachers in, 113, 117, 126–128, 132
role of reading in, 122, 128–129, 155
Devitt, Amy, 16, 138, 169
Dias, Patrick, 4, 15, 17, 170
Digital identity, 82
Disciplines
    boundaries of, 45–57
    compact, 14, 15, 19, 125
    defined, 4, 13–16
    diffuse, 14, 15, 125
    names of, 34–35
    quasi, 14, 52, 56
    student awareness of, 103–104
    student writing in (*See* writing, in majors)
Discourse
    African-American, 9, 12 (*See* also English, Black English Vernacular)
    alternative (*See* Alternative discourse)
    community, 16–18
    feminist, 9
    marginalized, 9

E

Early, Gerald, 42
Ecology
    of disciplines, 14, 101, 138
    local or institutional, 60, 170
Economics (major), 34, 49, 67–70, 111, 116, 122–123
Elbow, Peter, 23, 119, 165, 166–167
Emotion, 5, 36, 38–45, 47, 59, 75, 77–78, 89, 113
Engagement (by student writers), 66, 75, 87, 92, 120, 136, 150–152
Engestrom, Yrjo, 60
English
    as a discipline, 34, 37, 38, 42, 66–67, 114, 121
    Black English Vernacular, 12, 23
    correct (*See* Standard Edited American English)
    diversity of, 11
Environmental science, 34, 39, 61–63, 89, 119–120, 149
Epistemology, 59, 60, 65

Error (*See* Standard Edited American English)
Ethnography, 8, 44, 71, 106, 129, 144–145, 154
Ethos, 7, 73
Evaluation
criteria for, 80, 125
key terms for, 86, 89, 156
of arguments, 86–87
rubrics for, 85–88, 104, 158–159
Exigence, 46, 48, 59, 63–64, 68–80, 92–93, 101, 104, 106, 145
defined, 16
Experimental report (*See* Lab report)

F

Faculty development, 2, 149–150
workshops for, 59–60, 142, 152, 157–161
Feedback on writing (*See* Response to writing)
Feminist discourse (*See* Discourse, feminist)
Feminist theory and arguments, 3, 9, 20–22, 40–42
"Five contexts" (*See* Contexts for academic expectations)
Fleckenstein, Kristie, 21
Flynn, Elizabeth, 21
Focus groups, 25–26, 29–30, 99, 101–112
Format, 8, 59, 63, 64
alternative (*See* Alternative formats)
Foucault, Michel, 41
Fox, Helen, 10, 22, 23, 90
Freedman, Aviva, 15, 17, 170
Freud, Sigmund, 44

G

Gebhardt, Richard, 20
Gender, 9, 42, 43, 50
Genre, 8, 13, 55, 59, 63, 64, 117, 138, 141, 169
defined, 16–18
Geology (major), 123
George Mason University, 27
assessment website, 168
Gilyard, Keith, 21
Goswami, Dixie, 15

Graham, Joan, 164
Grant-Davie, Keith, 26
Grapholect, 10

H

Harding, Sandra, 21
Hawk, Byron, 169
Henry, James, 170
Herrington, Anne, 168
Herzberg, Bruce, 165
Hilgers, Thomas, 168
Hindman, Jane, 21
Hinds, John, 22
History, 34, 36, 37, 40, 42, 115, 123–124
Hocks, Mary, 53
Hooks, bell, 21
Huot, Brian, 99, 157
Hurlbert, Mark, 165
Hussey, Edna, 168
Hypermedia, 12, 46, 50–57, 80–83

I

"I," use of, 39–40, 54, 61, 149
Idiosyncracy (*See* Contexts for academic expectations, idiosyncratic or personal; Standards, idiosyncratic)
Individualized studies (major), 118–119, 140
Information technology (major), 122–124, 128
Informed consent, 26, 100
Interdisciplinary courses and writing, 50–57, 106, 140, 164–165
Interviews, 24, 25, 27
Intuition, 43, 77

J

Jarratt, Susan, 21
Johns, Ann, 22
Jolliffe, David, 15, 165
Jones, Chris, 28, 34, 39, 61–63, 89, 91, 92
Journals, 64–65, 73–74, 105, 153

K

Kairos, 51
Kirsch, Gesa, 21

L

Lab report, 15, 16, 63–64, 77, 87, 105, 127, 169
Lamb, Catherine, 21
Lancaster, Roger, 8, 28, 34, 37, 43, 61, 68, 89–90, 92, 136, 153
Learning communities, 51, 164
LeCourt, Donna, 22
Lu, Min-Zhan, 21, 23

M

Malinowitz, Harriet, 22
Malinowski, Bronislaw, 8, 44
Mathematics, 34, 37, 40, 43
Matsuda, Paul Kei, 24
McAdam, Doug, 45
McLeod, Susan, 59, 156
Media
    alternative (*See* Alternative media)
    new, 36, 50–57, 80–83, 168–169
Medway, Peter, 15, 17, 170
Mellix, Barbara, 21
Methodology, alternative (*See* Alternative methodologies)
Methods, 24–31
    replication of, 167–170
Miller, Carolyn, 16, 18, 42, 55, 168, 169
Miller, Linda, 28, 34, 36, 49–50, 52, 67
Miraglia, Eric, 156
Monroe, Jonathan, 164
Mortensen, Peter, 26
Mullin, Joan, 164
Multimedia, 50–57, 93
Music (major), 112, 113, 134

N

National Writing Project, 157
New Century College, 51, 81, 82, 99, 112, 119–120, 133, 140, 153, 164
Nursing, 20, 34, 43, 61, 75–78, 85, 89

O

Odell, Lee, 15
Originality, 94, 107, 115–117

P

Pare, Anthony, 15, 17, 170
Passion, 5, 6, 38, 96, 105, 112–115, 136–137, 139, 149–150, 157, 160
Pathos, 6
Pennycook, Alastair, 22
Perry, William, 109
Persona, 7, 46, 54
"Personal, the," 6, 45–47, 54, 74, 78–79
Petrosky, Anthony, 166
Phenomenology, 41, 43, 61, 77, 89
Philosophy, 34, 40–43, 61, 72–74, 89
Physics, 32, 35, 37, 47–49, 64–66
Political science, 34, 36, 39, 68–70, 84, 106, 108–110, 113–114, 116–117, 125–126
PopMatters, 55
Popular writing (*See* Audience, non-academic or popular)
Portfolios, 77–78, 125, 152
Postmodernism, 40–42, 44, 51
Powell, Malea, 5, 21, 23
Practices (teaching)
    cultivating student engagement, 150–152
    evaluation (*See* Evaluation)
    models for writing, 122, 125
    reflections on (by teachers), 151
    reflective writing by students, as, 153
    response (*See* Response to writing)
    revision, 127
    rubric for inquiry into disciplines, 154–156
    rubric for self-reflection, 147
    specifying expectations, 142–146
    writing guides in disciplines, 149
Principles for academic writing (*See* Academic writing)
Proficiency essays, 25, 30, 99, 101–112, 120–121
Program development, 2, 160–167
Psychology, 34, 38–39, 63–64, 86, 109, 116, 127

Q

Queer theory, 42
"Questioning Alternative Discourses: Reports from Across the Disciplines," 19

R

Rader, Victoria, 28, 34, 45–47, 76, 78–80, 91, 153
Reading, role of in development (*See* Development of disciplinary writers)
Reason, control by, 6, 38–45, 59, 113–115
Reagan, Priscilla, 28, 36, 37, 39, 68–70, 92
Religious studies (major), 106
Research, qualitative and quantitative, 43, 45–46, 106
Response to writing, 103, 122–128, 147–150
  on first paper, 124–126
Rhetoric
  alternative (*See* Alternative discourse)
  contrastive (*See* Contrastive rhetoric)
  epistemic, 17
Rich, Adrienne, 21
Ritchie, Joy, 21
Rose, Mike, 21
Royster, Jacqueline Jones, 21, 24
Rupiper, Amy, 161
Russell, David, 15, 17, 32, 59–60, 117, 169

S

Saltz, Laura, 168
Schick, Kurt, 161
Selber, Stuart, 168
Service learning, 112, 165
Shepherd, Dawn, 168
Smart, Graham, 16
Smith, Lesley, 28, 34, 36, 46, 50–57, 80–83, 90, 93, 133, 153, 168
Smith, Robert, 28, 36, 38–39, 63–64
Snyder, Mitch, 45
Sociology, 34, 45–47, 76, 78–80, 106, 117, 118–119
Sommers, Nancy, 168
Sorrell, Jeanne, 29, 34, 43, 61, 75–78, 89, 90, 92, 153
Soven, Margot, 156, 164
Stages of development (*See* Development of disciplinary writers)
Standard Edited American English, 1, 7, 10–12, 23, 66, 115, 127–128, 131–132, 148
Standards, 1–23, 35–36

academic, 36–38
contexts for (*See* Contexts for academic expectations)
disciplinary, 36–38
idiosyncratic, 7, 59, 101
Stitt-Bergh, Monica, 168
Struppa, Daniele, 29, 34, 35, 37, 40, 43, 92
Student writers
  confidence of, 114, 121–122, 126
  expectations by, 101–112, 115, 118–119, 122–124
  risks for, 72–75, 79–80, 83, 94
"Students' Right to Their Own Language," 19
Style, 8, 59, 127–128
  APA (American Psychological Association), 38, 63–64, 103–104, 127
  Chicago Manual of, 113
  non-linear, 33, 74–75
  of sentences, 71
  options for, 102, 107–108
Survey, 25, 29, 96–98, 101–112
Swales, John, 16
Syntax, alternative (*See* Alternative syntax)

T

Tate, Gary, 60, 161
Taxonomy of alternatives (*See* Alternative discourse, taxonomy of)
Templates, 15, 35, 40, 43
Tenure, 47, 48, 51, 54, 56–57
Thaiss, Chris, 1, 13, 15, 142, 156, 157, 164, 168
Tompkins, Jane, 21
Topics, choice of, 107
Toulmin, Stephen, 14, 19, 52, 56, 169
Townsend, Martha, 163
Transferability, 82
Transparency, myth of, 59, 71, 87, 89, 124
Trefil, James, 29, 32, 35, 37, 47–49, 64–66, 90, 91, 92

V

Villanueva, Victor, Jr., 21, 22
Voice, 8
  appropriate, 87
  original (*See* Originality)
  personal, 39–41, 54, 119
  woman's, 9

W

WAC (*See* Writing across the curriculum)
WAC Clearinghouse, 142, 165
Walvoord, Barbara, 142
WID (*See* Writing in the disciplines)
Williams, Ashley, 164
Williams, Patricia, 21
Williams, Walter, 29, 34, 36, 49, 67–70, 91, 92
Workplace writing, 4, 15, 144–146,
    151–153, 154, 169–170
    (*See Also* Audience, non-academic or
    popular)
Worsham, Lynn, 21
Writing
    academic (*See* Academic writing)
    across the curriculum (programs), 13,
        22, 142, 161
    amount of, 103
    autobiographical, 40–41
    creative, 55
    in double majors, 102, 106, 109, 111,
        117, 121, 128, 140

in interdisciplinary majors, 106
in majors, 95–135
in the disciplines (programs), 13, 22,
    103, 142, 161
in the workplace (*See* Workplace
    writing)
personal (*See* "Personal, the")
process(es), 54–55
reflection on, 105, 120–121, 140,
    146–147, 151–153
Writing centers, 164–165
Writing fellows, 164–165
Writing-intensive courses, 103, 163–165
Wysocki, Anne, 53, 166

Y

Yancey, Kathleen, 99, 157, 168
Yanez, Arturo, 17, 60, 117
Young, Art, 142

Z

Zawacki, Terry Myers, 9, 21, 164, 168